MYTH, LEGE...
FOLKLORE

The Book of Christmas

CHRISTMAS

THE BOOK OF CHRISTMAS.

Some say, that ever 'gainst that season comes
Wherein our Saviour's birth is celebrated,
This bird of dawning singeth all night long
Shakespeare

From the title page of the first edition — 1888

THE BOOK OF CHRISTMAS

Descriptive of the customs, ceremonies, traditions,
superstitions, fun, feeling and festivities
of the Christmas Season

Thomas K. Hervey

With Illustrations by
R. SEYMOUR

With an Introduction by
STEVE ROUD

WORDSWORTH EDITIONS
in association with
THE FOLKLORE SOCIETY

FLS
books

This edition published 2000 by Wordsworth Editions Limited
Cumberland House, Crib Street, Ware, Hertfordshire SG12 9ET
in association with The Folklore Society,
University College London, Gower Street, London WC1E 6BT

Editor FLS Books: Jennifer Chandler

ISBN 1 84022 506 8

Typeset by Antony Gray
Printed and bound in Great Britain by
Mackays of Chatham plc, Chatham, Kent

This exciting new series is made possible by a unique partnership between Wordsworth Editions and The Folklore Society.

Among the major assets of The Folklore Society is its unparalleled collection of books, in the making since 1878. The library and archives have, over the years, formed an invaluable specialist resource. Now, Wordsworth Editions, which is committed to opening up whole areas of culture through good-looking, good-value books and intelligent commentary, make these riches widely available.

Individual introductions by acknowledged experts place each work in historical context and provide commentaries from the perspective of modern scholarship.

PROFESSOR W. F. H. NICOLAISEN
President, The Folklore Society

Contents

THE SECOND PART

𝕿𝖍𝖊 𝕮𝖍𝖗𝖎𝖘𝖙𝖒𝖆𝖘 𝕯𝖆𝖞𝖘

Introduction

Any history of Christmas is necessarily a dialogue with the Victorians. When Hervey wrote his book, in 1888, Christmas had already undergone a process of change and innovation, encouraged by a combination of novelists, journalists, commercial interests and social reformers, and major developments continued after his time. The movement to reform Christmas had started early in the nineteenth century, but gathered rapid pace as the century progressed, and the Victorians turned out to be great reformers of traditional customs. Along with May Day, Christmas proved their greatest success. We owe many of the most widespread elements of the modern-day Christmas to their reforming zeal, and Hervey shows that he was perfectly aware of the trend of the time when he writes that he is deliberately 'mingling the customs of modern times with those of the past in our pages, as, in many respects, we wish our readers will do in practice' (p. 286).

It should be understood at the outset, however, that the history of Christmas is far more complex than can be adequately covered in this introduction, or even in an overview such as Hervey's. Different elements were introduced at different times, some with genuine antecedents, others completely new inventions, and most took decades to become widespread. There were vast class differences, and regional variations, all of which had their own history and were developing or declining at different speeds, and although the overall trend was towards homogenisation, the process was gradual and multifaceted. Even today, when we probably all have a basic idea of what belongs to Christmas, there are vast differences in the way each individual or family approaches the festival, and this has always been the case.

This is not to argue that the centuries before the nineteenth had no effect at all on the development of the festival. The roots of the wide difference in the relative weight given by the English to Christmas and the Scots to New Year, for example, can be explained by reference to the religious differences of the seventeenth century.

Recognisable elements of the pre-Victorian Christmas, all given their due space by Hervey, include: carol singers, Christmas puddings, mince pies, evergreen decorations, candles, ample food and drink, and hospitality to one's neighbours and the poor. But many of the ingredients of our modern Christmas had already been introduced by Hervey's time, and he seems unaware of them, or perhaps simply does not understand their developing importance. Christmas crackers were invented   in 1847, Christmas cards in 1843, and by 1888 the Christmas tree was becoming widespread. It had been introduced from Germany, being found in the Royal Family and others with German connections from the late eighteenth century and in occasional other families from the 1830s and 1840s, but really gaining popularity after the publication of popular engravings showing Victoria and Albert's trees from 1848. But it is indicative of the gradual nature of change, and the fact that Hervey had his eyes set firmly on the past, that he could write of a 'beautiful' German custom, in which 'a large bough is set up in the principal room, the smaller branches of which are hung with little presents suitable to the different members of the household' (p. 177), without commenting on this as the obvious precursor of the Christmas Tree.

Before the mid-nineteenth century, presents were given at New Year, not at Christmas itself, but the habit of giving presents on Christmas Day gradually gained ground, again based on German models. Hervey mentions both, but with clear emphasis on New Year. The history of hanging up a stocking is still unclear. A writer in 1866, referring to the northern counties of England, described it as an old custom, but others in the 1870s and 1880s wrote of the practice as unfamiliar to them. We can probably assume a Continental origin, but this has yet to be proved. The burgeoning capitalist industry quickly identified Christmas as a new market and was delighted to foster the increase in present-giving. Mass-produced toys flooded the market, and new forms such as the Christmas Annual were rapidly introduced. Mass-circulation magazines and cheap books, many with influential engravings, helped to spread the new fashions.

Father Christmas has developed largely since Hervey's time. Admittedly, since at least the fifteenth century, Christmas had been personified in various ways – Sir, Prince, and Lord Christmas among them – and the term Old Father Christmas was much used in the propaganda war against the Puritans, who banned the festival in 1647. But Father Christmas, the gift-bringer, developed only from about the 1870s, based on the Continental St Nicholas, either directly or, more probably, via the American version, Santa Claus. Father Christmas' physical characteristics and costume took a long time to stabilise, and in late Victorian illustrations he was quite likely to be dressed in green. His association with sleighs, reindeer and so on, also came from America. Modern attempts to postulate ancient origins in shamanism and other ritual practices are fanciful.

A major change since Hervey's time has been the drastic shortening of the Christmas period. From the sixth century onwards, the Christian church had decreed that the twelve days from the Nativity to the Epiphany would be held as sacred, and special activities and traditions took place throughout the period, which included both New Year and Twelfth Night. In modern times, Christmas celebrations are concentrated largely on Christmas Day and Boxing Day, with an almost separate festival on New Year's Eve. As indicated by Hervey, Twelfth Night was a very popular festival in former times, with its own traditions, but has virtually disappeared, except for being quoted as the day on which, or by which, the decorations should be removed, and for the all-important Twelfth Night cakes, which became our modern Christmas cake.

Christmas games and entertainments have also undergone major changes since high Victorian days. We still play board games, but card-playing, which was almost universal in previous times (even in families which would not allow it at other times of year) has almost disappeared. The increase in the number of toys, and the introduction of new forms such as television and computer-games, mean that few families now play the range of 'parlour games' such as Blind Man's Buff, Hot Cockles, and Hunt the Slipper, even though many of us feel we should. Even fewer would risk what was previously one of the most popular games of all – Snap-Dragon, described in 1813 as

a kind of play, in which brandy is set on fire, and raisins thrown into it, which those who are unused to the sport are afraid to take out, but which may be safely snatched by a quick motion and put blazing into the mouth, which being closed, the fire is at once extinguished [quoted by T. F. Thiselton Dyer, *British Popular Customs* (1876), pp. 462–3].

Many of us still feel that ghost stories round the fire would be appropriate, but we do not want to scare the children, and anyway the central-heating radiator is just not the same. Fire traditions in general have declined, although candles are still evident. Commercial decorations, made of all types of shiny materials, have largely replaced home-made paper chains, which in turn had replaced, or at least supplemented, evergreens. But we still try to have some natural decorations, and holly and mistletoe still hold their own. Calendar customs have declined throughout the year, and there are no mummers, wassailers, waits (perambulating musicians), sword dancers, hooden-horser, and so on, to visit and perform their songs or plays.

The restricted class view of most Victorian writers is obvious in *The Book of Christmas*. Hervey's families have servants to boil the Christmas pudding; they have children whose arrival home by coach from boarding-school is a major event of the season, and their dining-rooms are able to seat at least a dozen people, with plenty of food to go round. Ordinary working folk only have walk-on parts as servants, shopkeepers, and so on, and the poor only as carol-singers at the gate, or recipients of charity on St Thomas' Day. In some ways, however, this is a true reflection of Christmas in Victorian times. All the new introductions and reforms took hold first in the upper and middle classes and gradually filtered down the social scale, as standards of living rose and prices of particular items fell. Thus, in Hervey's time, the working folk, if they could afford anything special, would eat goose for Christmas, for which they might have saved for months in a 'goose club', while the middle classes increasingly ate the more expensive turkey. Eventually, it was the turkey which became the norm.

Christmas remains the most fascinating of modern festivals. It carries a huge burden of past traditions, or at least our perception of them, cloaked in warm memories of our own childhoods, but we still feel free to re-invent, to change the emphasis, to remodel as we think fit. Within the broad consensus of what we generally accept as 'normal' Christmas, there is a wide range of acceptable behaviour. But the principles which the Victorians fostered – a strong, family-oriented, child-centred festival, mostly secular with religious overtones, plenty of food and drink, in the cosiness of a family home on a winter's night, are as strong as ever.

The modern reader has to learn to treat Victorian writers like Hervey with caution, carefully separating the genuine from the spurious, the solid from the romantic. In particular, Victorians had an uncanny knack of clothing their inventions and remodelled traditions in an aura which implied that they were traditional and ancient. They conjured up a curiously timeless Merrie England in which the people were poor, but content, and were looked after by a benevolent local baron or lord of the manor and equally benevolent clergy. Everyone knew their place, and social hierarchies were not questioned. Such a time never existed, but in rewriting the history of our major festivals and traditions, it was this mythical Golden Age, which formed the backbone of the Victorian world-view, to which they aspired, and to which they returned again and again for ideas, ideals and legitimisation.

The Lord of Misrule is a good example of this revisionist vision of the past. This official, who planned and presided over the Christmas celebra-tions, existed only in the Royal court, some of the larger civic corporations, and wealthy institutions such as the universities. They are first mentioned in the fifteenth century and had virtually disappeared by mid-sixteenth century, but they are constantly referred to by Victorian writers as the central feature of the 'old Christmas'. Thus, a feature which lasted perhaps only a hundred years and affected a tiny proportion of the population became adopted as a major enduring symbol for all. Similarly, pictures of people dragging in impossibly large 'Yule logs' to be burnt in the impossibly large fireplaces of the baronial hall were reproduced over and over again to illustrate the Christmas of the mythical Golden Age.

In particular, Victorian writers like Hervey are not to be trusted on the question of origins. They were too willing to make assumptions and imply connections which did not exist, or for which there was no evidence The notion that much of our folklore and traditions survive directly from pagan times is now totally discredited.

Despite its period charm and its usefulness as a summing up, Hervey's book is essentially derivative in the manner of much folklore writing of the time. He shows no evidence of doing any original research, but bases his book solely on those of previous writers. His main fault, therefore, is a tendency to be a-historical – it is not always clear what period he is referring to, and, as already indicated, he irons out the complexities of the subject. As the book contains no bibliography, it would be useful for the modern reader to identify the following authorities on which he draws most heavily and refers to simply by surname: John Brand, *Observations on the Popular Antiquities of Great Britain* (first published 1777, but later in numerous editions including a 3-volume set of 1849 and a reorganised version by W. Carew Hazlitt, entitled *Dictionary of Faiths and Folklore* (1905), which is still in print); William Hone, *The Every-Day Book* (1827), *The Table Book* (1827), *The Year-Book* (1832); Robert Herrick, *Hesperides* (1648); Robert Nares, *A Glossary or Collection of Words, Phrases* . . . (new edition, 1888).

There have been countless books about Christmas published since Hervey's time, each covering the same ground to a large extent, and new ones are added every year. If only a few of them had concentrated on describing and analysing the Christmas of their own time rather than regurgitating the already well-trodden past, we would be in a much more informed position than we are. The Christmas researcher will find more real information in such contemporary sources as magazines, newspapers, diaries, and so on, than in a whole pile of retrospective books. Nevertheless, a handful of books of each generation contribute new insights and careful scholarship, and anyone who wants to follow up an interest in the subject is recommended to start with the following: J. M. Golby & A. W. Purdue, *The Making of Modern Christmas* (Batsford, 1986); Gavin Weightman & Steve Humphries, *Christmas Past* (Sidgwick & Jackson, 1987); Ronald Hutton, *The Stations of the Sun* (Oxford University Press, 1996); Jacqueline Simpson & Steve Roud, *Dictionary of English Folklore* (Oxford University Press, 2000).

STEVE ROUD
Joint-author of the *Oxford Dictionary of English Folklore*

A note on the text: Where there is anachronistic use of language or punctuation likely to be misunderstood by the general reader, some small changes to the text have been made.

Introductory Chapter

We take no note of time
But from its loss; to give it, then, a tongue
Is wise in man.   DR YOUNG

To give a language to time, for the preservation of its records and the utterance of its lessons, has been amongst the occupations of man from the day when first he found himself in its mysterious presence down to these latter ages of the world; and yet, all the resources of his ingenuity, impelled by all the aspirations of his heart, have succeeded only in supplying it with an imperfect series of hieroglyphics, difficult in their acquirement and uncertain in their use. Ages upon ages of the young world have passed away, of which the old has no chronicle. Generations after generations of men have 'made their bed in the darkness', and left no monuments. Of the crowded memorials reared by others along the stream of time, many (and those the mightiest) are written in a cipher of which the key is lost. The wrappings of the mummy are letters of a dead language; and no man can translate the ancient story of the pyramid!

We have learnt to speak of time, because it is that portion of eternity with which we have *presently* to do – as if it were a whit more intelligible (less vague, abstract, and unimaginable) than that eternity of which it is a part. He who can conceive of the one, must be able to embrace the awful image of the other. We think of time as of a section of eternity, separated and entrenched by absolute *limits;* and thus we seem to have arrived at a definite idea, surrounded by points on which the mind can rest. But when the imagination sets out upon the actual experiment, and discovers that those limits are not assignable, save only on one side, and finds but a single point on which to rest its failing wing, and looks from thence along an expanse whose boundaries are nowhere else within the range of its restricted vision – then does the mortal bird return into its mortal nest, wearied with its ineffectual flight, and convinced that a shoreless ocean and one whose shores it cannot see are alike formless and mysterious to its dim and feeble gaze.

And yet notwithstanding the connection of these two ideas – of time and of eternity – (the notion of the former being reached only through the latter) we deal familiarly, and even jestingly, with the one, while the mind approaches the other with reverential awe. Types, and symbols, and emblems – and those ever of a grave meaning – are the most palpable expressions which we venture to give to our conceptions of the one; whilst the other we figure and personify – and that, too often, after a fashion in which the better part of the moral is left unrepresented. Yet who shall personify time? And who that has ever tried it, in the silence of his chamber and the stillness of his heart, has not bowed down in breathless awe before the solemn visions which his conjuration has awakened? Oh, the mysterious shapes which Time takes, when it rises up into the mind as an image, at those hours of lonely inquisition! – 'And he said unto her, "What form is he of?" And she said, "An *old man* cometh up; and he is *covered with a mantle*." ' – The mysterious presence which it assumes 'in thoughts from the visions of the night, when deep sleep falleth on men'! Who, as he strove to collect the mournful attributes about which his fancy had been busy into an impersonation, has not suddenly felt as if 'a spirit passed before *his* face! . . . It stood still, but *he* could not discern the form thereof; an image was before his eyes, there was silence'; and out of that silence has seemed to come a voice like that which whispered to Job, 'They that dwell in houses of clay, whose foundation is in the dust, which are crushed before the moth, they are destroyed from morning to evening; they perish for ever, without any regarding it.'

Time, abstractedly considered as what in truth it is – a portion of the vast ocean of eternity, a river flowing from the sea and flowing to the sea, a channel leading from deep to deep through shores on which the races of the world are permitted to build for awhile, until the great waters shall once more cover all, and time, *as* time, 'shall be no more' – must long have defied the skill of man to map out its surface, and write his memorials upon its impalpable bosom. The thousand keels that sweep over the visible waters of the world leave on their face traces of their passage more legible and enduring than do the generations of men as they come and go on that viewless and voiceless stream. The ingenuity which has taught man to lay down the plan of the material ocean, to assign to each spot on its uniform surface its positive whereabouts and actual relation, and by a series of imaginary lines and figures to steer his way across its pathless solitudes with a knowledge as certain as that which guides him amidst the substantive and distinctive features of the solid earth, is scarcely more admirable than that which, by a similar device, has enabled him to measure out the expanse of the silent river, to cover, as it were, its surface with a crowd of imaginary latitudes and longitudes intersecting each other at all points, and to ascertain at any moment, by observation, his relative position on the great stream of time.

How long the unaided genius of man might have been ere it could have fallen upon a scheme for the one achievement or the other, if left to struggle with its own resources and unassisted by hints from without, we need not conjecture. But in each case, the solution of the problem was suggested to him, as the materials for working it are still furnished, by the finger of God himself. The great architect of the universe has planted in its frame all necessary models and materials for the guidance and use of its human inhabitants, leaving them to the exercise of those powers and capacities with which they have been furnished to improve the lessons and apply the examples thus conveyed. In each of the cases of which we have spoken, the constellations which surround the world and 'are the poetry of heaven' have been the sources of the inspiration, as they are still the lights by which that inspiration works. The hand that fashioned the 'two great lights', and appointed to them their courses, and gave them to be 'for signs and for seasons and for days and years', pointed out to man how he might, by the observation of their revolutions, direct his course along the unbroken stream of time or count its waves as they flowed silently and ceaselessly away. The sun and moon were the ancient and at first the only measures of time, as they are the essential foundations of all the modes by which man measures it now; and in the order of the world's architecture, the 'watches of the element' which guide us yet were framed and 'set in the firmament of heaven' at that distant and uncertain period whose 'evening and morning were the fourth day'.

Nor did the beneficent power which erected these great meters of time in the constitution of the universe leave the world without suggestions how their use might be improved in the business of more minute subdivision. The thousand natural inequalities of the earth's surface, and the vegetable columns which spring from its bosom, furnish – as do the spires and towers and columns which man rears thereon – so many gnomons of the vast dial on which are unerringly written with the finger of shadow the shining records of the sky. There is something unutterably solemn in watching the shade creep, day by day, round a circle whose diameter man might measure with his grave or even cover with his hand, and contrasting the limits within which it acts with the spaces of time which its stealing tread measures out, and feeling that it is the faithful index of a progress before which the individual being and the universal frame of things are alike hastening to rapid and inevitable decay. There are few types more awfully representative of that which they typify than is the shadow. It is Time almost made visible. Through it the mind reaches the most vivid impersonation of that mysterious idea which it is capable of containing. It seems as if flung directly from his present and passing wing. The silent and ceaseless motion – gliding for ever on and on, coming round again and again, but reverting never and tarrying never, blotting out the sunshine as it passes and leaving no trace where it has passed – make it the true and solemn symbol of him (the old unresting and unreturning one) who receded not, even when that same shadow went back on the dial of the king of Judah, nor paused when the sun stood still in the midst of heaven and the moon lingered over the valley of Ajalon! Of that mysterious type and its awful morals, a lost friend of ours has already spoken better than we can hope to speak; and as he is ('alas, that *he is* so!') already one whose 'sun shall no more go down, neither shall *his* moon withdraw itself', we will avail ourselves of a language which deserves to be better known, and sounds all the more solemnly that he who uttered it has since furnished in his own person a fresh verification of the solemn truths which he sung so well.

> Upon a dial-stone,
> Behold the shade of Time,
> For ever circling on and on
> In silence more sublime
> Than if the thunders of the spheres
> Pealed forth its march to mortal ears!
>
> It meets us hour by hour,
> Doles out our little span,
> Reveals a presence and a power
> Felt and confessed by man;
> The drop of moments, day by day,
> That rocks of ages wears away.
>
> Woven by a hand unseen
> Upon that stone, survey
> A robe of dark sepulchral green,
> The mantle of decay,
> The fold of chill oblivion's pall,
> That falleth with yon shadow's fall!
>
> Day is the time for toil,
> Night balms the weary breast,
> Stars have their vigils, seas awhile
> Will sink to peaceful rest;
> But round and round the shadow creeps
> Of that which slumbers not, nor sleeps!
>
> Effacing all that's fair,
> Hushing the voice of mirth

Into the silence of despair,
Around the lonesome hearth,
And training ivy-garlands green
O'er the once gay and social scene.

In beauty fading fast
Its silent trace appears,
And where – a phantom of the past,
Dim in the mist of years –
Gleams Tadmor o'er oblivion's waves,
Like wrecks above their ocean-graves.

Before the ceaseless shade
That round the world doth sail
Its towers and temples bow the head,
The pyramids look pale,
The festal halls grow hushed and cold,
The everlasting hills wax old!

Coeval with the sun
Its silent course began,
And still its phantom-race shall run,
Till worlds with age grow wan,
Till darkness spread her funeral pall,
And one vast shadow circle all!

To the great natural divisions of time (with their aid, and guided by these hints), the ingenuity of man, under the direction of his wants, has been busy since the world began in adding artificial ones, while his heart has been active in supplying impulses and furnishing devices to that end. Years, and months, and days – the periods marked out by the revolutions of our celestial guides – have been aggregated and divided after methods almost as various as the nations of the earth. Years have been composed into cycles and olympiads and generations and reigns, and months resolved into decades and weeks, days into hours, and hours into subdivisions which have been again subdivided almost to the confines of thought. Yet it is only in these latter ages of the world that a measurement has been attained, at once so minute and so closely harmonising with the motions and regulated by the revolutions of the dials of the sky, that, had the same machinery existed from the commencement of time – with the art of printing to preserve its results – the history of the past might be perused, with its discrepancies reconciled and many of its blanks supplied. And could the world agree upon its uniform adoption now, together with that of a common epoch to reckon from, comparative chronology would be no longer a science applicable to the future; and history, for the time to come (insofar as it is a mere record of facts), would present few problems but such as 'he who runs may read'.

But out of these conventional and multiplied divisions of time, these wheels within the great wheel, arise results far more important than the verification of a chronological series or the establishment of the harmonies of history. Through them not only may the ages of the world be said to intercommunicate, and the ends of the earth in a sense to meet, but by their aid the whole business of the life of nations and of individuals is regulated, and a set of mnemonics established upon which hinges the history of the human heart. By the multiplied but regular system of recurrences thus obtained, order is made to arise out of the web of duties and the chaos of events; and at each of the thousand points marked out on these concentric circles are written their appropriate duties and recorded their special memories. The calendar of every country is thus covered over with a series of events whose recollection is recalled and influence kept alive by the return of the cycles, in their ceaseless revolution, to those spots at which the record of each has been written; and acts of fasting or of festival, of social obligation or of moral observance – many of which would be surely lost or overlooked, amidst the inextricable confusion in which, without this systematic arrangement, they must be mingled – are severally pointed out by the moving finger of Time as he periodically reaches the place of each on his concentric dials.

But besides the calendar of general direction and national observance, where is the heart that has not a private calendar of its own? Long ere the meridian of life has been attained, the individual man has made many a memorandum of joy or pain for his periodic perusal, and established many a private celebration, pleasant or mournful, of his own. How many a lost hope and blighted feeling which the heart is the better for recalling, and would not willingly forget, would pass from the mind amid the crowd and noise and bustle of the world, but for these tablets on which it is ineffaceably written and yearly read! How many an act of memory, with its store of consolations and its treasure of warnings, would remain post-poned, amid the interests of the present, till it came to be forgotten altogether, but for that system which has marked its positive place upon the wheels of time, and brings the record certainly before the mental eye, in their unvarying revolution! Many are the uses of these diaries of the heart. By their aid something is saved from the wrecks of the past for the service of the present; the lights of former days are made to throw pleasant reflections upon many an after period of life; the weeds which the world and its cares had fostered are again and again cleared away from the sweet and wholesome fountain of tears; the fading inscriptions of other years are renewed, to yield their morals to the future; and the dead are restored, for a fleeting hour of sweet communion or hold high and solemn converse with us from the graves in which we laid them years ago.

And this result of the minute and accurate partitions of time, which consists in the establishment of a series of points for periodic celebration, is, as regards its public and social operation, more important than may at first sight appear. The calendar of almost every country is, as we have observed, filled with a series of anniversaries, religious or secular, of festival or abstinence, or instituted for the regulation of business or the operations of the law. In England, independently of those periods of observance which are common to the realm and written in her calendar, there are few districts which are without some festival peculiar to themselves, originating in the grant of some local charter or privilege, the establishment of some local fair, the influence of some ancient local superstition, or some other cause, of which, in many cases, the sole remaining trace is the observance to which it has given rise – and which observance does not always speak in language sufficiently clear to give any account of its parent. Around each of these celebrations has grown up a set of customs and traditions and habits, the examination into which has led to many a useful result, and which are for the most part worth preserving, as well for their picturesque aspect and social character as for the sake of the historic chambers which they may yet help us to explore. Their close resemblance, as existing amongst different nations, has formed an element in the solution of more than one problem which had for its object a chapter of the history of the world; and they may be said, in many cases, to furnish an apparent link of connection between generations of men long divided and dwelling far apart. They form, too, amid the changes which time is perpetually effecting in the structure of society, a chain of connection between the present and former times of the same land, and prevent the national individuality from being wholly destroyed. They tend to preserve some similarity in the moral aspect of a country from epoch to epoch, and, without having force enough to act as drags on the progress of society towards improvement, they serve for a feature of identification amid all its forms. Curious illustrations they are, too, of national history; and we learn to have confidence in its records when we find in some obscure nook the peasant of today, who troubles himself little with the lore of events and their succession, doing that which some ancient chronicler tells us his ancestors did a thousand years ago, and keeping in all simplicity some festival, the story of whose origin we find upon its written page.

To the philosophic inquirer, few things are more important in the annals of nations than their festivals, their anniversaries, and their public celebrations of all kinds. In nothing is their peculiar character more strikingly exhibited. They show a people in its undress, acting upon its impulses, and separated from the conventions and formalities of its everyday existence. We may venture to say that could we, in the absence of every other record, be furnished with a complete account of the festivals, traditions, and anniversaries of any given nation now extinct, not only might a correct estimate be therefrom made of their progress in morals and civilisation, but a conjectural history of their doings be hazarded, which should bear a closer resemblance to the facts than many an existing history constructed from more varied materials.

For these reasons – and some others, which are more personal and less philosophical – we love all old traditions and holiday customs. Like honest Sir Andrew Aguecheek, we 'delight in masques and revels, sometimes altogether'. Many a happy chance has conducted us unpremeditatedly into the midst of some rustic festival, whose recollection is amongst our pleasant memories yet – and many a one have we gone venturously forth to seek – when we dwelt in the more immediate neighbourhood of the haunts to which, one by one, these traditional observances are retiring before the face of civilisation! The natural tendency of time to obliterate ancient customs and silence ancient sports, is too much promoted by the utilitarian spirit of the day; and they who would have no man enjoy without being able to give a reason for the enjoyment which is in him, are robbing life of half its beauty and some of its virtues. If the old festivals and hearty commemorations in which our land was once so abundant – and which obtained for her, many a long day since, the name of 'merrie England' – had no other recommendation than their *convivial* character, the community of enjoyment which they imply, they would on that account alone be worthy of all promotion, as an antidote to the cold and selfish spirit which is tainting the life-blood and freezing the pulses of society. ' 'Tis good to be merry and wise'; but the wisdom which eschews mirth, and holds the time devoted to it as so much wasted by being taken from the schoolmaster, is very questionable wisdom in itself, and assuredly not made to promote the happiness of nations. We love all commemorations. We love these anniversaries, for their own sakes, and for their uses. We love those Lethes of an hour which have a virtue beyond their gift of oblivion, and while they furnish a temporary forgetfulness of many of the ills of life, revive the memory of many a past enjoyment, and reawaken many a slumbering affection. We love those milestones on the journey of life beside which man is called upon to pause, and take a reckoning of the distance he has passed, and of that which he may have yet to go. We love to reach those free, open spaces at which the crossroads of the world converge, and where we are sure to meet, as at a common rendezvous, with travellers from its many paths. We love to enter those houses of refreshment by the wayside of existence, where we know we shall encounter with other wayfarers like ourselves – perchance with friends long separated, and whom the chances of the world keep far apart – and whence, after a sweet communion and lusty festival and needful rest, we may go forth upon our journey new fortified against its accidents, and strengthened for its toils. We love those festivals which have been made, as Washington Irving says, 'the season for gathering together of family connections, and drawing closer again those bonds of kindred hearts which the cares and pleasures and sorrows of the world are continually operating to cast loose; of calling back the children of a family who have launched forth in life and wandered widely asunder, once more to assemble about the paternal hearth, that rallying place of the affections, there to grow young and loving again among the endearing mementos of childhood.' Above all, we love those seasons ('for pity is not common!' says the old ballad) which call for the exercise of a general hospitality, and give the poor man his few and precious glimpses of a plenty which, as the world is managed, his toil cannot buy; which shelter the houseless wanderer, and feed the starving child, and clothe the naked mother, and spread a festival for all – those seasons which in their observance by our ancestors, kept alive, by periodical reawakenings, that flame of charity which thus had scarcely time wholly to expire during all the year. We love all which tends to call man from the solitary and chilling pursuit of his own separate and selfish views into the warmth of a common sympathy, and within the bands of a common brotherhood. We love these commemorations, as we have said, for themselves; we love them for their uses; and still more we love them for the memories of our boyhood! Many a bright picture do they call up in our minds, and in the minds of most who have been amongst their observers; for with these festivals of the heart are inalienably connected many a memory for sorrow or for joy, many a scene of early love, many a merry meeting which was yet the last, many a parting of those who shall part no more, many a joyous group composed of materials which separated only too soon and shall never be put together again on earth, many a lost treasure and many a perished hope –

> Hopes that were angels in their birth,
> But perished young, like things of earth.

Happy, happy days were they! – 'Oh, their record is lively in my soul!' – and there is a happiness, still, in looking back to them:

> Ye are dwelling with the faded flowers
> Ye are with the suns long set,
> But oh, your memory, gentle hours,
> Is a living vision yet!

Yet are they, for the most part, eras to count our losses by. Beside them, in the calendar of the heart, is written many a private note, not to be read without bitter tears:

> There's many a lad I loved is gone,
> And many a lass grown old;
> And when, at times, I think thereon,
> My weary heart grows cold.

'Oh, the mad days that I have spent,' says old Justice Shallow, 'and to see how many of mine old acquaintance are dead!' Yet still we love these commemorations and hail them, each and all, as the year restores them to us, shorn and scarred as they are. And though many and many a time the welcome has faltered on our lips as we 'turned from all they brought to all they could not bring', still by God's help we will enjoy them, as yet we may – drawing closer to us, and with the more reason, the friends that still remain, and draining to the last –

> One draught, in memory of many
> A joyous banquet past.

The revels of merry England are fast subsiding into silence, and her many customs wearing gradually away. The affectations and frivolities of society, as well as its more grave and solemn pursuits – the exigences of fashion, and the tongue of the pedagogue – are alike arrayed against them; and, one by one, they are retreating from the great assemblies where mankind 'most do congregate', to hide themselves in remote solitudes and rural nooks. In fact, that social change which has enlarged and filled the towns at the expense of the country, which has annihilated the yeomanry of England, and drawn the estated gentleman from the shelter of his ancestral oaks, to live upon their produce in the haunts of dissipation, has been, in itself, the circumstance most unfavourable to the existence of many of them, which delight in byways and sheltered places, which had their appropriate homes in the old manor house or the baronial hall. Yet do they pass lingeringly away. Traces of most of them still exist, and from time to time reappear even in our cities and towns; and there are probably scarcely any which have not found some remote district or other of these islands in which their influence is still acknowledged, and their rites duly performed. There is something in the mind of man which attaches him to ancient superstitions even for the sake of their antiquity, and endears to him old traditions even because they are old. We cannot readily shake off our reverence for that which our fathers have reverenced so long, even where the causes in which that reverence originated are not very obvious or not very satisfactory. We believe that he who shall aid in preserving the records of these vanishing observances, ere it be too late, will do good and acceptable service in his generation; and such contribution to that end as we have in our power it is the purpose of these volumes to bestow. Of that taste for hunting out the obsolete which originates in the mere dry spirit of antiquarianism, or is pursued as a display of gladiatorial skill in the use of the intellectual weapons, we profess ourselves no admirers. But he who pursues in the track of a receding custom – which is valuable either as a historical illustration or because of its intrinsic beauty, moral or pictur-esque – is an antiquary of the beneficent kind; and he who assists in restoring observances which had a direct tendency to propagate a feeling of brotherhood and a spirit of benevolence, is a higher benefactor still. Right joyous festivals there have been amongst us, which England will be none the merrier – and kindly ones which she will be none the better – for losing. The following pages will give some account of that season which has, at all times since the establishment of Christianity, been most crowded with observances, and whose celebration is still the most con-spicuous and universal with us, as well as throughout the whole of Christendom.

The First Part

The Christmas Season

'Merry Christmas to you!'

The Christmas Season

This Book of Christmas is a sound and good persuasion for
gentlemen, and all wealthy men, to keep a good Christmas.

A ha! Christmas! T. H. LONDON, 1647

Any man or woman . . . that can give any knowledge, or tell any
tidings, of an old, old, very old gray-bearded gentleman, called
Christmas, who was wont to be a verie familiar ghest, and visite all
sorts of people both pore and rich, and used to appeare in glittering
gold, silk, and silver, in the Court, and in all shapes in the Theatre in
Whitehall, and had ringing, feasts, and jollitie in all places, both in the
citie and countrie, for his comming . . . whosoever can tel what is
become of him, or where he may be found, let them bring him back
againe into England.

An Hue and Cry after Christmas.

In Ben Jonson's *Mask of Christmas*, presented before the court in 1616 –
wherein the ancient gentleman so earnestly inquired after in one of the
quotations which head this chapter, and a number of his children,
compose the *dramatis personæ* – that venerable personage (who describes
himself as 'Christmas, Old Christmas, Christmas of London, and Captain
Christmas') is made to give a very significant hint to some parties who fail
to receive him with due ceremony, which hint we will, in all courtesy,
bestow upon our readers. 'I have seen the time you have wished for me,'
says he . . . 'and now you have me, they would not let me in. I must come
another time! – a good jest! *As if I could come more than once a year!*' Over
and over again, too, has this same very pregnant argument been enforced
in the words of the old ballad, quoted in the 'Vindication of Christmas':

> Let's dance and sing, and make good cheer,
> For *Christmas comes but once a year!*

Now if this suggestion was full of grave meaning in the days of Jonson –
when the respectable old man was for the most part well received and
liberally feasted, when he fed with his laughing children at the tables of
princes, and took tribute at the hands of kings, when he showed beneath
the snows of his reverend head a portly countenance (the result of much

revelling), an eye in which the fire was unquenched, and a frame from which little of the lustihood had yet departed – we confess that we feel its import to be greatly heightened in these our days, when the patriarch himself exhibits undeniable signs of a failing nature, and many of his once rosy sons are evidently in the different stages of a common decline. A fine and a cheerful family the old man had; and never came they within any man's door without well repaying the outlay incurred on their account. To us, at all times, their 'coming was a gladness'; and we feel that we could not, without a pang, see their honest and familiar faces rejected from our threshold, with the knowledge that the course of their wanderings could not return them to us under a period so protracted as that of twelve whole months.

In that long space of time, besides the uncertainty of what may happen to ourselves, there is but too much reason to fear that, unless a change for the better should take place, some one or more of the neglected children may be dead. We could not but have apprehensions that the group might never return to us entire. Death has already made much havoc amongst them, since the days of Ben Jonson. Alas for Baby-cocke! And woe is me for Post-and-paire! And although Carol and Minced-pie, and New-year's Gift, and Wassail, and Twelfth-cake, and some others of the children, appear still to be in the enjoyment of a tolerably vigorous health, yet we are not a little anxious about Snap-dragon, and our mind is far from being easy on the subject of Hot-cockles. It is but too obvious that, one by one, this once numerous and pleasant family are falling away; and as the old man will assuredly not survive his children, we may yet, in our day, have to join in the heavy lamentation of the lady at the sad result of the above 'Hue and Cry'. 'But is old, old, good old Christmas gone? – nothing but the hair of his good, grave old head and beard left!' For these reasons, he and his train shall be welcome to us as often as they come. It shall be a heavy dispensation under which we will suffer them to pass by our door unhailed; and if we can prevail upon our neighbours to adopt our example, the veteran and his offspring may yet be restored. They are dying for lack of nourishment. They have been used to live on most bountiful fare – to feed on chines and turkeys and drink of the wassail bowl. The rich juices of their constitution are not to be maintained, far less re-established, at a less generous rate; and though we will, for our parts, do what lies in our power, yet it is not within the reach of any private gentleman's exertions or finances to set them on their legs again. It should be made a national matter; and as the old gentleman, with his family, will be coming our way soon after the publication of the present volume, we trust we may be the means of inducing some to receive them with the ancient welcome and feast them after the ancient fashion.

To enable our readers to do this with due effect, we will endeavour to

Snap-dragon

furnish them with a programme of some of the more important ceremonies observed by our hearty ancestors on the occasion, and to give them some explanation of those observances which linger still, although the causes in which their institution originated are becoming gradually obliterated, and although they themselves are falling into a neglect which augurs too plainly of their final and speedy extinction.

It is, alas, but too true that the spirit of hearty festivity in which our ancestors met this season has been long on the decline; and much of the joyous pomp with which it was once received has long since passed away. Those 'divers plente of plesaunces', in which the genius of mirth exhibited himself –

> About yule, when the wind blew cule,
> And the round tables began –

have sent forward to these dull times of ours but few, and those sadly degenerated, representatives. The wild, barbaric splendour; the unbridled 'mirth and princely cheare' with which, upon the faith of ancient ballads, we learn that 'ages long ago' King Arthur kept Christmas 'in merry Carleile' with Queen Guenever, 'that bride soe bright of blee'; the wholesale hospitality; the royal stores of 'pigs' heads and gammons of bacon' for a Christmas largesse to the poor, at which we get glimpses in the existing records of the not over-hospitable reign of King John; the profuse expenditure and stately ceremonial by which the season was illustrated in the reign of the vain and selfish Elizabeth; and the lordly wassailings and antic mummings, whose universal prevalence, at this period of the year, furnished subjects of such holy horror to the Puritans in the time of the first Charles – have gradually disappeared before the philosophic pretensions and chilling pedantry of these sage and self-seeking days. The picturesque effects of society – its strong lights and deep shadows – are rapidly passing away; as the inequalities of surface from which they were projected are smoothed and polished down. From a period of high ceremonial and public celebration, which it long continued to be in England, the Christmas-tide has tamed away into a period of domestic union and social festivity; and the ancient observances which covered it all over with sparkling points are now rather perceived – faintly and distantly and imperfectly – by the light of the still surviving spirit of the season than contribute anything to that spirit, or throw as of old any light over that season from themselves.

Of the various causes which contribute to the mingled festival of the Christmas-tide, there are some which have their origin in feelings, and are the remains of observances that existed previously to that event from which the season now derives its name. After the establishment of Christianity, its earliest teachers, feeling the impossibility of replacing at once those pagan commemorations which had taken long and deep root in the constitution of society and become identified with the feelings of nations, endeavoured rather to purify them from their uncleanness, and adapt them to the uses of the new religion. By this arrangement, many an object of pagan veneration became an object of veneration to the early Christians; and the polytheism of papal Rome (promoted, in part, by this very compromise, working in the stronghold of the ancient superstition) became engrafted upon the polytheism of the heathen. At a later period, too, the Protestant reformers of that corrupted worship found themselves, from a similar impossibility, under a similar necessity of retaining a variety of Catholic observances; and thus it is that festival customs still exist amongst us which are the direct descendants of customs connected with the classic or druidical superstitions, and sports which may be traced to the celebrations observed of old in honour of Saturn or of Bacchus.

Amongst those celebrations which have thus survived the decay of the religions with which they were connected, by being made subservient to the new faith (or purified forms) which replaced them, that which takes place at the period of the new year – placed as that epoch is in the neighbourhood of the winter solstice – stands conspicuous. Bequeathed as this ancient commemoration has been, with many of its forms of rejoicing, by the pagan to the Christian world, it has been by the latter thrown into close association with their own festival observances in honour of the first great event in the history of their revelation; and while the old observances and the feelings in which they originated have thus been preserved to swell the tide of Christian triumph, their pedigree has been overlooked amid the far higher interest of the observances by whose side they stand, and their ancient titles merged in that of the high family into which they have been adopted.

In most nations of ancient or modern times, the period of what is popularly called the winter solstice appears to have been recognised as a season of rejoicing. The deepening gloom and increasing sterility which have followed the downward progress of the sun's place in heaven would generally dispose the minds of men to congratulation at the arrival of that period when, as experience had taught them, he had reached his lowest point of influence with reference to *them;* and the prospects of renewed light, and warmth, and vegetation offered by what was considered as his returning march, would naturally be hailed by the signs of thanksgiving and the voice of mirth. The Roman Saturnalia, which fell at this period, were accordingly a season of high festivity, honoured by many privileges and many exemptions from ill. The spirit of universal mirth and un-bounded licence was abroad, and had a free charter. Friends feasted together, and the quarrels of foes were suspended. No war was declared and no capital executions were permitted to take place during this season of general goodwill; and the very slave, beneath its genial influence, regained for a moment the moral attitude of a man, and had a right to use the tongue which God had given him, for its original purpose of expressing his thoughts. Not only in the spirit of the time but in many of the forms which it took, may a resemblance be traced to the Christmas rejoicings of later days. The hymns in honour of Saturn were the Roman representatives of the modern carol; and presents passed from friend to friend, as Christmas gifts do in our day. (It may be observed here that the inter-change of gifts and the offering of donations to the poor appear to have been, at all periods of rejoicing or delivery, from the earliest times, one of the modes by which the heart manifested its thankfulness; and our readers may be referred for a single example, where examples abound, to the directions recorded in the Book of Esther, as given by Mordecai to the Jews in Shushan, for celebrating their escape from the conspiracy of Haman: that on the anniversaries of 'the days wherein the Jews rested from their enemies, and the month which was turned unto them from sorrow to joy and from mourning into a goodday, they should make them days of feasting and joy, and of sending portions one to another and gifts to the poor.') But a more striking resemblance still between the forms observed during the days of the Saturnalia and those by which the Christmas festival was long illustrated may be noticed in the ruler, or king, who was appointed, with considerable prerogatives, to preside over the sports of the former. He is the probable ancestor of that high potentate who, under the title of Christmas Prince, Lord of Misrule, or Abbot of Unreason, exercised a similar sway over the Christmas games of more recent times, and whose last descendant – the Twelfth Night King – still rules with a diminished glory over the lingering revelries of a single night.

In the northern nations of ancient Europe the same period of the year was celebrated by a festival in honour of the god, Thor, which, like the Roman Saturnalia and the festival of our own times, was illustrated by the song, the dance, and the feast, executed after their barbarous fashion, and mingled with the savage rites of their own religion. The name of this celebration – Yule, Jule, Iul, or Iol – has given rise to many disputes amongst antiquaries as to its derivation, whose arguments, however, we need not report for the benefit of our readers till judgment shall have been finally pronounced. When that time shall arrive, we undertake to publish a new edition of the present work, for the purpose of giving our readers an abstract of the pleadings and acquainting them with the ultimate decision. In the meantime, we will let Sir Walter Scott inform them how –

> The savage Dane,
> At Iol, more deep the mead did drain;
> High on the beach his galleys drew,
> And feasted all his pirate-crew;
> Then, in his low and pine-built hall,
> Where shields and axes decked the wall,
> They gorged upon the half-dressed steer,
> Caroused in sea of sable beer –
> While round, in brutal jest, were thrown
> The half-gnawed rib and marrow-bone;
> Or listened all, in grim delight,
> While Scalds yelled out the joys of fight.
> Then forth in frenzy would they hie,
> While wildly loose their red locks fly,
> And, dancing round the blazing pile,
> They made such barbarous mirth the while,
> As best might to the mind recall
> The boisterous joys of Odin's hall.

Amongst other traces of the northern observances which have descended to our times, and of which we shall have occasion hereafter to speak, the name of the festival itself has come down, and is still retained by our Scottish brethren, as well as in some parts of England.

The Christian festival of the Nativity, with which these ancient celebrations have been incorporated, appears to have been appointed at a very early period after the establishment of the new religion. Its first positive footsteps are met with in the second century, during the reign of the Emperor Commodus; but the decretal epistles furnish us with traces of it more remote. At whatever period, however, its formal institution is to be placed, there can be no doubt that an event so striking in its manner and so important in itself would be annually commemorated amongst Christians from the days of the first apostles, who survived our Lord's resurrection. As to the actual year of the birth of Christ, as well as the *period* of the year at which it took place, great uncertainty seems to exist, and many controversies have been maintained. One of the theories on the subject, held to be amongst the most probable, places that event upwards of five years earlier than the vulgar era, which latter, however, both as regards the year and *season* of the year, was a tradition of the primitive Church. In the first ages of that Church, and up till the Council of Nice, the celebration of the Nativity and that of the Epiphany were united on the 25th of December, from a belief that the birth of Christ was simultaneous with the appearance of the star in the East which revealed it to the Gentiles. The time of the year at which the Nativity fell has been placed, by contending opinions, at the period of the Jewish Feast of Tabernacles, at that of the Passover, and again at that of the Feast of the Expiation, whose date corresponds with the close of our September. Clemens Alexandrinus informs us that it was kept by many Christians in April, and by others in the Egyptian month Pachon, which answers to our May. Amongst the arguments which have been produced against the theory that places its occurrence in the depth of winter, one has been gathered from that passage in the sacred history of the event which states that 'there were shepherds abiding in the field, keeping watch over their flocks by night'. It is an argument, however, which does not seem very conclusive in a pastoral country and Eastern climate. Besides the employment which this question has afforded to the learned, it has, in times of religious excitement, been debated with much Puritanical virulence and sectarian rancour. For the purposes of commemoration, however, it is unimportant whether the celebration shall fall or not at the precise anniversary period of the event commemorated; and the arrangement which assigns to it its place in our calendar fixes it at a season when men have leisure for a lengthened festivity, and when their minds are otherwise wholesomely acted upon by many touching thoughts and solemn considerations.

From the first introduction of Christianity into these islands, the period of the Nativity seems to have been kept as a season of festival, and its observance recognised as a matter of state. The Wittenagemots of our

Saxon ancestors were held under the solemn sanctions and beneficent influences of the time; and the series of high festivities established by the Anglo-Saxon kings appear to have been continued, with yearly increasing splendour and multiplied ceremonies, under the monarchs of the Norman race. From the court the spirit of revelry descended by all its thousand arteries throughout the universal frame of society, visiting its furthest extremities and most obscure recesses, and everywhere exhibiting its action, as by so many pulses, upon the traditions and superstitions and customs which were common to all or peculiar to each. The pomp and ceremonial of the royal observance were imitated in the splendid establishments of the more wealthy nobles, and more faintly reflected from the diminished state of the petty baron. The revelries of the baronial castle found echoes in the hall of the old manor-house; and these were, again, repeated in the tapestried chamber of the country magistrate or from the sanded parlour of the village inn. Merriment was everywhere a matter of public concernment; and the spirit which assembles men in families now congregated them by districts then.

Neither, however, were the feelings wanting which connected the superstitions of the season with the tutelage of the rooftree, and mingled its ceremonies with the sanctities of home. Men might meet in crowds to feast beneath the banner of the baron, but the mistletoe hung over each man's own door. The black-jacks might go round in the hall of the lord of the manor; but they who could had a wassail bowl of their own. The pageantries and high observances of the time might draw men to common centres or be performed on a common account, but the flame of the Yule log roared up all the individual chimneys of the land. Old Father Christmas, at the head of his numerous and uproarious family, might ride his goat through the streets of the city and the lanes of the village, but he dismounted to sit for some few moments by each man's hearth; while some one or another of his merry sons would break away, to visit the remote farmhouses or show their laughing faces at many a poor man's door. For be it observed, this worthy old gentleman and his kind-hearted children were no respecters of persons. Though trained to courts, they had ever a taste for a country life. Though accustomed in those days to the tables of princes, they sat freely down at the poor man's board. Though welcomed by the peer, they showed no signs of superciliousness when they found themselves cheek-by-jowl with the pauper. Nay, they appear even to have preferred the less exalted society, and to have felt themselves more at ease in the country mansion of the private gentleman than in the halls of kings. Their reception in those high places was accompanied, as royal receptions are apt to be, by a degree of state repugnant to their frank natures; and they seem never to have been so happy as when they found

The Baronial Hall

themselves amongst a set of free and easy spirits – whether in town or country – unrestrained by the punctilios of etiquette, who had the privilege of laughing just when it struck them to do so, without inquiring wherefore, or caring how loud.

Then, what a festival they created! The land rang with their joyous voices, and the frosty air steamed with the incense of the good things provided for their entertainment. Everybody kept holiday but the cooks; and all sounds known to the human ear seemed mingled in the merry pæan, save the gobble of the turkeys. *There were no turkeys* – at least they had lost their 'most sweet voices'. The turnspits had a hard time of it, too. That quaint little book which bears the warm and promising title of 'Round about our Coal Fire' tells us that 'by the time dinner was over they would look as black and as greasy as a Welsh porridge-pot'. Indeed, the accounts of that time dwell with great and savoury emphasis upon the prominent share which eating and drinking had in the festivities of the season. There must have been sad havoc made amongst the livestock. That there are turkeys at all in our days is only to be accounted for upon the supposition of England having been occasionally replenished with that article from the East; and our present possession of geese must be explained by the well-known impossibility of extinguishing the race of the goose. It is difficult to imagine a consumption equal to the recorded provision. Men's gastronomic capacities appear to have been enlarged for the occasion, as the energies expand to meet great emergencies. 'The tables,' says the same racy authority above quoted, 'were all spread from the first to the last; the sirloyns of beef, the minc'd-pies, the plumb-porridge, the capons, turkeys, geese, and plumb-puddings were all brought upon the board; and all those who had sharp stomachs and sharp knives eat heartily and were welcome, which gave rise to the proverb –

Merry in the hall, when beards wag all!'

Now, *all* men in those days appear to have had good stomachs, and, we presume, took care to provide themselves with sharp knives. The only recorded instance in which we find a failure of the latter is that portentous one which occurred, many a long day since, in the court of King Arthur, when the Christmas mirth was so strangely disturbed by the mischievous interference of the Boy with the Mantle. Under the test introduced by that imp of discord and which appears to have 'taken the shine out of' the monarch's own good sword Excalibur itself, there was found but one knight, of all the hungry knights who sat at that Round Table, whose weapon was sharp enough to carve the boar's head or hand steady enough to carry the cup to his lip without spilling the lamb's wool; and even he had a very narrow escape from the same incapacities. But then, as we have said, this was at court, and under the influence of a spell (with whose nature we take it for granted that our readers are acquainted – and, if not, we refer them to the Percy Ballads); and it is probable that, in those early as in later days, tests of such extreme delicacy were of far more dangerous introduction in the courts of kings than amongst assemblies of more mirth and less pretension. We could by no means feel sure that the intrusion, in our own times, of a similar test into a similar scene might not spoil the revels.

But to return. The old ballads which relate to this period of the year are redolent of good things, and not to be read by a hungry man with any degree of equanimity. Of course, they are *ex post facto* ballads, and could have been written only under the inspiration of memory, at a time when men were at leisure to devote their hands to some other occupation than that of cooking or carving. But it is very difficult to understand how they ever found – as it appears they did – their mouths in a condition to sing them at the season itself. There is one amongst those ballads, of a comparatively modern date, printed in Evans's collection, which we advise no man to read fasting. It is directed to be sung to the tune of 'The Delights of the Bottle', and contains in every verse a vision of good things, summed up by the perpetually recurring burden of

Plum-pudding, goose, capon, minc'd-pies, and roast beef.

Our readers had better take a biscuit and a glass of sherry before they venture upon the glimpses into those regions of banqueting which we are tempted to lay before them. The ballad opens like the ringing of a dinner-bell, and, we conceive, should be sung to some such accompaniment:

Enjoying Christmas

All you that to feasting and mirth are inclin'd,
Come here is good news for to pleasure your mind –
Old Christmas is come for to keep open house,
He scorns to be guilty of starving a mouse:
Then come, boys, and welcome for diet the chief,
Plum-pudding, goose, capon, minc'd-pies, and roast beef.

'Diet *the chief*'! – by which we are to understand that this promising muster-roll merely includes the names of some of the principal viands – the high-commissioned dishes of the feast – leaving the subalterns, and the entire rank and file which complete the goodly array, unmentioned. It must have been a very ingenious or a very strong-minded mouse which could contrive to be starved under such circumstances. The ballad is long, and we can afford to give our readers only 'tastings' of its good things. It is everywhere full of most gracious promise:

The cooks shall be busied, by day and by night,
In roasting and boiling, for taste and delight,
Their senses in liquor that's nappy they'll steep,
Though they be afforded to have little sleep;
They still are employed for to dress us, in brief,
Plum-pudding, goose, capon, minc'd-pies, and roast beef.

Although the cold weather doth hunger provoke,
'Tis a comfort to see how the chimneys do smoke;
Provision is making for beer, ale, and wine,
For *all that are willing or ready to dine:*
Then haste to the kitchen for diet the chief,
Plum-pudding, goose, capon, minc'd-pies, and roast beef.

All travellers, as they do pass on their way,
At gentlemen's halls are invited to stay,
Themselves to refresh and their horses to rest,
Since that he must be old Christmas's guest;
Nay, the poor shall not want, but have for relief
Plum-pudding, goose, capon, minc'd-pies, and roast beef.

And so on, through a variety of joyous and substantial anticipations, from which the writer draws an inference, which we think is most satisfactorily made out:

Then *well may we welcome* old Christmas to town,
Who brings us good cheer, and good liquor so brown;
To pass the cold winter away with delight,
We feast it all day, and we frolick all night.

In Ellis's edition of Brand's *Popular Antiquities,* an old Christmas song is quoted from 'Poor Robin's Almanack' for 1695, which gives a similar enumeration of Christmas dainties, but throws them into a form calculated for more rapid enunciation, as if with a due regard to the value of those moments at which it was probably usual to sing it. The measure is not such a mouthful as that of the former one which we have quoted. It comes trippingly off the tongue; and it is not impossible that, in those days of skilful gastronomy, it might have been sung eating. We will quote a couple of the verses, though they include the same commissariat truths as that from which we have already extracted; and our readers will observe, from the ill-omened wish which concludes the second of these stanzas, in what horror the mere idea of *fasting* had come to be held, since it is the heaviest curse which suggested itself to be launched against those who refused to do homage to the spirit of the times:

> Now thrice welcome Christmas,
>   Which brings us good cheer,
> Minc'd pies and plumb-porridge,
>   Good ale and strong beer;
>
> With pig, goose, and capon,
>   The best that may be,
> So well doth the weather
>   And our stomachs agree.
>
> Observe how the chimneys
>   Do smoak all about,
> The cooks are providing
>   For dinner no doubt;
> But those on whose tables
>   No victuals appear,
> *O may they keep Lent*
> *All the rest of the year!*

The same author quotes, from a manuscript in the British Museum, an Anglo-Norman carol of the early date of the thirteenth century, and appends to it a translation by the late Mr Douce, the following verse of which translation informs us (what, at any rate, might well be supposed, namely) that so much good eating on the part of the ancient gentleman, Christmas, would naturally suggest the propriety of good drinking, too:

> Lordings, Christmas loves good drinking,
>   Wines of Gascoigne, France, Anjou,
> English ale, that drives out thinking,
>   Prince of liquors old or new.
> Every neighbour shares the bowl,
>   Drinks of the spicy liquor deep,
> Drinks his fill without controul,
>   Till he drowns his care in sleep.

In a "Christmas Carroll", printed at the end of Wither's *Juvenilia*, a graphic account is given of some of the humours of Christmas, among which the labours of the kitchen are introduced in the *first* verse, with a due regard to their right of precedency, and in words which, if few, are full of suggestion:

> Lo, now is come our joyful'st feast!
>   Let every man be jolly.
> Each roome with yvie leaves is drest,
>   And every post with holly.

Now, all our neighbour's chimneys smoke,
    And Christmas Blocks are burning;
Their ovens they with bak't-meats choke,
    And all their spits are turning.

We must present our readers with another quotation from an old ballad, entitled 'Time's Alteration; or, The Old Man's Rehearsal, what brave dayes he knew a great while agone, when his old cap was new', which appears to have been written after the times of the Commonwealth. And this extract we are induced to add to those which have gone before, because, though it deals with precisely the same subjects, it speaks of them as of things gone by, and is written in a tone of lamentation, in which it is one of the purposes of this chapter to call upon our readers to join. We are sorry we cannot give them directions as to the tune to which it should be sung – further than that it is obviously unsuited to that of the 'Delights of the Bottle', prescribed for the joyous ballad from which we first quoted on this subject; and that, whatever may be the *tune*, we are clear that the direction as to *time* should be the same as that which Mr Hood prefixes to his song of the Guildhall Giants; namely, 'Dinner-time and mournful':

A man might then behold,
    At Christmas in each hall,
Good fires to curb the cold,
    And meat for great and small;
The neighbours were friendly bidden,
    And all had welcome true,
The poor from the gates were not chidden,
    When this old cap was new.

Black-jacks to every man
    Were fill'd with wine and beer;
No pewter pot nor can
    In those days did appear;
Good cheer in a nobleman's house
    Was counted a seemly shew;
We wanted no brawn nor souse,
    When this old cap was new.

Can our readers bear, after this sad ditty, to listen to the enumeration of good things described by Whistlecraft to have been served up at King Arthur's table on Christmas day? If the list be authentic, there is the less reason to wonder at the feats of courage and strength performed by the Knights of the Round Table.

They served up salmon, venison, and wild boars,
By hundreds, and by dozens, and by scores.

Hogsheads of honey, kilderkins of mustard,
   Muttons, and fatted beeves, and bacon swine;
Herons and bitterns, peacocks, swan, and bustard,
   Teal, mallard, pigeons, widgeons, and, in fine,
Plum-puddings, pancakes, apple-pies, and custard.
   And therewithal they drank good Gascon wine,
With mead, and ale, and cider of our own;
For porter, punch, and negus were not known.

But we cannot pursue this matter further. It is not to be treated with any degree of calmness before dinner, and we have not dined. We must proceed to less trying parts of our subject.

Of the earnest manner in which our ancestors set about the celebration of this festival, the mock ceremonial with which they illustrated it, the quaint humours which they let loose under its inspiration, and the spirit of fellowship which brought all classes of men within the range of its beneficent provisions, we have a large body of scattered evidence, to be gleaned out of almost every species of existing record, from the early days of the Norman dynasty down to the times of the Commonwealth. The tales of chroniclers, the olden ballads, the rolls of courts, and the statute-book of the land, all contribute to furnish the materials from which a revival of the old pageantry must be derived, if men should ever again find time to be as merry as their fathers were.

The numberless *local* customs of which the still remaining tradition is almost the sole record, and which added each its small contingent to the aggregate of commemoration, would certainly render it a somewhat difficult matter to restore the festival in its integrity; and, to be very candid with our readers, we believe we may as well confess, at the onset, what will be very apparent to them before we have done, that many of the Christmas observances (whether general or local) are to be recommended to their notice rather as curious pictures of ancient manners than as being at all worthy of imitation by us who 'are wiser in our generation'. Sooth to say, we dare not let our zeal for our subject lead us into an unqualified approbation of all the doings which it will be our business to record in these pages, though they seem to have made all ranks of people very happy in other days – and that is no mean test of the value of any institution. Really earnest as we are in the wish that the *sentiment* of the season could be restored in its amplitude, we fear that many of the fooleries by which it exhibited itself could not be gravely proposed as worthy amusements for a nation of philosophers.

Still these very absurdities furnish the strongest evidences of the right goodwill with which men – ay, grave and learned men – surrendered themselves to the merry spirit of the time, of that entire abandonment which forgot to make a reservation of their outward dignities and gave them courage to 'play the fool'. Our readers need scarcely be told that it must be a man of a very strong mind, or a man who could not help it, who should dare to make a Jack-pudding of himself in these days, when all his fellows are walking about the world with telescopes in their hands and quadrants in their pockets. No doubt it would have a somewhat ridiculous effect today to see the members of the bar dancing a galliard or a coranto, in full costume, before the Benchers, notwithstanding that certain ancient forms are still retained in their halls which have all the absurdity of the exploded ones without any of their fun; and unquestionably we should think it rather strange to see a respectable gentleman capering through the streets on a pasteboard hobby-horse – in lieu of the figurative hobby-horses on which most men still exhibit – although even that, we think, would offer an object less ungracious than a child with an anxious brow and 'spectacles on nose'. The great wisdom of the world is, we presume, one of the natural consequences of its advancing age; and though we are quite conscious that some of its former pranks would be very unbecoming, now that it is getting into years, and 'knows so much as it does', yet we are by no means sure that we should not have been well content to have our lot cast in the days when it was somewhat younger. They must have been very pleasant times! Certain it is that the laugh of the humbler classes, and of the younger classes, would be all the heartier, that it was echoed by the powerful and the aged; the mirth of the ignorant more free and genial, that the learned thought no scorn of it. For all that appears, too, the dignities of those days suffered no detriment by their surrender to the spirit of the times, but seem to have resumed all their functions and privileges, when it had exhausted itself, with unimpaired effect. Philosophers had due reverence, without erecting themselves always on stilts for the purpose of attracting it; and names have come down to us which are esteemed the names of grave and learned and wise men – even in this grave and learned and wise age – who, nevertheless, appear in their own to have conducted themselves at times very like children.

From the royal Household-Books which exist, and from the Household-Books of noble families (some of which have been printed for better preservation), as also from the other sources to which we have alluded, Mr Sandys, in the very valuable introduction to his collection of Christmas carols, already mentioned, has brought together a body of valuable information – both as to the stately ceremonies and popular observances by which the season continued to be illustrated, from an early period up to the time of its decline, amid the austerities of the civil war. To this careful compilation we shall be occasionally indebted for some curious particulars which had escaped ourselves, amid the multiplied and unconnected sources from which our notes for this volume had to be made. To those who would go deeper into the antiquarian part of the subject than suits the purpose of a popular volume, we can recommend that work, as containing the most copious and elaborate synopsis of the existing information connected therewith which we have found in the course of our own researches. It would be impossible, however, in a paper of that length – or, indeed, in a volume of any moderate size – to give an account of all the numerous superstitions and observances of which traces are found, in an extended inquiry, to exist – throwing light upon each other and contributing to the complete history of the festival. We have therefore gleaned from all quarters those which appear to be the most picturesque and whose relation is the most obvious, with a view, as much as possible, of generalising the subject and presenting its parts in relation to an intelligible whole.

As we shall have occasion, in our second part, to speak of those *peculiar* feelings and customs by which each of the several days of the Christmas festival is specially illustrated, we shall not at present pause to go into any of the details of the subject, although continually tempted to do so by their connection with the observations which we are called upon to make. The purpose of the present chapter is rather to insist generally, and by some of its more striking features, upon the high and lengthened festivity with which this portion of the year was so long and so universally welcomed, and to seek some explanation of the causes to which the diminution of that spirit, and the almost total neglect of its ancient forms, are to be ascribed.

As early as the twelfth century we have accounts of the spectacles and pageants by which Christmas was welcomed at the court of the then monarch Henry II; and from this period the wardrobe rolls and other Household-Books of the English kings furnish continual evidences of the costly preparations made for the festival. Many extracts from these books have been made by Mr Sandys and others, from which it appears that the mirth of the celebration, and the lavish profusion expended upon it, were on the increase from year to year, excepting during that distracted period of England's history when these, like all other gracious arrangements and social relations, were disturbed by the unholy contests between the houses of the rival roses. There is, however, a beautiful example of the sacred influence of this high festival mentioned by Turner in his *History of England*, showing that its hallowed presence had power, even in those warlike days, to silence even the voice of war – of all war save that most impious of (what are almost always impious) wars, civil war. During the siege of Orleans, in 1428, he says: 'The solemnities and festivities of

Christmas gave a short interval of repose. The English lords requested of the French commanders that they might have a night of minstrelsy, with trumpets and clarions. This was granted; and the horrors of war were suspended by melodies, that were felt to be delightful.'

In the peaceful reign of Henry VII, the nation, on emerging from that long and unnatural struggle, appears to have occupied itself, as did the wise monarch, in restoring as far as was possible, and by all means, its disrupted ties, and rebaptising its apostate feelings; and during this period the festival of Christmas was restored with revived splendour and observed with renewed zeal. The Household-Book of that sovereign, preserved in the chapterhouse at Westminster, contains numerous items for disbursements connected with the Christmas diversions, in proof of this fact.

The reign of Henry VIII was a reign of jousts and pageants till it became a reign of blood; and accordingly the Christmas pageantries prepared for the entertainment of that execrable monarch were distinguished by increased pomp and furnished at a more profuse expenditure. The festivities of Eltham and Greenwich figure in the pages of the old chroniclers; and the account books at the chapterhouse abound in payments made in this reign, for purposes connected with the revels of the season.

We shall by and by have occasion to present our readers with some curious particulars, illustrative of the cost and pains bestowed upon this court celebration during the short reign of the young monarch Edward VI.

Not all the gloom and terror of the sanguinary Mary's reign were able entirely to extinguish the spirit of Christmas rejoicing throughout the land, though the court itself was too much occupied with its auto-da-fé spectacles to have much time for pageants of less interest.

Our readers, we think, need scarcely be told that the successor of this stern and miserable queen (and, thank God, the last of that bad family) was sure to seize upon the old pageantries, as she did upon every other vehicle which could in any way be made to minister to her intolerable vanity, or by which a public exhibition might be made, before the slaves whom she governed, of her own vulgar and brutal mind. Under all the forms of ancient festival observance, some offering was presented to this insatiable and disgusting appetite – and that, too, by men entitled to stand erect, by their genius or their virtues, yet whose knees were rough with kneeling before as worthless an idol as any wooden god that the most senseless superstition ever set up for worship. From all the altars which the court had reared to old Father Christmas of yore, a cloud of incense was poured into the royal closet, enough to choke anything but a woman – that woman a queen, and that queen a Tudor. The festival was preserved, and even embellished; but the saint, as far as the court was concerned, was changed. However, the example of the festivity to the people was the same; and the land was a merry land, and the Christmas time a merry time, throughout its length and breadth, in the days of Queen Elizabeth.

Nay, out of this very anxiety to minister to the craving vanity of a weak and worthless woman – the devices to which it gave rise and the labourers whom it called into action – have arisen results which are not amongst the least happy or important of those by its connection with which the Christmas festival stands recommended. Under these impulses, the old dramatic entertainments – of which we shall have occasion to speak more at large hereafter – took a higher character and assumed a more consistent form. The first regular English tragedy, called 'Ferrex and Porrex', and the entertainment of 'Gammer Gurton's Needle', were both productions of the early period of this queen's reign; and amid the crowd of her worshippers (alas that it is so!) rose up – with the star upon his forehead which is to burn for all time – the very first of all created beings, William Shakespeare. These are amongst the strange anomalies which the world, as it is constituted, so often presents, and *must* present at times, constitute it how we will. Shakespeare doing homage to Queen Elizabeth! The loftiest genius and the noblest heart that have yet walked this earth, in a character merely human, bowing down before this woman with the soul of a milliner and no heart at all! The 'bright particular star' humbling itself before the temporal crown! The swayer of hearts, the ruler of all men's minds, in virtue of his own transcendent nature, recognising the supremacy of this overgrown child, because she presided over the temporalities of a half emancipated nation, by rights derived to her from others and sanctioned by no qualities of her own!

And yet if to the low passions of this vulgar queen, and the patronage which they led her to extend to all who could best minister to their gratification, we owe any part of that development by which this consummate genius expanded itself, then do we stand in some degree indebted to her for one of the greatest boons which has been bestowed upon the human race; and as between her and mankind in general (for the accounts between her and individuals, and still more that between her and God, stand uninfluenced by this item), there is a large amount of good to be placed to her credit. Against her follies of a day there would have to be set her promotion of a wisdom whose lessons are for all time; against the tears which she caused to flow, the human anguish which she inflicted, and the weary, pining hours of the captives whom she made, would stand the tears of thousands dried away, many and many an aching heart beguiled of its sorrow, and many a captive taught to feel that

> Stone walls do not a prison make,
> Nor iron bars a cage;

all the chords of human feeling touched with a hand that soothes as did the harp of David, all the pages of human suffering stored with consolations!

To anyone who will amuse himself by looking over the Miracle Plays and Masques, which were replaced by the more regular forms of dramatic entertainment, and will then regale himself by the perusal of 'Gammer Gurton's Needle' or 'Ferrex and Porrex', which came forward with higher pretensions in the beginning of this reign, there will appear reason to be sufficiently astonished at the rapid strides by which dramatic excellence was attained before its close and during the next, even without taking Shakespeare into the account at all. But when we turn to the marvels of this great magician, and find that in his hands not only were the forms of the drama perfected, but that, without impeding the action or impairing the interest invested in those forms, and besides his excursions into the regions of imagination and his creations *out of* the natural world, he has touched every branch of human knowledge and struck into every train of human thought; that without learning, in the popular sense, he has arrived at all the results and embodied all the wisdom which learning is only useful if it teaches; that we can be placed in no imaginable circumstances and under the influence of no possible feelings of which we do not find exponents – and *such* exponents! – 'in sweetest music', on his page; and above all, when we find that all the final morals to be drawn from all his writings are hopeful ones, that all the lessons which all his agents – joy or sorrow, pain or pleasure – are made alike to teach are lessons of goodness – it is impossible to attribute all this to aught but a revelation, or ascribe to him any character but that of a prophet. Shakespeare knew more than any other mere man ever knew; and none can tell how that knowledge came to him. 'All men's business and bosoms' lay open to him. We should not like to have him quoted against us on *any* subject. Nothing escaped him, and he never made a mistake (we are not speaking of technical ones). He was the universal interpreter into language of the human mind, and he knew all the myriad voices by which nature speaks. He reminds us of the vizier in the Eastern story, who is said to have understood the languages of all animals. The utterings of the elements, the voices of beasts and of birds, Shakespeare could translate into the language of men; and the thoughts and sentiments of men he rendered into words as sweet as the singing of birds. If the reign of Elizabeth had been illustrated only by the advent of this great spirit, it might itself have accounted for some portion of that prejudice which (illustrated, as in fact it was, by much that was great and noble) blinds men still – or induces them to shut their eyes – to the true personal claims and character of that queen.

But we are digressing, again, as who does not when the image of Shakespeare comes across him? To return.

Mummers

The court celebrations of Christmas were observed throughout the reign of the first James; and the Prince Charles himself was an occasional performer in the pageantries prepared for the occasion, at great cost. But at no period do they appear to have been more zealously sought after, or performed with more splendour, than during that which immediately preceded the persecution, from whose effects they have never since recovered into anything like their former lustihood. In the early years of Charles the First's reign, the court pageants of this season were got up with extraordinary brilliancy – the king with the lords of his court, and the queen with her ladies, frequently taking parts therein. This was the case in 1630-31; and at the Christmas of 1632–3 the queen, says Sandys, 'got up a pastoral in Somerset House, in which it would seem she herself took a part. There were masques at the same time, independent of this perform-ance, the cost of which considerably exceeded £2,000, besides that portion of the charge which was borne by the office of the revels and charged to the accounts of that department.' In the same year, we learn that a grant of £450 was made to George Kirke, Esq., gentleman of the robes, for the *masking attire* of the king and his party. In 1637 there is a warrant, under the privy seal, to the same George Kirke for £150, to provide the masking dress of the king; and, in the same year, another to Edmund Taverner for £1,400 towards the expenses of a masque to be presented at Whitehall on the ensuing Twelfth Night. We have selected these from similar examples furnished by Sandys, in order to give our readers some idea of the sums expended in these entertainments, which sums will appear very considerable when estimated by the difference between the value of money in our days and that of two hundred years ago. Several of the masques presented at court during this reign, and the preceding ones, were written by Ben Jonson.

During the whole of this time, the forms of court ceremonial appear to have been aped, and the royal establishments imitated as far as possible, by the more powerful nobles; and the masques and pageantries exhibited for the royal amusement were accordingly reproduced or rivalled by them at their princely mansions in the country. Corporate and other public bodies caught the infection all over the land; and each landed proprietor and country squire endeavoured to enact such state in the eyes of his own retainers, as his means would allow. The sports and festivities of the season were everywhere taken under the protection of the lord of the soil; and all classes of his dependants had a customary claim upon the hospitalities which he prepared for the occasion. The masques of the court and of the nobles were imitated in the mummings of the people – of which we give a representation here, and which we shall have occasion particularly to describe hereafter – they having survived the costly pageants of which they were the humble representatives. The festival was thus rendered a universal one, and its amusements brought within the reach of the indigent and the remote. The peasant, and even the pauper, were made, as it were, once a year sharers in the mirth of their immediate lord, and even of the monarch himself. The labouring classes had enlarged privileges during this season, not only by custom, but by positive enactment; and restrictive Acts of Parliament, by which they were prohibited from certain games at other periods, contained exceptions in favor of the Christmas-tide. Nay, folly was, as it were, crowned, and disorder had a licence! Sandys quotes from Leland the form of a proclamation given in his 'Itinerary' as having been made by the sheriff of York, wherein it is declared that all 'thieves, dice-players, carders' (with some other characters by name that are usually repudiated by the guardians of order) '*and all other unthrifty folke*, be welcome to the towne, whether they come late or early, att the reverence of the high feast of Youle, till the twelve dayes be passed'. The terms of this proclamation were, no doubt, not intended to be construed in a grave and literal sense, but were probably meant to convey something like a satire upon the unbounded licence of the season which they thus announce.

There are very pleasant evidences of the care which was formerly taken, in high quarters, that the poor should not be robbed of their share in this festival. The yearly increasing splendour of the royal celebrations appears at one time to have threatened that result, by attracting the country gentlemen from their own seats, and thereby withdrawing them from the presidency of those sports which were likely to languish in their absence.

Accordingly, we find an order, in 1589, issued to the gentlemen of Norfolk and Suffolk, commanding them 'to depart from London before Christmas, and to repair to their countries, there to keep hospitality amongst their neighbours'. And similar orders appear to have been from time to time necessary, and from time to time repeated.

Amongst those bodies who were distinguished for the zeal of their Christmas observances, honourable mention may be made of the two English universities; and we shall have occasion hereafter to show that traces of the old ceremonials linger still in those their ancient haunts. But the reader who is unacquainted with this subject would scarcely be prepared to look for the most conspicuous celebration of these revels, with all their antics and mummeries, in the grave and dusty retreats of the law. Such, however, was the case. The lawyers beat the doctors hollow. Their ancient halls have rung with the sounds of a somewhat barbarous revelry; and the walls thereof, had they voices, could tell many an old tale, which the present occupants might not consider as throwing any desirable light upon the historical dignities of the body to which they belong. Our readers, no doubt, remember a certain scene in *Guy Mannering*, wherein the farmer Dinmont and Colonel Mannering are somewhat inconsiderately intruded upon the carousals of Mr Counsellor Pleydell at his tavern in the city of Edinburgh and find that worthy lawyer in what are called his 'altitudes', being deeply engaged in the ancient and not very solemn pastime of 'High Jinks'. Their memory may probably present the counsellor 'enthroned as a monarch in an elbow-chair placed on the dining-table, his scratch-wig on one side, his head crowned with a bottle-slider, his eye leering with an expression betwixt fun and the effects of wine', and recall, assisted by the jingle, some of the high discourse of his surrounding court:

'Where is Gerunto now? and what's become of him?'
'Gerunto's drowned, because he could not swim,' etc.

Now, if our readers shall be of opinion – as Colonel Mannering and the farmer were – that the attitude and the occupation were scarcely consistent with the dignity of a gentleman whom they had come to consult on very grave matters, we may be as much to blame as was the tavern-waiter on that occasion, in introducing them to the revels of the Inns of Court. We will do what we can to soften such censure by stating that there certainly appears at times to have arisen a suspicion, in the minds of a portion of the profession, that the wig and gown were not figuring to the best possible advantage on these occasions. For, in the reign of the first James, we find an order issued by the benchers of Lincoln's Inn, whereby the 'under barristers were, by decimation, put out of commons because the whole bar offended by not dancing on Candlemas Day preceding, according to the ancient order of the society, when the judges were present'; and this order is accompanied by a threat 'that, if the fault were repeated, they should be fined or disbarred'.

There seems to have been a contest between the four Inns of Court as to which should get up these pageantries with the greatest splendour, and occasionally a struggle between the desire of victory and the disinclination, or perhaps inability, to furnish the heavy cost at which that victory was to be secured. Most curious particulars on these subjects are furnished by the account-books of the houses: by the *Gesta Grayorum* (which was published for the purpose of describing a celebrated Christmas kept at Gray's Inn in 1594, and had its title imitated from the then popular work called the *Gesta Romanorum*); by Dugdale, in his *Origines Juridiciales*; and by Nichols, in his *Progresses of Queen Elizabeth*. For some time Lincoln's Inn appears to have carried it all its own way, having been first on the ground. The Christmas celebrations seem to have been kept by this society from as early a period as the reign of Henry VI; although it was not until the reign of Henry VIII that they began to grow into celebrity, or at least that we have any account of their arrangements. When, however, the societies of the two Temples, and that of Gray's Inn, began, with a laudable jealousy, to contest the palm of splendour, the necessary expenditure appears occasionally to have 'given them pause'. Accordingly, they held anxious meetings, at the approach of the season, to decide the important question whether Christmas should be kept that year or not; and one of the registers of the society of Lincoln's Inn, bearing date the 27 November, in the twenty-second year of the reign of Henry VIII, contains the following order: 'Yt is agreed that if the two Temples do kepe Chrystemas, then Chrystemas to be kept here; and to know this, the Steward of the House ys commanded to get knowledge, and to advertise my master by the next day at night.'

There is a curious story told in Baker's Chronicle of an awkward predicament into which the society of Gray's Inn brought themselves by a play which they enacted amongst their Christmas revels of 1527. The subject of this play was to the effect that 'Lord Governance was ruled by Dissipation and Negligence; by whose evil order Lady Public-Weal was put from Governance.' Now, if these gentlemen did not intend, by this somewhat delicate moral, any insinuation against the existing state of things (which, being lawyers, and therefore courtiers, there is good motive to believe they did not), it is, at all events, certain that, *as* lawyers, they ought to have known better how to steer clear of all offence to weak consciences. That respectable minister, Cardinal Wolsey, felt himself (as we think he had good right to do) greatly scandalised at what, if not designed, was, by accident, a palpable hit; and, in order to teach the gentlemen of Gray's Inn that they were responsible for wounds given, if they happened to shoot arrows in the dark, he divested the ingenious author, Sergeant Roe, of his coif, and committed him to the Fleet, together with one of the actors, of the name of Moyle – in order to afford them leisure for furnishing him with a satisfactory explanation of the matter.

In Dugdale's *Origines Juridiciales*, we have an account of a magnificent Christmas which was kept at the Inner Temple, in the fourth year of Queen Elizabeth's reign; at which the Lord Robert Dudley, afterwards Earl of Leicester, presided, under the mock-title of Palaphilos, Prince of Sophie, High Constable Marshal of the Knights Templar, and Patron of the honourable order of Pegasus. A potentate with such a title would have looked very foolish without a 'tail'; and accordingly he had for his master of the game no less a lawyer than Christopher Hatton, afterwards Lord Chancellor of England, with four masters of the revels, a variety of other officers, and fourscore persons forming a guard. Gerard Leigh, who was so fortunate as to obtain the dignity of a knight of Pegasus, describes, as an eye-witness, in his *Accidence of Armorie*, the solemn fooleries which were enacted on the occasion by these worthies of the sword and of the gown.

Of course, it was not to be expected that such shrewd courtiers as lawyers commonly are, if they had ever kept Christmas at all, should fail to do so during the reign of this virgin queen, when its celebration offered them such admirable opportunities for the administration of that flattery which was so agreeable to her Majesty, and might possibly be so profitable to themselves. We have great pleasure in recording a speech made by her Majesty on one of these occasions, nearly so much as two centuries and a half ago, but which for its great excellence has come down to our days. The gentlemen of Gray's Inn (their wits, probably, a little sharpened by the mistake which they had made in her father's time) had ventured upon a dramatic performance again; and, in the course of a masque which they represented before the queen's Majesty, had administered to her copious draughts of that nectar on which her Majesty's vanity was known to thrive so marvellously. They appear, however, with a very nice tact, to have given her no more of it on this occasion than was sufficient to put her Majesty into spirits, without intoxicating her, for by this period of her life it took a great deal of that sort of thing to intoxicate the queen's Majesty; and the effect was of the pleasantest kind, and could not fail to be most satisfactory to the gentlemen of Gray's Inn. For after the masque was finished (in which we presume there had been a little dancing by the lawyers, who would, as in duty bound, have stood on their wigs to please her Majesty), and on the courtiers attempting, in *their* turn, to execute a dance, her Majesty was most graciously pleased to exclaim, 'What! Shall we have bread and cheese after a banquet?' – meaning thereby, we presume, to imply that the courtiers could not hope to leap as high or, in any respect, to cut such capers as the lawyers had done. Now, this speech of the virgin queen we have reported here less for the sake of any intrinsic greatness in the thought or elegance in the form than because, out of a variety of speeches by her Majesty, which have been carefully preserved, we think this is about as good as any other, and has the additional recommendation (which so few of the others have) of exhibiting the virgin queen in a good humour. And, further, because having recorded the disgrace into which the gentlemen of Gray's Inn danced themselves, in the lifetime of her illustrious father, it is but right that we should likewise record the ample indemnification which they must have considered themselves to have received at the lips of his virgin daughter.

The celebrations at the Inns of Court were from time to time continued, down to the period of the civil troubles which darkened the reign of Charles I; and so lately as the year 1641, when they had already commenced, we find it recorded by Evelyn, in his memoirs, that he was elected one of the comptrollers of the Middle Temple revellers, 'as the fashion of the young students and gentlemen was, the Christmas being kept this yeare with greate solemnity'. During this reign, we discover the several societies lessening their expenses by a very wise compromise of their disputes for supremacy; for in the eighth year thereof the four Inns of Court provided a Christmas masque in conjunction, for the entertainment of the court, which cost the startling sum of £ 24,000 of the money of that day, and in return King Charles invited one hundred and twenty gentlemen of the four Inns to a masque at Whitehall on the Shrove Tuesday following.

That our readers may form some idea of the kind of sports which furnished entertainment to men of no less pretension than Hatton and Coke and Crewe, we will extract for them a few more particulars of the ceremonies usually observed at the grand Christmases of the Inner Temple, before quitting this part of the subject.

In the first place, it appears that on Christmas Eve there was a banquet in the hall, at which three masters of the revels were present, the oldest of whom, after dinner and supper, was to sing a carol, and to command other gentlemen to sing with him; and in all this we see nothing which is not perfectly worthy of all imitation now. Then, on each of the twelve nights, before and after supper were revels and dancing; and if any of these revels and dancing were performed in company with the fair sex (which, on the face of the evidence, does not appear), then we have none of the objections to urge against them which we have ventured to insinuate against the solemn buffooneries, for which the bar was fined for refusing to surrender itself, in the time of James I. Neither do we find anything repugnant to our modern tastes in the announcement that the breakfasts of the following mornings were very substantial ones, consisting of brawn, mustard, and malmsey, which the exhaustion of the previous night's dancing might render necessary; nor that all the courses were served with music, which we intend that some of our own shall be this coming Christmas. But against most of that which follows we enter our decided protest, as not only very absurd in itself, but eminently calculated to spoil a good dinner.

On St Stephen's Day, we learn that, after the first course was served in, the constable marshal was wont to enter the hall (and we think he had much better have come in, and said all he had to say beforehand) bravely arrayed with 'a fair rich compleat harneys, white and bright and gilt, with a nest of fethers, of all colours, upon his crest or helm, and a gilt pole ax in his hand', and, no doubt, thinking himself a prodigiously fine fellow. He was accompanied by the lieutenant of the Tower, 'armed with a fair white armour', also wearing 'fethers', and 'with a like pole ax in his hand', and of course also thinking himself a very fine fellow. With them came sixteen trumpeters, preceded by four drums and fifes, and attended by four men clad in white 'harneys', from the middle upwards, having halberds in their hands, and bearing on their shoulders a model of the Tower, and each and every one of these latter personages, in his degree, having a consciousness that he, too, was a fine fellow. Then all these fine fellows, with the drums and music, and with all their 'fethers' and finery, went three times round the fire, whereas, considering that the boar's head was cooling all the time, we think once might have sufficed. Then the constable marshal, after three courtesies, knelt down before the Lord Chancellor, with the lieutenant doing the same behind him, and then and there deliberately proceeded to deliver himself of an 'oration of a quarter of an hour's length', the purport of which was to tender his services to the Lord Chancellor, which, we think, at such a time he might have contrived to do in fewer words. To this the Chancellor was unwise enough to reply that he would 'take farther advice therein', when it would have been much better for him to settle the matter at once, and proceed to eat his dinner. However, this part of the ceremony ended at last by the constable marshal and the lieutenant obtaining seats at the Chancellor's table, upon the former giving up his sword; and then enter, for a similar purpose, the master of the game, apparelled in green velvet, and the ranger of the forest, in a green suit of 'satten', bearing in his hand a green bow, and 'divers' arrows, 'with either of them a hunting-horn about their necks, blowing together three blasts of venery'. These worthies, also, thought it necessary to parade their finery three times around the fire; and having then made similar obeisances, and offered up a similar petition in a similar posture, they were finally inducted into a similar privilege.

But though seated at the Chancellor's table, and no doubt sufficiently roused by the steam of its good things, they were far enough as yet from getting anything to eat, as a consequence; and the next ceremony is one which strikingly marks the rudeness of the times. 'A huntsman cometh into the hall, with a fox, and a purse-net with a cat, both bound at the end of a staff, and with them nine or ten couple of hounds, with the blowing of hunting-horns. And the fox and the cat are set upon by the hounds, and killed beneath the fire.' 'What this "merry disport" signified (if practised) before the Reformation,' says a writer in Mr Hone's *Year Book*, 'I know not. In "Ane compendious boke of godly and spiritual songs, Edinburgh, 1621, printed from an old copy", are the following lines, seemingly referring to some such pageant:

> The hunter is Christ that hunts in haist,
> The hunds are Peter and Pawle,
> The paip is the fox, Rome is the Rox
> That rubbis us on the gall.'

After these ceremonies, the welcome permission to betake themselves to the far more interesting one of an attack upon the good things of the feast appears to have been at length given; but at the close of the second course the subject of receiving the officers who had tendered their Christmas service was renewed. Whether the gentlemen of the law were burlesquing their own profession intentionally or whether it was only an awkward *hit*, like that which befell their brethren of Gray's Inn, does not appear. However, the common sergeant made what is called 'a plausible speech', insisting on the necessity of these officers 'for the better reputation of the Commonwealth'; and he was followed, to the same effect, by the king's sergeant-at-law till the Lord Chancellor silenced them by desiring a respite of further advice, which it is greatly to be marvelled he had not done sooner. And thereupon he called upon the 'ancientest of the masters of the revels' for a song – a proceeding to which we give our unqualified approbation.

So much for the dinner. After supper, the constable marshal again presented himself, if possible finer than before, preceded by drums – as so fine a man ought to be – and mounted on a scaffold borne by four men. After again going thrice round the hearth, he dismounted from his elevation, and having set a good example by first playing the figurant himself for the edification of the court, called upon the nobles, by their respective Christmas names, to do the same. Of the styles and titles which it was considered humorous to assume on such occasions, and by which he called up his courtiers to dance, our readers may take the following for specimens:

Sir Francis Flatterer, of Fowlehurst, in the county of Buckingham.
Sir Randle Rackabite, of Rascall Hall, in the county of Rabchell.
Sir Morgan Mumchance, of Much Monkery, in the county of
    Mad Popery.

And so on, with much more of the same kind, which we are sure our readers will spare us, or rather thank us for sparing them. The ceremonies of St John's Day were, if possible, more absurd than those by which St Stephen was honoured; but, that we may take leave of the lawyers on good terms, and with a word of commendation, we will simply add that the concluding one is stated to be that on the Thursday following 'the Chancellor and company partook of dinner of roast beef and venison pasties, and at supper of mutton and hens roasted', which we take to have been not only the most sensible proceeding of the whole series, but about as sensible a thing as they or anybody else could well do.

So important were these Christmas celebrations deemed by our ancestors, and such was the earnestness bestowed upon their preparation, that a special officer was appointed for that purpose, and to preside over the festival with large privileges, very considerable appointments, and a retinue which in course of time came to be no insignificant imitation of a prince's. We are of course speaking at present of the officer who was appointed to the superintendence of the Christmas ceremonials *at court*. The title by which this potentate was usually distinguished in England was that of 'Lord of Misrule', 'Abbot of Misrule', or 'Master of Merry Disports'; and his office was, in fact, that of a temporary 'Master of the Revels' (which latter title was formerly that of a permanent and distinguished officer attached to the household of our kings). Accordingly we find that amongst those of the more powerful nobles who affected an imitation of the royal arrangements in their Christmas establishments, this Christmas officer (when they appointed one to preside over their private Christmas celebrations) was occasionally nominated as *their* 'Master of the Revels'. In the Household-Book of the Northumberland family, amongst the directions given for the order of the establishment, it is stated that 'My lorde useth and accustomyth yerly to gyf hym which is ordynede to be the MASTER OF THE REVELLS yerly in my lordis hous in cristmas for the overseyinge and orderinge of his lordschips Playes, Interludes, and Dresinge that is plaid befor his lordship in his hous in the xijth dayes of Cristenmas, and they to have in rewarde for that caus yerly, xxs.' In the Inns of Court, where this officer formed no part of a household, but was a member elected out of their own body for his ingenuity, he was commonly dignified by a title more appropriate to the extensive authority with which he was invested, and the state with which he was furnished for its due maintenance; namely, that of 'Christmas Prince', or sometimes 'King of Christmas'. He is the same officer who was known in Scotland as the 'Abbot of Unreason', and bears a close resemblance to the 'Abbas Stultorum', who presided over the Feast of Fools in France, and the 'Abbé de la Malgourverné', who ruled the sports in certain provinces of that kingdom. In a note to Ellis's edition of Brand's *Popular Antiquities*, we find a quotation from Mr Warton (whose *History of English Poetry* we have not at hand) in which mention is made of an 'Abbé de Liesse', and a reference given to Carpentier's Supplement to Du Cange, for the title 'Abbas Lætitiæ'. We mention these, to enable the antiquarian portion of our readers to make the reference for themselves. Writing in the country, we have not access to the works in question, and could not, in these pages, go farther into the matter if we had.

We have already stated that the 'Lord of Misrule' appears to bear a considerable resemblance to that ruler or king who was anciently appointed to preside over the sports of the Roman Saturnalia; and we find on looking further into the subject, that we are corroborated in this view by one who, of course, asserts the resemblance for the purpose of making it a matter of reproach. The notorious Prynne, in his *Histrio-Mastix*, affirms (and quotes Polydore Virgil to the same effect) that 'our Christmas lords of Misrule, together with dancing, masques, mummeries, stage-players, and such other Christmas disorders, now in use with Christians, were derived from these Roman Saturnalia and Bacchanalian festivals; which,' adds he, 'should cause all pious Christians eternally to abominate them.' We should not, however, omit to mention that by some this officer has been derived from the ancient ceremony of the Boy-Bishop. Faber speaks of him as originating in an old Persico-Gothic festival in honor of Buddha: and Purchas, in his *Pilgrimage*, as quoted in the Aubrey manuscripts, says, that the custom is deduced from the 'Feast in Babylon, kept in honour of the goddess Dorcetha, for five dayes together; during which time the masters were under the dominion of their servants, one of which is usually sett over the rest, and royally cloathed, and was called Sogan, that is, Great Prince.'

The title, however, by which this officer is most generally known is that of Lord of Misrule. 'There was,' says Stow, 'in the feast of Christmas, in the king's house, wheresoever he was lodged, a Lord of Misrule, or Master of merry Disports; and the like had ye for the house of every nobleman of honour or good worship, were he spiritual or temporal. Among the which the Mayor of London and either of the Sheriffs had their several Lords of Misrule ever contending, without quarrel or offence, which should make the rarest pastimes to delight the beholders.'

Of the antiquity of this officer in England, we have not been able to find any satisfactory account; but we discover traces of him almost as early as we have any positive records of the various sports by which the festival of this season was supported. Polydore Virgil speaks of the splendid spectacles, the masques, dancings, etc., by which it was illustrated as far back as the close of the twelfth century; and it is reasonable to suppose that something in the shape of a master of these public ceremonies must have existed then, to preserve order as well as furnish devices, particularly as the hints for the one and the other seem to have been taken from the celebrations of the heathens. As early as the year 1489 Leland speaks of an Abbot of Misrule 'that made much sport, and did right well his office'. Henry VII's 'boke of paymentis', preserved in the Chapter House, is stated by Sandys to contain several items of disbursement to the Lord of Misrule (or Abbot, as he is therein sometimes called) for different years 'in rewarde for his besynes in Christenmes holydays', none of which exceeded the sum of £6 13s. 4d. This sum – multiplied as we imagine it ought to be by something like fifteen, to give the value thereof in our days – certainly affords no very liberal remuneration to an officer whose duties were of any extent; and we mention it that our readers may contrast it with the lavish appointments of the same functionary in after times. Henry, however, was a frugal monarch, though it was a part of his policy to promote the amusements of the people; and from the treasures which that frugality created, his immediate successors felt themselves at liberty to assume a greater show. In the subsequent reign, the yearly payments to the Lord of Misrule had already been raised as high as £15 6s. 8d.; and the entertainments over which he presided were furnished at a proportionably increased cost.

It is not, however, until the reign of the young monarch, Edward the Sixth, that this officer appears to have attained his highest dignities; and during the subsequent reign we find him playing just such a part as might be expected from one whose business it was to take the lead in revels such as we have had occasion to describe; namely, that of arch-buffoon.

In Hollinshed's *Chronicle*, honorable mention is made of a certain George Ferrers, therein described as a 'lawyer, a poet, and an historian', who supplied the office well in the fifth year of Edward VI, and who was rewarded by the young king with princely liberality. This George Ferrers was the principal author of that well-known work, the *Mirrour for Magistrates*; and Mr Kempe, the editor of the recently published *Loseley Manuscripts*, mentions his having been likewise distinguished by military services, in the reign of Henry VIII. It appears that the young king having fallen into a state of melancholy after the condemnation of his uncle, the Protector, it was determined to celebrate the approaching Christmas festival with more than usual splendour, for the purpose of diverting his mind; and this distinguished individual was selected to preside ever the arrangements.

The publication of the *Loseley Manuscripts* enables us to present our readers with some very curious particulars, illustrative at once of the nature of those arrangements, and of the heavy cost at which they were furnished. By an order in council – dated 30 September, 1552, and addressed to Sir Thomas Cawarden, at that time Master of the King's

Revels – after reciting the appointment of the said George Ferrers, the said Sir Thomas is informed that it is his Majesty's pleasure 'that you se hym furneshed for hym and his bande, as well in apparell as all other necessaries, of such stuff as remayneth in your office. And whatsoever wanteth in the same, to take order that it be provided accordinglie by yor discretion.'

For the manner in which the Lord of Misrule availed himself of this unlimited order, we recommend to such of our readers as the subject may interest a perusal of the various estimates and accounts published by Mr Kempe from the manuscripts in question. Were it not that they would occupy too much of our space, we should have been glad to introduce some of them here, for the purpose of conveying to the reader a lively notion of the gorgeousness of apparel and appointment exhibited on this occasion. We must, however, present them with some idea of the train for whom these costly preparations were made, and of the kind of mock court with which the Lord of Misrule surrounded himself.

Amongst these we find mention made of a chancellor, treasurer, comptroller, vice-chamberlain, lords-councillors, divine, philosopher, astronomer, poet, physician, apothecary, master of requests, civilian, disard (an old word for clown), gentleman-ushers, pages of honour, sergeants-atarms, provost-marshal, under-marshal, footmen, messengers, trumpeter, herald, orator; besides hunters, jugglers, tumblers, band, fools, friars (a curious juxtaposition, which Mr Kempe thinks might intend a satire), and a variety of others. None seem in fact to have been omitted who were usually included in the retinue of a prince; and over this mock court the mock monarch appears to have presided with a sway as absolute, as far as regarded the purposes of his appointment, as the actual monarch himself over the weightier matters of the state. But the most curious part of these arrangements is that by which (as appears from one of the lists printed from these manuscripts) he seems to have been accompanied in his processions by an heir-at-law, and three other children, besides two *base sons*. These two base sons, we presume, are bastards; and that the establishment of a potentate could not be considered complete without them. The editor also mentions that he was attended by an almoner, who scattered amongst the crowd during his progresses, certain coins made by the wiredrawers; and remarks that if these bore the portrait and superscription of the Lord of Misrule, they would be rare pieces in the eye of a numismatist.

The following very curious letter, which we will give entire, will furnish our readers with a lively picture of the pageantries of that time, and of the zeal with which full-grown men set about amusements of a kind which are now usually left to children of a smaller growth. Playing at kings is in our day one of the sports of more juvenile actors. The letter is addressed by Master George Ferrers to Sir Thomas Cawarden; and gives some account of his intended entry at the court at Christmas, and of his devices for furnishing entertainment during the festival.

SIR — Whereas you required me to write, for that y^r busynes is great, I have in as few wordes as I maie signefied to you such things as I thinke moste necessarie for my purpose.

ffirst, as towching my Introduction. Whereas the laste yeare my devise was to cum of oute of the mone (moon) this yeare I imagine to cum oute of a place called *vastum vacuum*, the great waste, as moche to saie as a place voide or emptie wthout the worlde, where is neither fier, ayre, nor earth; and that I have bene remayning there sins the last yeare. And, because of certaine devises which I have towching this matter, I wold, yf it were possyble, have all myne apparell blewe, the first daie that I p'sent my self to the King's Matie; and even as I shewe my self that daie, so my mynd is in like order and in like suets (suits) to shew myself at my comyng into London after the halowed daies.

Againe, how I shall cum into the Courte, whether under a canopie, as the last yeare, or in a chare triumphall, or uppon some straunge beaste – that I reserve to you; but the serpente with sevin heddes, cauled hidra, is the chief beast of myne armes, and wholme[1] (holm) bushe is the devise of my crest, my worde[2] is *semper ferians*, I alwaies feasting or keping holie daies. Uppon Christmas daie I send a solempne ambassad^e to the King's Ma^{ie} by an herrald, a trumpet, an orator speaking in a straunge language, an interpreter or a truchman with hym, to which p'sons ther were requiset to have convenient farnyture, which I referre to you.

I have provided one to plaie uppon a kettell drom with his boye, and a nother drome wth a fyffe, whiche must be apparelled like turkes garments, according to the paternes I send you herewith. On St Stephen's daie, I wold, if it were possyble, be with the King's Matie before dynner. Mr Windham, being my Admyrall, is appointed to receive me beneth the bridge with the King's Brigandyne, and other vessells apointed for the same purpose; his desire is to have the poope of his vessell covered wth white and blew, like as I signefie to you by a nother 1re.

Sir George Howard, being my M^r of the Horsis, receiveth me at my landing at Grenwiche with a spare horse and my pages of hono^r, one

---

1 The evergreen holly is meant, a bearing peculiarly appropriate to the lord of Christmas sports.
2 His motto or impress.

carieng my hed pece, a nother my shelde, the thirde my sword, the fourth my axe. As for their furniture I know nothing as yet provided, either for my pages or otherwise, save a hed peece that I caused to be made. My counsailo^{rs}, with suche other necessarie psons y^t attend uppon me that daie, also must be consydered. There maie be no fewer than sixe counsailo^{rs} at the least; I must also have a divine, a philosopher, an astronomer, a poet, a phisician, a potecarie, a m^r of requests, a sivilian, a disard, John Smyth, two gentlemen ushers, besides juglers, tomblers, fooles, friers, and suche other.

The residue of the wholie daies I will spend in other devises: as one daie in feats of armes, and then wolde I have a challeng pformed with hobbie horsis, where I purpose to be in pson. Another daie in hunting and hawking, the residue of the tyme shalbe spent in other devisis, which I will declare to you by mouth to have yor ayde and advice therin.

S^r, I know not howe ye be provided to furnish me, but suer methinks I shold have no lesse than five suets of apparell, the first for the daie I come in, which shall also serve me in London, and two other suets for the two halowed daies folowing, the fourth for newe yeares daie, and the fifte for XIIth daie.

Touching my suet of blew, I have sent you a pece of velvet which hath a kinde of powdered ermaines in it, vearie fytt for my wering, yf you so thynke good. All other matters I referre tyll I shall speake with you.

GEORGE FERRERS

In other letters from this Lord of Misrule to the Master of the Revels he applies for eight visors for a drunken masque, and eight swords and daggers for the same purpose; twelve hobby-horses, two Dryads, and Irish dresses for a man and woman; and seventy jerkins of buckram, or canvas painted like mail, for seventy 'hakbuturs', or musketeers of his guard.

Such are some of the testimonies borne by the parties themselves to their own right pleasant follies, and the expense at which they maintained them; and to these we will add another, coming from an adverse quarter, and showing the light in which these costly levities had already come to be regarded by men of sterner minds so early as the reign of Elizabeth. The following very curious passage is part of an extract made by Brand, from a most rare book entitled *The Anatomie of Abuses* – the work of one Phillip Stubs, published in London in 1585 – and gives a quaint picture of the Lord of Misrule and his retainers, as viewed through Puritan optics.

'Firste,' says Master Stubs, 'all the wilde heades of the parishe conventynge together, chuse them a grand Capitaine (of mischeef) whom they innoble with the title of my *Lorde of Misserule*, and hym they crown with great solemnitie, and adopt for their kyng. This kyng anoynted, chuseth for the twentie, fourtie, three score, or a hundred lustie guttes like to hymself, to waite uppon his lordely majestie, and to guarde his noble persone. Then every one of these his menne he investeth with his liveries of greene, yellowe or some other light wanton colour. And as though that were not (baudie) gaudy enough I should saie, they bedecke themselves with scarffes, ribons, and laces, hanged all over with golde rynges, precious stones, and other jewelles: this doen, they tye about either legge twentie or fourtie belles with rich handkercheefes in their handes, and sometymes laied acrosse over their shoulders and neckes, borrowed for the moste parte of their pretie Mopsies and loovyng Bessies, for bussyng them in the darcke. Thus thinges sette in order, they have their hobbie horses, dragons, and other antiques, together with their baudie pipers, and thunderyng drommers, to strike up the Deville's Daunce withall' (meaning the Morris Dance), 'then marche these heathen companie towardes the church and churche yarde, their pipers pipyng, drommers thonderyng, their stumppes dauncyng, their belles iynglyng, their handkerchefes swyngyng about their heades like madmen, their hobbie horses and other monsters skyrmishyng amongst the throng: and in this sorte they goe to the churche (though the minister bee at praier or preaçhyng) dauncyng and swingyng their handkercheefes over their heades, in the churche, like devilles incarnate, with suche a confused noise that no man can heare his owne voice. Then the foolishe people, they looke, they stare, they laugh, they fleere, and mount upon formes and pewes, to see these goodly pageauntes, solemnised in this sort.'

At the Christmas celebration held at Gray's Inn in 1594, to which we have already alluded, the person selected to fill the office of Christmas Prince was a Norfolk gentleman of the name of Helmes, whose leg, like that of Sir Andrew Aguecheek, appears 'to have been formed under the star of a galliard'. He is described as being 'accomplished with all good parts, fit for so great a dignity, and also a very proper man in personage, and very active in dancing and revelling'. The revels over which this mock monarch presided were, as our readers will remember, exhibited before Queen Elizabeth; and it was the exquisite performance of this gentleman and his court which her Majesty described as bearing the same relation for excellence to those of her own courtiers which a banquet does to bread and cheese. We must refer such of our readers as are desirous of informing themselves as to the nature and taste of the devices which could make her Majesty so eloquent, to the *Gesta Grayorum*; contenting ourselves with giving them such notion thereof, as well as of the high dignities which appertained to a Lord of Misrule, as may be conveyed by a perusal of the magnificent style and titles assumed by Mr Henry Helmes on his accession. They were enough to have made her Majesty jealous, if she had not been so good-natured a queen; for looking at the *philosophy* of the thing, she was about as much a mock monarch as himself, and could not dance so well. To be sure, she was acknowledged by this potentate as Lady Paramount; and to a woman like Elizabeth, it was something to receive personal homage from:

> The High and Mighty Prince Henry, Prince of Purpoole, Archduke of Stapulia and Bernardia; Duke of High and Nether Holborn; Marquis of St Giles and Tottenham; Count Palatine of Bloomsbury and Clerkenwell; Great Lord of the Cantons of Islington, Kentish Town, Paddington, and Knightsbridge; Knight of the most Heroical Order of the Helmet, and Sovereign of the same!

It is admitted that no man can be a great actor who has not the faculty of divesting himself of his personal identity, and persuading himself that he really is, for the time, that which he represents himself to be; his doing which will go far to persuade others into the same belief. Now as her Majesty has pronounced upon the excellence of Mr Henry Helmes's acting, and if we are therefore to suppose that that gentleman had contrived to mystify both himself and her, she would naturally be not a little vain of so splendid a vassal. But seriously, it is not a little amusing to notice the good faith with which these gentlemen appear to have put on and worn their burlesque dignities, and the real homage which they not only expected, but actually received. If the tricks which they played during their 'brief authority', were not of that mischievous kind which 'make the angels weep', they were certainly fantastic enough to make those who are 'a little lower than the angels' smile. A Lord Mayor in his gilt coach seems to be a trifle compared with a Lord of Misrule entering the city of London in former days; and the following passage from Warton's *History of English Poetry*, exhibits amusingly enough the sovereign functions seriously exercised by this important personage, and the homage, both ludicrous and substantial, which he sometimes received:

> At a Christmas celebrated in the hall of the Middle Temple, in the year 1635, the jurisdiction privileges and parade of this mock monarch are thus circumstantially described. He was attended by his Lord Keeper, Lord Treasurer with eight white staves, a Captain of his Band of Pensioners and of his guard, *and with two Chaplains who were so seriously impressed with an idea of his regal dignity that, when they preached before him on the preceding Sunday in the Temple Church, on ascending the pulpit they saluted him with three low bows.* He dined both in the Hall and in his Privy Chamber under a cloth of Estate. The pole-axes for his Gentlemen Pensioners were borrowed of Lord Salisbury.

Lord Holland, his temporary justice in Eyre, supplies him with venison on demand; and the Lord Mayor and Sheriffs of London with wine. On Twelfth Day, at going to Church, he received many petitions which he gave to his Master of Requests; and like other kings he had a favourite, whom – with others, gentlemen of high quality – he knighted at returning from Church.

The Christmas Prince on this occasion was Mr Francis Vivian, who expended from his own private purse the large sum of £2,000 in support of his dignities. Really, it must have tried the philosophy of these gentlemen to descend from their temporary elevation, into the ranks of ordinary life. A deposed prince like that high and mighty prince, Henry, Prince of Purpoole, must have felt, on getting up on the morrow of Candlemas-day, some portion of the sensations of Abou Hassan on the morning which succeeded his caliphate of a day, when the disagreeable conviction was forced upon him that he was no longer Commander of the Faithful, and had no further claim to the services of Cluster-of-Pearls, Morning-Star, Coral-Lips or Fair-Face. In the case, however, of Mr Francis Vivian, it is stated that after his deposition he was knighted by the king – by way, we suppose, of breaking his fall.

In Wood's *Athenæ Oxonienses*, mention is made of a very splendid Christmas ceremonial observed at St John's College, Oxford, in the reign of our first James, which was presided over by a Mr Thomas Tooker, whom we elsewhere find called 'Tucker'. From a manuscript account of this exhibition, Wood quotes the titles assumed by this gentleman in his character of Christmas Prince; and we will repeat them here, for the purpose of showing that the legal cloisters were not the only ones in which mirth was considered as no impeachment of professional gravity, and that humour (such as it is) was an occasional guest of the wisdom which is proverbially said to reside in wigs – of *all* denominations. From a comparison of these titles with those by which Mr Henry Helmes illustrated his own magnificence at Gray's Inn, our readers may decide for themselves upon the relative degrees of the wit which flourished beneath the shelter of the respective gowns. Though ourselves a Cantab, we have no skill in the measurement of the relations of small quantities. Of the hearty mirth in each case there is little doubt; and humour of the finest quality could have done no more than produce that effect, and might probably have failed to do so much. The appetite is the main point. 'The heart's all,' as Davy says. A small matter made our ancestors laugh, because they brought stomachs to the feast of Momus. And, Heaven save the mark, through how many national troubles has that same joyous temperament (which is the farthest thing possible from levity – one of the phases of deep feeling) helped to bring the national mind? The 'merry days' of England were succeeded by what may be called her 'age of tears' – the era of the sentimentalists, when young gentlemen ceased to wear cravats, and leaned against pillars in drawing-rooms in fits of moody abstraction or under the influence of evident inspiration, and young ladies made lachrymatories of their boudoirs, and met together to weep, and in fact went through the world weeping. Amid all its absurdity, there was some real feeling at the bottom of this, too; and therefore it, too, had its pleasure. But there is to be an end of this also. Truly are we falling upon the 'evil days' of which we may say we 'have no pleasure in them'. Men are neither to laugh nor smile, now, without distinctly knowing why. We are in the age of the philosophers. All this time, however, Mr Thomas Tucker is waiting to have his style and titles proclaimed; and thus do we find them duly set forth:

> The most magnificent and renowned Thomas, by the favor of Fortune, Prince of Alba Fortunata, Lord of St John's, High Regent of the Hall, Duke of St Giles's, Marquis of Magdalen's, Landgrave of the Grove, Count Palatine of the Cloysters, Chief Bailiff of Beaumont, High Ruler of Rome, Master of the Manor of Walton, Governor of Gloucester Green, sole Commander of all Titles, Tournaments, and Triumphs, Superintendent in all Solemnities whatever.

From these titles – as well as from those which we have already mentioned as being assumed by the courtiers of the illustrious Prince of Sophie, our readers will perceive that alliteration was an esteemed figure in the rhetoric of the revels.

In order to give our readers a more lively idea of this potentate, we have, as the frontispiece to our second part, introduced a Lord of Misrule to preside over the Christmas sports therein described. Although the titles with which we have there invested him are taken from the *Gesta Grayorum*, the dress in which the artist has bestowed him is not copied from any one of the particular descriptions furnished by the different records. He is intended to represent the ideal of a Christmas prince, and not the portrait of any particular one of whom we have accounts. The artist's instructions were therefore confined to investing him with a due magnificence (referring to the records only so far as to keep the costume appropriate) and with a complacent sense of his own finery and state, and we think that Mr Seymour has succeeded very happily in catching and embodying the mock heroic of the character. The Prince of Purpoole, or His Highness of Sophie, must have looked just such a personage as he has represented.

We must not omit to observe that a corresponding officer appears to have formerly exercised his functions at some of the colleges at Cambridge, under the more classical title of Imperator. And we must further state that at Lincoln's Inn, in the early times of their Christmas celebrations, there appear to have been elected (besides the Lord of Misrule, and, we presume, in subordination to him) certain dignitaries exercising a royal sway over the revelries of particular days of the festival. In the account given by Dugdale of the Christmas held by this society in the ninth year of the reign of Henry VIII, mention is made – besides the Marshal and (as he is there called) the Master of the Revels – of a King chosen for Christmas day, and an officer for Childermas day having the title of King of the Cockneys. A relic of this ancient custom exists in the Twelfth Night King, whom it is still usual to elect on the festival of the Epiphany, and of whom we shall have occasion to speak at length in his proper place.

The length of the period over which the sway of this potentate extended does not seem to be very accurately defined, or rather it is probable that it varied with circumstances. Strictly speaking, the Christmas season is in our day considered to terminate with Twelfth Night, and the festival itself to extend over that space of time of which this night on one side and Christmas eve on the other are the limits. In ancient times, too, we find frequent mention of the *twelve* days of Christmas. Thus the George Ferrers of whom we have spoken, is appointed 'to be in his hyness household for the twelve days'; and he dates one of his communications to Sir Thomas Cawarden, 'From Greenwich ye second of January and ye ixth day of o^r rule'. In the extract from the Household-Book of the Northumberland family which we have already quoted, mention is also made of the 'Playes, Interludes and Dresinge that is plaid befor his lordship in his hous in the xijth dayes of Christenmas'. Stow, however, says that 'these Lords beginning their rule at Allhallond Eve, continued the same till the morrow after the Feast of the Purification, commonly called Candlemas day'; and that during all that time there were under their direction 'fine and subtle disguisings, masks and mummeries, with playing at cards for counters, nayles and points in every house, more for pastimes than for gaine'. This would give a reign of upwards of three months to these gentlemen. Dugdale, in describing the revels of the Inner Temple, speaks of the three principal days being All-Hallows, Candlemas, and Ascension days – which would extend the period to seven months; and the masque of which we have spoken as forming the final performance of the celebrated Christmas of 1594, described in the *Gesta Grayorum*, is stated to have been represented before the queen at Shrovetide. At the Christmas exhibition of St John's college, Oxford, held in 1607, Mr Thomas Tucker did not resign his office till Shrove Tuesday; and the costly masque of which we have spoken as being presented by the four Inns of Court to Charles I, and whose title was 'The Triumph of Peace', was exhibited in February of 1633. In

Scotland, the rule of the Abbot of Unreason appears to have been still less limited in point of time; and he seems to have held his court and made his processions at any period of the year which pleased him. These processions, it appears, were very usual in the month of May (and here we will take occasion to observe parenthetically, but in connection with our present subject, that the practice at *all* festival celebrations of selecting some individual to enact a principal and presiding character in the ceremonial is further illustrated by the ancient May King, and by the practice, not yet wholly forgotten, of crowning on the first of that month a Queen of the May. This subject we shall have occasion to treat more fully when we come to speak in some future volume of the beautiful customs of that out-of-doors season).

From what we have stated, it appears probable that the officer who was appointed to preside over the revels so universally observed at Christmas time, extended, as a matter of course, his presidency over all those which – either arising out of them or unconnected therewith – were performed at more advanced periods of the succeeding year; that in fact, the Christmas prince was, without new election, considered as special master of the revels till the recurrence of the season. It is not necessary for us to suppose that the whole of the intervals lying between such stated and remote days of celebration were filled up with festival observances; or that our ancestors, under any calenture of the spirits, could aim at extending Christmas over the larger portion of the year. It is, however, apparent that although the common observances of the season were supposed to fall within the period bounded by the days of the Nativity and the Epiphany, the special pageantries with a view to which the Lords of Misrule were appointed in the more exalted quarters were in years of high festival spread over a much more extended time, and that their potential dignities were in full force, if not in full display, from the eve of All-Hallows to the close of Candlemas day. It is stated in Drake's *Shakspeare and his Times*, that the festivities of the season, which were appointed for at least twelve days, were frequently extended over a space of six weeks; and our readers know from their own experience that, even in these our days of less prominent and ceremonial rejoicing, the holiday spirit of the season is by no means to be restrained within the narrower of those limits. The Christmas feeling waits not for Christmas day. The important preparations for so great a festival render this impossible. By the avenues of most of the senses, the heralds of old Father Christmas have long before approached to awake it from its slumber. Signal notes which there is no mistaking, have been played on the visual and olfactory organs for some time past, and the palate itself has had foretastes of that which is about to be. From the day on which his sign has been seen in the heavens, the joyous influences of the star have been felt and the moment the schoolboy arrives at his home he is in the midst of Christmas. And if the 'coming events' of the season 'cast their shadows before', so, amid all its crosslights it would be strange if there were no reflections flung behind. The merry spirit which has been awakened and suffered to play his antics so long is not to be laid by the exorcism of a word. After so very absolute and unquestioned a sway, it is not to be expected that Momus should abdicate at a moment's notice. Accordingly, we find that, anything enacted to the contrary notwithstanding, the genial feelings of the time and the festivities springing out of them contrive to maintain their footing throughout the month of January; and Christmas keeps lingering about our homes till he is no longer answered by the young glad voices to whom he has not as yet begun to utter his solemn warnings and expound his sterner morals, and for whom his coming is hitherto connected with few memories of pain. Till the merry urchins have gone back to school there will continue to be willing subjects to the Lord of Misrule.

In Scotland, the Abbot of Unreason was frequently enacted by persons of the highest rank; and James V is himself said to have concealed his crown beneath the mitre of the merry abbot. As in England, his revels were shared by the mightiest of the land; but they appear to have been of a less inoffensive kind and to have imitated more unrestrainedly the licence of the Roman Saturnalia than did the merrymakings of the South. The mummeries of these personages (a faint reflection of which still exists in the Guisars whom we shall have to mention hereafter), if less costly than those of their brethren in England, were not less showy; and though much less quaint, were a great deal more free. 'The bodyguards of the Abbot of Unreason were all arrayed in gaudy colors bedecked with gold or silver lace, with embroidery and silken scarfs, the fringed ends of which floated in the wind. They wore chains of gold or baser metal gilt that glittered with mock jewels. Their legs were adorned and rendered voluble by links of shining metal hung with many bells of the same material twining from the ankle of their buskins to their silken garters, and each flourished in his hand a rich silk handkerchief brocaded over with flowers. This was the garb of fifty or more youths, who encircled the person of the leader. They were surrounded by ranks, six or more in depth, consisting of tall, brawny, fierce-visaged men covered with crimson or purple velvet bonnets, and nodding plumes of the eagle and the hawk, or branches of pine, yew, oak, fern, boxwood, or flowering heath. Their jerkins were always of a hue that might attract the eye of ladies in the bower or serving-damsels at the washing-green. They had breeches of immense capacity so padded or stuffed as to make each man occupy the space of five in their natural proportions; and in this seeming soft raiment they concealed weapons of defence or offence, with which to arm themselves and the bodyguard if occasion called for resistance. To appearance, they had no object but careless sport and glee – some playing on the Scottish harp, others blowing the bagpipes or beating targets for drums, or jingling bells. Whenever the procession halted they danced, flourishing about the banners of their leader. The exterior bands perhaps represented in dumb show or panto- mime the actions of warriors or the wildest buffoonery; and these were followed by crowds who, with all the grimaces and phrases of waggery, solicited money or garniture from the nobles and gentry that came to gaze upon them. Wherever they appeared, multitudes joined them, some for the sake of jollity, and not a few to have their fate predicted by spae-wives, warlocks, and interpreters of dreams, who invariably were found in the train of the Abbot of Unreason.'

In England, not only was this merry monarch appointed over the revelries of the great and the opulent, but – as of most of the forms of amusement over which he presided, so of the president himself – we find a rude imitation in the Christmas celebrations of the commonalty. Nor was the practice confined to towns or left exclusively in the hands of corporate or public bodies. The quotation which we have already made from Stubs's *Anatomie of Abuses*, refers to a rustic Lord of Misrule; and while the antics which took place under his governance do not seem to have risen much above the performances of the morris-dancers, the gaudiness of the tinsel attire paraded by him and his band forms an excellent burlesque of the more costly finery of their superiors. Nay; the amusements themselves exhibit nearly as much wisdom as those of the court (with less of pretension), and we dare say created a great deal more fun at a far less cost. As to the Scottish practices, our readers will not fail to observe from our last quotation that the lordly Abbot and his train were little better than a set of morris-dancers themselves, and that so much of their practices as was innocent differed nothing from those which Stubs and his brother Puritans deemed so ridiculous in a set of parish revellers. In fact, the Lord of Misrule seems to have set himself up all over the land; and many a village had its master Simon who took care that the sports should not languish for want of that unity of purpose and concentration of mirth to which some directing authority is so essential.

We have already stated, and have made it quite apparent in our descriptions, that the Christmas celebrations of the more exalted classes are not put forward for the consideration of our readers on the ground of any great wisdom in the matter or humour in the manner of those celebrations themselves. But we claim for them serious veneration, in right of the excellence of the spirit in which they originated, and the excellence of the result which they produced. The very extravagance of the court pageantries – their profuse expenditure and grotesque displays – were so many evidences of the hearty reception which was given to the season in the highest places, and so many conspicuous sanctions under which the spirit of unrestrained rejoicing made its appeals in the lowest. This ancient festival of all ranks, consecrated by all religious feelings and all moral influences; this privileged season of the lowly; this Sabbath of the poor man's year – was recognised by his superiors with high observance and honoured by his governors with ceremonious state. The mirth of the humble and uneducated man received no check from the assumption of an unseasonable gravity or ungenerous reserve on the part of those with whom fortune had dealt more kindly, and to whom knowledge had opened her stores. The moral effect of all this was of the most valuable kind. Nothing so much promotes a reciprocal kindliness of feeling as a community of enjoyment; and the bond of good will was thus drawn tighter between those remote classes, whose differences of privilege, of education, and of pursuit, are perpetually operating to loosen it, and threatening to dissolve it altogether. There was a great deal of wisdom in all this; and the result was well worth producing even at the cost of much more folly than our ancestors expended on it. We deny that spectacles and a wig are the inseparable symbols of sapience; and we hold that portion of the world to be greatly mistaken which supposes that wisdom may not occasionally put on the cap and bells, and under that disguise be wisdom still! The ancient custom which made what was called a fool a part of the establishment of princes, and gave him a right in virtue of his bauble to teach many a wise lesson and utter many a wholesome truth – besides its practical utility, contained as excellent a moral and was conceived in as deep a spirit as the still more ancient one of the skeleton at a feast. '*Cucullus non facit monachum*', says one of those privileged gentry, in the pages of one who, we are sure, could have enacted a Christmas foolery with the most foolish, and yet had 'sounded all the depths and shallows' of the human mind, and was himself the wisest of modern men. 'Better a witty fool than a foolish wit.' There is a long stride from the wisdom of that sneering philosopher who laughed *at* his fellows to his who on proper occasions can laugh *with* them; and in spite of all that modern philosophy may say to the contrary, there was in the very extravagances of Coke and Hatton, and other lawyers and statesmen of past times – if they aimed at such a result as that which we have mentioned, and insofar as they contributed thereto – more real wisdom than all which they enunciated in their more solemn moods, or have put upon record in their books of the law.

In the same excellent spirit, too, everything was done that could assist in promoting the same valuable effect; and while the pageantries which were prepared by the court and by other governing bodies furnished a portion of the entertainments by which the populace tasted the season in towns, and sanctioned the rest, care was taken in many ways (of which we have given an example) that the festival should be spread over the country, and provision made for its maintenance in places more secluded and remote. A set of arrangements sprang up which left no man without their influence; and figuratively and literally, the crumbs from the table of the rich man's festival were abundantly enjoyed by the veriest beggar at his gate. The kindly spirit of Boaz was abroad in all the land, and every Ruth had leave to 'eat of the bread and dip her morsel in the vinegar'. At that great harvest of rejoicing, all men were suffered to glean; and they with whom at most other seasons the world had 'dealt very bitterly' – whose names were Mara, and who ate sparingly of the bread of toil – gleaned 'even among its sheaves', and no man reproached them. The old English gentleman, like the generous Bethlehemite in the beautiful story, even scattered that the poor might gather, and 'commanded his young men saying . . . "Let fall also some of the handfuls of purpose for them and leave them, that they may glean them, and rebuke them not." ' And the prayer of many a Naomi went up in answer, 'Blessed be he that did take knowledge of thee'; 'blessed be he of the Lord!'

In a word, the blaze of royal and noble celebration was as a great beacon to the land, seen afar off by those who could not share in its warmth or sit under the influence of its immediate inspirations. But it was answered from every hilltop and repeated in every valley of England; and each man flung the Yule log on his own fire at the cheering signal. The hearth, according to Aubrey, at the first introduction of coals, was usually in the middle of the room; and he derives from thence the origin of the saying, 'round about our coal fire'. But whether the huge fagot crackled and flustered within those merry circles or flared and roared up the ample chimneys – all social feelings, and all beautiful superstitions and old traditions and local observances awoke at the blaze; and from their thousand hiding-places crept out the customs and ceremonials which crowd this festal period of the year, and of which it is high time that we should proceed to give an account in these pages. The charmed log that (duly lighted with the last year's brand, which, as we learn from Herrick, was essential to its virtue) scared away all evil spirits, attracted all beneficent ones. The squire sat in the midst of his tenants as a patriarch might amid his family, and appears to have had no less reverence, though he compounded the wassail bowl with his own hands and shared it with the meanest of his dependants. The little book from which we have more than once quoted by the title of *Round about our Coal-fire*, furnishes us with an example of this reverence too ludicrous to be omitted. Its writer tells us that if the squire had occasion to ask one of his neighbours what o'clock it was, he received for answer a profound bow and an assurance that it was

Gate of the 'Old English Gentleman'

what o'clock his worship pleased – an answer, no doubt, indicative of profound respect, but not calculated to convey much useful information to the inquirer. In fine, however, while the glad spirit of the season covered the land, hospitality and harmony were everywhere a portion of that spirit. The light of a common festival shone for once upon the palace and the cottage, and the chain of a universal sympathy descended unbroken through all ranks, from the prince to the peasant and the beggar.

> The damsel donned her kirtle sheen;
> The hall was dress'd with holly green;
> Forth to the wood did merry men go,
> To gather in the misletoe.
> Then opened wide the baron's hall,
> To vassall, tenant, serf and all;
> Power laid his rod of rule aside,
> And ceremony doffed his pride.
> The heir, with roses in his shoes,
> *Those nights* might village partner chuse;
> The lord, underogating, share
> The vulgar game of 'post-and-pair'.
>
> The fire with well-dried logs supplied,
> Went roaring up the chimney wide;
> The huge hall-table's oaken face,

Scrubbed till it shone, the *time* to grace,
Bore then upon its massive board
No mark to part the squire and lord.
Then was brought in the lusty brawn,
By old blue-coated serving-man;
Then the grim boar's head frowned on high,
Crested with bays and rosemary.
Well can the green-garbed ranger tell,
How, when, and where, the monster fell;
What dogs, before his death, he tore,
And all the batings of the boar.
The wassail round, in good brown bowls,
Garnished with ribbons, blithely trowls.
There the huge sirloin reeked; hard by
Plumb-porridge stood, and Christmas pye;
Nor failed old Scotland to produce,
At such high-tide, her savoury goose.
Then came the merry masquers in,
And carols roared with blithesome din;
If unmelodious was the song,
It was a hearty note, and strong.
Who lists may, in their mumming, see
Traces of ancient mystery;
White shirts supplied the masquerade,
And smutted cheeks the visors made:
But, Oh! what masquers, richly dight,
Can boast of bosoms half so light?
England was merry England, when
Old Christmas brought his sports again.
'Twas Christmas broached the mightiest ale,
'Twas Christmas told the merriest tale,
A Christmas gambol oft would cheer
The poor man's heart through half the year.

The ceremonies and superstitions and sports of the Christmas season are not only various in various places, but have varied from time to time in the same. Those of them which have their root in the festival itself are for the most part common to all, and have dragged out a lingering existence even to our times. But there are many which, springing from other sources, have placed themselves under its protection or, naturally enough, sought to associate themselves with merry spirits like their own. Old Father Christmas has had a great many children in his time, some of whom he has survived; and not only so, but in addition to his own lawful offspring the generous old man has taken under his patronage and adopted into his family many who have no legitimate claim to that distinction by any of the wives to whom he has been united – neither by the Roman lady, his lady of the Celtic family, nor her whom he took to his bosom and converted from the idolatry of Thor. His family appears to have been generally far too numerous to be entertained at one time in the same establishment, or indeed by the same community, and to have rarely travelled therefore in a body.

In Ben Jonson's Masque of Christmas, to which we have already alluded, the old gentleman is introduced 'attired in round hose, long stockings, a close doublet, a high-crowned hat with a broach, a long thin beard, a truncheon, little ruffs, white shoes, his scarfs and garters tied cross, and his drum beaten before him', and is accompanied by the following members of his fine family: MISSRULE, CAROLL, MINCED-PIE, GAMBOLL, POST-AND-PAIR (since dead), NEW YEAR'S GIFT, MUMMING, WASSAIL, OFFERING, and BABY-CAKE – or BABY-COCKE, as we find him elsewhere called, but who we fear is dead, too, unless he may have changed his name, for we still find one of the family bearing some resemblance to the description of him given by Ben Jonson.

In the frontispiece to this volume the artist has represented the old man like another magician, summoning his spirits from the four winds for a general muster; and we hope that the greater part of them will obey his conjuration. The purpose, we believe, is to take a review of their condition and see if something cannot be done to amend their prospects – in which it is our purpose to assist him. Already some of the children have appeared on the stage; and the rest, we have no doubt, are advancing in all directions. We are glad to see amongst the foremost, as he ought to be, Roast Beef – that English 'champion bold' who has driven the invader hunger from the land in many a well-fought fray, and for his doughty deeds was created a knight banneret on one of his own gallant fields so long ago as King Charles's time. We suppose he is the same worthy who, in the Romish calendar, appears canonised by the title of Saint George, where his great adversary Famine is represented under the figure of a dragon. Still following Roast Beef, as he has done for many a long year, we perceive his faithful squire (bottle-holder if you will) PLUM PUDDING, with his rich round face and rosemary cockade. He is a blackamoor, and derives his extraction from the spice lands. His Oriental properties have however received an English education and taken an English form, and he has long ago been adopted into the family of Father Christmas. In his younger days his name was 'PLUMB-PORRIDGE'; but since he grew up to be the substantial man he is, it has been changed into the one he now bears, as indicative of greater consistency and strength. His master treats him like a brother; and he has, in return, done good service against the enemy in many a hard-fought field, cutting off all straggling detachments or flying parties from the main body, which the great champion had previously routed. Both these individuals, we think, are looking as vigorous as they can ever have done in their lives, and offer in their well-maintained and portly personages a strong presumption that *they* at least have at no time ceased to be favourite guests at the festivals of the land.

Near them stands, we rejoice to see, their favourite sister Wassail. She was of a slender figure in Ben Jonson's day, and is so still. If the garb in which she appears has a somewhat antiquated appearance, there is a play of the lip and a twinkle of the eye which prove that the glowing and joyous spirit which made our ancestors so merry 'ages long ago', and helped them out with so many a pleasant fancy and quaint device, is not a day older than it was in the time of King Arthur. How should she grow old who bathes in such a bowl? It is her fount of perpetual youth! Why, even mortal hearts grow younger, and mortal spirits lighter, as they taste of its charmed waters. There it is, with its floating apples and hovering inspirations! We see, too, that the 'tricksy spirit', whose head bears it (and that is more than every head could do) has lost none of his gambols, and that he is still on the best of terms with the Turkey who has been his playfellow at these holiday-times for so many years. The latter, we suppose, has just come up from Norfolk, where Father Christmas puts him to school; and the meeting on both sides seems to be of the most satisfactory kind.

Mumming also, we see, has obeyed the summons, although he looks as if he had come from a long distance and did not go about much now. We fancy he has become something of a student. Misrule too, we believe, has lost a good deal of his mercurial spirit, and finds his principal resource in old books. He has come to the muster, however, with a very long 'feather in his cap', as if he considered the present summons portentous of good fortune. He looks as if he were not altogether without hopes of taking office again. We observe with great satisfaction, that the Lord of Twelfth Night has survived the revolutions which have been fatal to the King of the Cockneys and so many of his royal brethren; and that he is still 'every inch a king'. Yonder he comes under a state canopy of cake, and wearing yet his ancient crown. The lady whom we see advancing in the distance we take to be Saint Distaff. She used to be a sad romp; but her merriest days we fear are over, for she is looking very like an old maid. Not far behind her we fancy we can hear the clear voice of Caroll singing as he comes along; and if our ears do not deceive us, the Waits are coming up in another direction. The children are dropping in on all sides.

But what is he that looks down from yonder pedestal in the background upon the merry muster, with a double face? And why, while the holly and the mistletoe mingle with the white tresses that hang over the brow of the one, is the other hidden by a veil? The face on which we gaze is the face of an old man, and a not uncheerful old man – a face marked by many a scar, by the channels of tears that have been dried up and the deep traces of sorrows passed away. Yet does it look placidly down from beneath its crown of evergreens on the joyous crew who are assembled at the voice of Christmas. But what aspect has that other face which no man can see? Why does our flesh creep and the blood curdle in our veins as we gaze? What awful mystery does that dark curtain hide? What may be written on that covered brow, that the old man dare not lift the veil and show it to those laughing children? Much, much, much that might spoil the revels. Much that man might not know and yet bear to abide. That twin face is Janus, he who shuts the gates upon the old year and opens those of the new, he who looks into the past and into the future, and catches the reflections of both, and has the tales of each written on his respective brows. For the past, it is known and has been suffered; and even at a season like this we can pause to retrace the story of its joys and of its sorrows as they are graven on that open forehead – and from that retrospect, glancing to the future for hope, can still turn to the present for enjoyment. But oh, that veil and its solemn enigmas! On that other brow may be written some secret which, putting out the light of hope, should add the darkness of the future to the darkness of the past, until, amid the gloom before and the gloom behind, the festal lamps of the season, looked on by eyes dim with our own tears, should show as sad as tapers lighted up in the chamber of the dead. God in mercy keep down that veil!

> Such foresight who on earth would crave,
> Where knowledge is not power to save?

It will be our business to introduce to our readers each of the children of old Christmas as they come up in obedience to the summons of their father, reserving to ourselves the right of settling the order of their precedence; and we will endeavor to give some account of the part which each played of old in the revelries of the season peculiarly their own, and of the sad changes which time has made in the natural constitutions, or animal spirits, of some of them. Preparatory, however, to this we must endeavour to give a rapid glance at the causes which contributed to the decay of a festival so ancient and universal and uproarious as that which we have described, and brought into the old man's family that disease to which some of them have already fallen victims, and which threatens others with an untimely extinction.

We have already shown that so early as the reign of Elizabeth the Puritans had begun to lift up their testimony against the pageantries of the Christmas-tide; and the Lord of Misrule, even in that day of his potential ascendancy, was described as little better than the great Enemy of Souls himself. Our friend Stubs (whose denunciations were directed against *all* amusements which from long usage and established repetition had assumed anything like a form of ceremonial, and who is quite as angry with those who 'goe some to the woodes and groves and some to the hilles and mountaines . . . where they spende all the night in pastymes, and in the mornyng they return bringing with them birch bowes and braunches of ` trees to deck their assemblies withall', in the sweet month of May, as he could possibly be with the Christmas revellers, although the very language in which he is obliged to state the charge against the former was enough to tempt people out 'a Maying', and might almost have converted himself) assures the reader of his 'Anatomie' that all who contribute 'to the maintenaunce of these execrable pastymes' do neither more nor less than 'offer sacrifice to the devill and Sathanas'. It is probable, however, that the people of those days, who were a right loyal people and freely acknowledged the claim of their sovereigns to an absolute disposition of all their temporalities (any of the common or statute laws of the land notwithstanding), considered it a part of their loyalty to be damned in company with their sovereigns, too, and resolved that so long as these iniquities obtained the royal patronage it was of their allegiance to place themselves in the same category of responsibility. Or perhaps their notion of regal prerogative, which extended so far as to admit its right to mould the national law at its good pleasure, might go the further length of ascribing to it a controlling power over the moral statutes of right and wrong, and of pleading its sanction against the menaces of Master Stubs. Or it may be that Master Stubs had failed to convince them that they were wrong, even without an appeal to the royal dispensation. Certain it is that, in spite of all that Master Stubs and his brethren could say, the sway of the Lord of Misrule, and the revels of his court continued to flourish with increasing splendour during this reign, and, as we have seen, lost no portion of their magnificence during the two next, although in that time had arisen the great champion of the Puritans, Prynne, and against them and their practices had been directed whole volumes of vituperation, and denounced large vials of wrath.

In Scotland, however, where the reformation took a sterner tone than in the southern kingdom, and where, as we have said, the irregularities committed under cover of the Christmas and other ceremonials laid them more justly open to its censure, the effect of this outcry was earlier and far more sensibly felt; and even so early as the reign of Queen Mary an act passed the Scottish Parliament whereby the Abbot of Unreason and all his 'merrie disports' were suppressed.

In England, it is true that, according to Sandys, an order of the common council had issued as early as the beginning of *our* Mary's reign prohibiting the Lord Mayor or Sheriffs from entertaining a Lord of Misrule in any of their houses; but this appears to have been merely on financial grounds, with a view of reducing the corporation expenditure, and to have extended no further.

It was not, however, until after the breaking out of the Civil War that the persecution of the Puritans (who had long and zealously laboured not only to resolve the various ceremonials of the season into their pagan elements, but even to prove that the celebration of the Nativity at all was in itself idolatrous) succeeded to any extent in producing that result which the war itself and the consequent disorganisation of society must in a great measure have effected even without the aid of a fanatical outcry. In the very first year of that armed struggle, the earliest successful blow was struck against the festivities with which it had been usual to celebrate this period of the year, in certain ordinances which were issued for suppressing the performance of plays and other diversions; and in the following year some of the shops in London were for the first time opened on Christmas day, in obedience to the feelings which connected any observance of it with the spirit of popery. By the year 1647 the Puritans had so far prevailed that in various places the parish officers were subjected to penalties for encouraging the decking of churches and permitting divine service to be performed therein on Christmas morning; and in the same year the observance of the festival itself, with that of other holidays, was formally abolished by the two branches of the legislature.

It was found impossible, however, by all these united means, to eradicate the Christmas spirit from the land; and many of its customs and festivities continued to be observed, not only in obscure places, but even in towns, in spite of prohibition and in spite of the disarrangement of social ties. The contest between the Puritan spirit and the ancient spirit of celebration led to many contests; and we have an account – in a little book of which we have seen a copy in the British Museum, entitled *Canterbury Christmas, or a True Relation of the Insurrection in Canterbury* – of the disturbances which ensued in that city upon the Mayor's proclamation, issued in consequence of that Parliamentary prohibition at the Christmas which followed. This said proclamation, it appears, which was made by the city crier, was to the effect 'that Christmas day and all other superstitious festivals should be put downe and that a market should be kept upon Christmas day'. This order, it goes on to state, was 'very ill taken by the country', the people of which neglected to bring their provisions into the town, and gave other tokens of their displeasure of a less negative kind. For, a few of the shopkeepers in the city, 'to the number of twelve at the most', having ventured to open their shops in defiance of the general feeling, 'they were commanded by the multitude to shut up again; but refusing to obey, their ware was thrown up and down and they at last forced to shut in.'

Nor were the revilings of the Puritans against the lovers of Christmas observances suffered to remain unanswered. Many a squib was directed against the Roundheads; and the popular regret for the suppression of their high festival was skilfully appealed to by Royalist politicians and favourers of the ancient religion. The connection between the new condition of things in Church and State and the extinction of all the merriment of the land was carefully suggested in publications that stole out in spite of penalties and were read in defiance of prohibitions. As an example, that curious little tract from which we have more than once quoted under the title of *An Hue and Cry after Christmas*, bears the date of 1645; and we shall best give our readers an idea of its character by setting out that title at length, as the same exhibits a tolerable abstract of its contents. It runs thus: 'The arraignment, conviction, and imprisoning of Christmas on St Thomas day last, and how he broke out of prison in the holidayes and got away, onely left his hoary hair and gray beard sticking between two iron bars of a window. With an Hue and Cry after Christmas, and a letter from Mr Woodcock, a fellow in Oxford, to a malignant lady in London. And divers passages between the lady and the cryer about Old Christmas; and what shift he was fain to make to save his life, and great stir to fetch him back again. Printed by Simon Minc'd Pye for Cissely Plum-Porridge, and are to be sold by Ralph Fidler Chandler at the signe of the Pack of Cards in Mustard Alley in Brawn Street.' Besides the allusions contained in the latter part of this title to some of the good things that follow in the old man's train, great pains are taken by the 'cryer' in describing him, and by the lady in mourning for him, to allude to many of the cheerful attributes that made him dear to the people. His great antiquity and portly appearance are likewise insisted upon. 'For age this hoarie-headed man was of great yeares, and as white as snow. He entered the Romish Kallendar, time out of mind, as o'd or very neer as Father Mathusalem was – one that looked fresh in the Bishops' time, though their fall made him pine away ever since. He was full and fat as any divine doctor on them all; he looked under the consecrated lawne sleeves as big as Bul-beefe – just like Bacchus upon a tunne of wine, when the grapes hang shaking about his eares; but since the Catholike liquor is taken from him he is much wasted, so that he hath looked very thin and ill of late.' 'The poor,' says the 'cryer' to the lady, 'are sory for' his departure; 'for they go to every door a-begging, as they were wont to do (*good Mrs, Somewhat against this good time*); but Time was transformed, *Away, be gone; here is not for you*.' The lady, however, declares that she for one will not be deterred from welcoming old Christmas. 'No, no!' says she; 'bid him come by night over the Thames, and we will have a back-door open to let him in;' and ends by anticipating better prospects for him another year.

And by many a back door was the old man let in to many a fireside during the heaviest times of all that persecution and disgrace. On the establishment of the Commonwealth, when the more settled state of things removed some of the causes which had opposed themselves to his due reception, the contests of opposition between the revived spirit of festival and the increased sectarian austerity became more conspicuous. There is an order of the Parliament in 1652 again prohibiting the observance of Christmas day, which proves that the practice had revived; and there are examples of the military having been employed to disperse congregations assembled for that purpose. In the *Vindication of Christmas*, published about this time, the old gentleman, after complaining bitterly of the manner in which he was 'used in the city, and wandering into the country up and down from house to house, found small comfort in any', asserts his determination not to be so repulsed: 'Welcome or not welcome,' says he, 'I am come.' In a periodical publication of that day entitled 'Mercurius Democritus, or a True and Perfect Nocturnall, communicating many strange wonders out of the World in the Moon, etc.,' the public are encouraged to keep Christmas, and promised better days. No. 37 contains some verses to that effect, of which the following are the first two:

> Old Christmass now is come to town,
>   Though few do him regard;
> He laughs to see them going down,
>   That have put down his Lord.

> Cheer up, sad heart, crown Christmass bowls,
>   Banish dull grief and sorrow;
> Though you want cloaths, you have rich souls,
>   The *sun* may shine tomorrow.

And again in No. 38:

> A gallant crew, stir up the fire,
>   The other winter tale,
> Welcome, Christmass, 'tis our desire
>   To give thee more spic'd ale.

On the return of the royal family to England, the court celebrations of Christmas were revived both there and at the Inns of Court; and the Lord of Misrule came again into office. We have allusions to the one and the other in the writings of Pepys and of Evelyn. The nobles and wealthy gentry, too, once more at their country seats, took under their protection such of the ancient observances as had survived the persecution, and from time to time stole out of their hiding-places under the encouragement of the new order of things. But in none of its ancient haunts did the festival ever again recover its splendour of old. The condition of Charles's exchequer, and the many charges upon it – arising as well out of the services of his adherents as from his own dissolute life – left him little chance of imitating the lavish appointments of the court pageantries in the days of Elizabeth and James; and the troubles out of which the nation had emerged had made changes as well in the face of the country as in the condition and character of society, alike opposed to anything like a general and complete revival of the merry doings of yore. In the country, estates had passed into new hands, and the immemorial ties between the ancient families and the tenants of the soil had been rudely severed. Many of the old establishments in which these celebrations had been most zealously observed, were finally broken up; and friends who had met together from childhood around the Christmas fire, and pledged each other year by year in the wassail bowl, were scattered by the chances of war. But out of this disturbance of the old localities and disruption of the ancient ties of the land, a result still more fatal to these old observances had arisen, promoted besides by the dissipation of manners which the restored monarch had introduced into the country. Men rooted out from their ancestral possessions and looking to a licentious king for compensation, became hangers-on about the court; and others who had no such excuse, seduced by their example and enamoured of the gaieties of the metropolis and the profligacies of Whitehall, abandoned the shelter of the old trees beneath whose shade their fathers had fostered the sanctities of life, and from 'country gentlemen' became 'men about town'. The evils of this practice, at which we have before hinted as one of those to which the decay of rural customs is mainly owing, began to be early felt, and form the topic of frequent complaint and the subject of many of the popular ballads of that day. The song of the 'Old and Young Courtier' was written for the purpose of contrasting the good old manners with those of Charles's time; and the effects of the change upon the Christmas hospitalities has due and particular notice therein. We extract it from the Percy collection for our readers, as appropriate to our subject and a sample of the ballads of the time:

The Old and Young Courtier

An old song made by an aged old pate,
Of an old worshipful gentleman who had a greate estate,
That kept a brave old house at a bountifull rate,
And an old porter to relieve the poor at his gate;
      Like an old courtier of the Queen's,
      And the Queen's old courtier.

With an old lady, whose anger one word assuages;
They every quarter paid their old servants their wages,
And never knew what belong'd to coachmen, footmen, nor pages,
But kept twenty old fellows with blue coats and badges;
      Like an old courtier, etc.

With an old study fill'd full of learned old books,
With an old reverend chaplain – you might know him by his looks –
With an old buttery hatch worn quite off the hooks,
And an old kitchen, that maintained half-a-dozen old cooks;
      Like an old courtier, etc.

With an old hall, hung about with pikes, guns, and bows,
With old swords, and bucklers that had borne many
                         shrewde blows,
And an old frize coat, to cover his worship's trunk hose,
And a cup of old sherry to comfort his copper nose;
      Like an old courtier, etc.

With a good old fashion, when Christmasse was come,
To call in all his old neighbours with bagpipe and drum,
With good chear enough to furnish every old room,
And old liquor able to make a cat speak, and man dumb;
      Like an old courtier, etc.

With an old falconer, huntsman, and a kennel of hounds,
That never hawked, nor hunted, but in his own grounds,
Who, like a wise man, kept himself within his own bounds,
And when he dyed gave every child a thousand good pounds;
      Like an old courtier, etc.

But to his eldest son his house and land he assign'd,
Charging him in his will to keep the old bountifull mind,
To be good to his old tenants, and to his neighbours be kind;
But in the ensuing ditty you shall hear how he was inclined;
      Like a young courtier, etc.

Like a flourishing young gallant, newly come to his land,
Who keeps a brace of painted madams at his command,
And takes up a thousand pound upon his father's land,
And gets drunk in a tavern, till he can neither go nor stand;
      Like a young courtier, etc.

With a new-fangled lady, that is dandy, nice, and spare,
Who never knew what belong'd to good housekeeping or care,
Who buys gaudy-color'd fans to play with wanton air,
And seven or eight different dressings of other women's hair;
      Like a young courtier, etc.

With a new-fashion'd hall, built where the old one stood,
Hung round with new pictures, that do the poor no good,
With a fine marble chimney, wherein burns neither coal nor wood,
And a new smooth shovelboard, whereon no victuals ne'er stood;
      Like a young courtier, etc.

With a new study, stuff'd full of pamphlets and plays,
And a new chaplain, that swears faster than he prays,
With a new buttery-hatch that opens once in four or five days,
And a new French cook, to devise fine kickshaws and toys;
      Like a young courtier, etc.

With a new fashion, when Christmasse is drawing on,
On a new journey to London straight we all must begone,
And leave none to keep house, but our new porter John,
Who relieves the poor with a thump on the back with a stone;
      Like a young courtier, etc.

With a new gentleman usher, whose carriage is compleat,
With a new coachman, footmen, and pages to carry up the meat,
With a waiting-gentlewoman, whose dressing is very neat,
Who when her lady has din'd, lets the servants not eat;
      Like a young courtier, etc.

With new titles of honour bought with his father's old gold,
For which sundry of his ancestors' old manors are sold;
And this is the course most of our new gallants hold,
Which makes that good housekeeping is now grown so cold,
       Among the young courtiers of the King,
       Or the King's young courtiers.

In a word, the old English feeling seemed nearly extinct for a time; and the ancient customs which had connected themselves therewith, one by one fell more or less into disuse. The chain of *universal* sympathy and *general* observance, which had long kept the festival together in all its parts, was broken; and the parts fell asunder, and were by degrees lost or overlooked. Let no man say that this is scarcely worth lamenting! Let none imagine that, in the decay of customs useless or insignificant in themselves, there is little to regret! 'The affections,' says Sterne, 'when they are busy that way, will build their structures, were it but on the paring of a nail'; and there is no practice of long observance and ancient veneration – whether among nations or individuals – round which the affections have not in some degree twined themselves, and which are not therefore useful as supports and remembrancers to those affections. There are few of the consequences springing from civil war more lamentable than the disturbance which it gives to the social arrangements, were it but to the meanest of them. It is impossible that customs long identified with the feelings should perish without those feelings (though from their own eternal principle they will ultimately revive and find new modes of action) suffering some temporary injury. It was a beautiful assertion of Dr Johnson that his feelings would be outraged by seeing an old post rooted up from before his door which he had been used to look at all his life – even though it might be an encumbrance there. How much more would he have grieved over the removal of a village Maypole, with all its merry memories and all its ancient reverence!

The Christmas festival has languished from those days to this, but never has been, and never will be extinct. The stately forms of its celebration in high places have long since (and, in all probability, forever) passed away. The sole and homely representative of the gorgeous Christmas prince is the mock-monarch of the Epiphany – the laureate of our times, with his nominal duties, in the last faint shadow of the court bards and masque-makers of yore; and the few lingering remains of the important duties once confided to the master of the royal revels are silently and unostentatiously performed in the office of the Lord Chamberlain of today. But the spirit of the season yet survives, and, for reasons which we shall proceed to point out, *must* survive. True, the uproarious merriment, the loud voice which it sent of old throughout the land, have ceased; and while the ancient sports and ceremonies are widely scattered, many of them have retreated into obscure places, and some perhaps are lost. Still, however, this period of commemoration is everywhere a merry time; and we believe, as we have already said, that most of the children of Father Christmas are yet wandering up and down in one place or another of the land. We call upon all those of our readers who know anything of the 'old, old, very old, gray-bearded gentleman' or his family to aid us in our search after them; and with their good help we will endeavour to restore them to some portion of their ancient honours in England.

Feelings of the Season

Of all the festivals which crowd the Christian calendar there is none that exercises an influence so strong and universal as that of Christmas; and those varied superstitions, and quaint customs, and joyous observances, which once abounded throughout the rural districts of England, are at no period of the year so thickly congregated or so strongly marked as at this season of unrestrained festivity and extended celebration. The reasons for this are various and very obvious. In the case of a single celebration, which has to support itself by its own solitary influence long, perchance, after the feeling in which it originated has ceased to operate, whose significance is perhaps dimly and more dimly perceived (through the obscurity of a distance, year after year receding further into shadow) by its own unaided and unreflected light, the chances are many that the annually increasing neglect into which its observance is likely to fall, shall finally consign it to an entire obliteration. But a cluster of festivals, standing in a proximate order of succession, at once throwing light upon each other and illustrated by a varied and numerous host of customs, traditions, and ceremonies – of which, as in a similar cluster of stars, the occasional obscuration of any one or more would not prevent their memory being suggested and their place distinctly indicated by the others – present greatly multiplied probabilities against their existence being ever entirely forgotten or their observation wholly discontinued. The arrangement by which a series of celebrations – beautiful in themselves, and connected with the paramount event in which are laid the foundations of our religion – are made to fall at a period otherwise of very solemn import (from its being assumed as the close of the larger of those revolutions of time into which man measures out the span of his transitory existence), and the chance which has brought down to the same point and thrown together the traces of customs and superstitions both of a sacred and secular character, uniting with the crowd of Catholic observances, offshoots from the ancient Saturnalia, remains of old Druidical rites, and glimpses into the mythology of the Northern nations, have written a series of hieroglyphics upon that place of the calendar, which, if they cannot be deciphered in every part, are still, from their number and juxtaposition, never likely to be overlooked.

Family Congratulations

But though these causes are offered as accounting for the preservation of many customs which, without them, would long since have passed into oblivion, which exist by virtue of the position they occupy on the calendar, yet the more conspicuous celebrations of this season need no such aid and no such arguments. Nothing can be added to their intrinsic interest, and they are too closely connected with the solemn warnings of man's temporal destiny, and linked with the story of his eternal hopes, ever to lose any portion of that influence, a share of which (without thereby losing, as light is communicated without diminution) they throw over all the other celebrations that take shelter under their wing.

In every way, and by many a tributary stream, are the holy and beneficent sentiments which belong to the period increased and refreshed. Beautiful feelings, too apt to fade within the heart of man amid the chilling influences of worldly pursuit, steal out beneath the sweet religious warmth of the season, and the pure and holy amongst the hopes of earth assemble, to place themselves under the protection of that eternal hope whose promise is now, as it were, yearly renewed. Amid the echoes of that song which proclaimed peace on earth and goodwill towards men, making no exclusions, and dividing them into no classes, rises up a dormant sense of universal brotherhood in the heart; and something like a distribution of the good things of the earth is suggested in favour of those, destitute here, who are proclaimed as joint participators in the treasure thus announced from heaven. At no other period of the year are the feeling of a universal benevolence and the sense of a common Adam so widely awakened; at no season is the predominant spirit of selfishness so effectually rebuked; never are the circles of love so largely widened.

The very presence of a lengthened festivity – for festivity can never be *solitary* – would, apart from its sacred causes, promote these wholesome effects. The extended space of time over which this festival is spread, the protracted holiday which it creates, points it out for the gathering together of distant friends whom the passing nature of an occasional and single celebration would fail to collect from their scattered places of the world. By this wise and beautiful arrangement the spell of home is still made to cast its sweet and holy influence along the sterile regions as along the bright places of after-life, and from the dark valleys and the sunny hilltops of the world to call back alike the spoiled of fortune and the tired and travel-stained to refresh themselves again and again at the fountain of their calmer hopes and purer feelings. A wise and beautiful arrangement this would be, in whatever season of the year it might be placed! Wise and beautiful is any institution which sets up a rallying-place for the early affections and reawakens the sacred sympathies of youth – which, from that wellhead of purity and peace, sends forth, as it were, a little river of living waters, to flow with revivifying freshness and soothing murmur along the wastes and wildernesses of after years; which makes of that springtime of the heart a reservoir of balm, to which in hours of sorrow it can return for joy, and in years of guilt for regeneration; and which, like the widow's cruse of oil, wasteth not in all the ages of the mind's dearth. But how greatly are the wisdom and the beauty of this arrangement increased by the sacred season at which it has been placed! Under the sanctions of religion the covenants of the heart are renewed. Upon the altars of our faith the lamps of the spirit are rekindled. The loves of earth seem to have met together at the sound of the 'glad tidings' of the season, to refresh themselves for the heaven which those tidings proclaim. From 'Abana and Pharpar' and all the 'rivers of Damascus' the affections are returned to bathe in 'the waters of Israel'. In many a peaceful spot and lowly home,

> Wi' joy unfeigned, brothers and sisters meet,
> An' each for other's welfare kindly spiers;

and as the long-separated look once more into the 'sweet, familiar faces', and listen in that restored companionship to strains such as 'once did sweet in Zion glide' (even as they listened long ago, and, it may be, with some who are gone from them for ever) –

> Hope springs, 'exulting on triumphant wing'
> That thus they all shall meet in future days,
> There ever bask in uncreated rays,
> No more to sigh or shed the bitter tear,
> Together hymning their Creator's praise
> In such society, yet still more dear,
> While ceaseless time moves round in an eternal sphere.

To this tone of feeling the services of the Church have for some time previously been gradually adapting the mind. During the whole period of Advent a course of moral and religious preparation has been going on, and a state of expectation is by degrees excited, not unlike that with which the Jews were waiting for the Messiah, of old. There is, as it were, a sort of watching for the great event, a questioning where Christ shall be born, and an earnest looking out for his star in the East that we may 'come to worship him'. The feeling awakened by the whole series of these services – unlike that suggested by some of those which commemorate other portions of the same sacred story – is entirely a joyous one. The lowly manner of the Saviour's coming, the exceeding humiliation of his appointments, the dangers which beset his infancy, and his instant rejection by those to whom he came, are all forgotten in the fact of his coming itself, in the feeling of a mighty triumph and the sense of a great deliverance, or only so far remembered as to temper the triumph and give a character of tenderness to the joy. 'The services of the Church about this season,' says Washington Irving, 'are extremely tender and inspiring. They dwell on the beautiful story of the origin of our faith, and the pastoral scenes that accompanied its announcement. They gradually increase in fervor and pathos during the season of Advent, until they break forth in full jubilee on the morning that brought "peace and good-will to men".' 'I do not know,' he adds, 'a grander effect of music on the moral feelings than to hear the full choir and the pealing organ performing a Christmas anthem in a cathedral, and filling every part of the vast pile with triumphant harmony.' We confess that, for ourselves, very sensible as we are to the grander and more complicated effects of harmony, we have, on the occasion in question, been more touched by the simple song of rejoicing as it rang in its unaided sweetness through the aisles of some village church. We have felt ourselves more emphatically reminded, amid pastoral scenes and primitive choirs, of the music of congratulation which was uttered through the clear air to men 'abiding in the field, keeping watch over their flocks by night':

The hallowed anthem sent to hail
Bethlehem's shepherds in the lonely vale
When Jordan hushed his waves, and midnight still
Watched on the holy towers of Zion's hill.

Nor is the religious feeling which belongs to this season suffered to subside with the great event of the Nativity itself. The incidents of striking interest which immediately followed the birth of the Messiah, the persecutions which were directed against His life, and the starry writing of God in the sky, which, amid the rejection of 'His own', drew to him witnesses from afar, all contribute to keep alive the sense of a sacred celebration to the end of the period usually devoted to social festivity, and send a wholesome current of religious feeling through the entire season, to temper its extravagancies and regulate its mirth. The worship of the shepherds; the lamentation in Rama, and the weeping of Rachel for the murder of the innocents; the miraculous escape from that massacre of the Saviour, and the flight of His parents into Egypt with the rescued child; and the manifestation of Christ to the Gentiles, which is indeed the day of His Nativity to *us* – are all commemorated in the Christian Church, and illustrated by the series of services distributed through that period of religious worship which bears the general title of Christmas.

There is, too, in the lengthened duration of this festival a direct cause of that joyous and holiday spirit which, for the most part (after the first tenderness of meeting has passed away, and a few tears perhaps been given, as the muster-roll is perused, to those who answer to their names no more), pervades all whom that same duration has tempted to assemble.

Regrets there will no doubt, in most cases, be, for these distant and periodical gatherings together of families but show more prominently the blanks which the long intervals have created; this putting on anew, as it were, of the garment of love but exposes the rents which time has made since it was last worn; this renewing of the chain of our attachments but displays the links that are broken! The Sybil has come round again, as year by year she comes, with her books of the affections; but new leaves have been torn away. 'No man,' says Shakespeare, 'ever bathed twice in the same river'; and the home-Jordan to which the observers of the Christmas festival come yearly back to wash away the leprous spots contracted in the world never presents to them again the identical waters in which last they sported, though it be Jordan still. Amid these jubilant harmonies of the heart there will be parts unfilled up, voices wanting. 'This young gentle-woman,' says the Countess of Rousillon to Lafeu, 'had a father (oh that *had!* how sad a passage 'tis!).' And surely, with such changes as are implied in that past tense, some of the notes of life's early music are silenced forever. 'Would they were with us still!' says the old ballad; and in the first hour of these reunions many and many a time is the wish echoed in something like the words! And if these celebrations have been too long disused, and the wanderer comes rarely back to the birthplace of the affections, the feeling of sadness may be too strong for the joyous influences of the season –

> A change *he may find* there, and many a change!
> Faces and footsteps and all things strange!
> Gone are the heads of the silvery hair,
> And the young that were, have a brow of care,
> And the place is hushed where the children played!

till, amid the bitter contrasts of the past with the present, and thoughts of 'the loved, the lost, the distant, and the dead', something like

> A pall,
> And a gloom o'ershadowing the banquet-hall,
> And a mark on the floor as of life-drops spilt,

may spoil his ear for the voice of mirth, and darken all the revels of the merry Christmas-tide.

To few assemblages of men is it given to come together in the scene of ancient memories without having to 'remember such things were that were most precious'. But excepting in those cases in which the suffering is extreme or the sorrow immediate, after a few hours given to a wholesome and perhaps mournful retrospect, the mind readjusts itself to the tone of the time, and men for the most part seem to understand that they are met for the purpose of being as merry as it is in their natures to be. And to the attainment of this right joyous frame of mind we have already said that a sense of the duration of the festival period greatly contributes. In the case of a single holiday, the mind has scarcely time to take the appropriate tone before the period of celebration has passed away; and a sense of its transitoriness tends often to prevent the effort being made with that heartiness which helps to insure success.

But when the holiday of today terminates only that it may make way for the holiday of tomorrow, and gladness has an ancient charter in virtue of which it claims dominion over a series of days so extended that the happy schoolboy (and some who are quite as happy as schoolboys, and as merry, too) cannot see the end of them for the blaze of joyous things that lies between – then does the heart surrender itself confidently to the genius of the time, and lets loose a host of cheerful and kindly feelings, which it knows will not be suddenly thrown back upon it, and heaps up pleasant devices upon the glowing flame of mirth, as we heap up logs on the roaring fire, laying them decently aside at the end of the season, as we lay aside the burned-out brand of the Yule log to rekindle the Christmas fire and the Christmas feeling of another year.

But there is yet another reason, in aid of those which we have enumerated, accounting for an observance of the Christmas festivities more universal, and a preservation of its traditions more accurate and entire, than are bestowed in England upon the festival customs of any other period of the year. This reason, which might not at first view seem so favourable to that end as in truth it is, is to be found in the outward and natural aspects of the season. We have been watching the year through the period of its decline, are arrived at the dreary season of its old age, and stand near the edge of its grave. We have seen the rich sunshines and sweet but mournful twilights of autumn, with their solemn inspirations, give place to the short days and gloomy evenings which usher in the coming solstice. One by one the fair faces of the flowers have departed from us, and the sweet murmuring of 'shallow rivers, by whose falls melodious birds sing madrigals', has been exchanged for the harsh voice of the swollen torrent and the dreary music of winds that 'rave through the naked tree'. Through many a chilling sign of 'weary winter comin' fast', we have reached the

> Last of the months, severest of them all.

> For lo! the fiery horses of the Sun
> Through the twelve signs their rapid course have run;
> Time, like a serpent, bites his forked tail,
> And Winter, on a goat, bestrides the gale;
> Rough blows the North-wind near Arcturus' star,
> And sweeps, unreined, across the polar bar.

The halcyon days, which sometimes extend their southern influence even to our stern climate, and carry an interval of gloomy calm into the heart of this dreary month, have generally ere its close given place to the nipping frosts and chilling blasts of mid-winter. 'Out of the South' has come 'the whirlwind, and cold out of the North'. The days have dwindled to their smallest stature, and the long nights, with their atmosphere of mist, shut in and circumscribe the wanderings of man. Clouds and shadows surround us. The air has lost its rich echoes, and the earth its diversified aspects; and to the immediate threshold of the house of feasting and merriment we have travelled through those dreary days which are emphatically called 'the dark days before Christmas'. Of one of the gloomy mornings that usher in these melancholy days, Ben Jonson gives the following dismal description:

It is, methinks, a morning full of fate!
It riseth slowly, as her sullen car
Had all the weights of sleep and death hung at it!
She is not rosy-fingered, but swoln black!
Her face is like a water turned to blood,
And her sick head is bound about with clouds,
As if she threatened night, ere noon of day!
It does not look as it would have a hail
Or health wished in it – as of other morns!

And the general discomforts of the season are bemoaned by old Sackville, with words that have a wintry sound, in the following passage, which we extract from *England's Parnassus*:

The wrathfull winter, proching on a pace,
With blustring blast had all ybard the treene;
And old Saturnus, with his frosty face,
With chilling cold had pearst the tender greene;
The mantle rent wherein inwrapped beene
The gladsome groves that now lay over-throwne,
The tapers torne, and every tree downe blowne;
The soyle, that erst so seemely was to seeme,
Was all dispoiled of her beauties hewe,
And stole fresh flowers (wherewith the Somer's queene
Had clad the earth), now Boreas blast downe blew;
And small fowles flocking, in their songs did rew
The Winter's wrath, where with each thing defast,
In wofull wise bewayl'd the Sommer past:
Hawthorne had lost his motley liverie,
The naked twigs were shivering all for cold,
And, dropping down the teares aboundantlie,
Each thing, methought, with weeping eye me told
The cruell season, bidding me withhold
Myselfe within.

The feelings excited by this dreary period of transition, and by the desolate aspect of external things to which it has at length brought us, would seem, at first view, to be little in harmony with a season of festival, and peculiarly unpropitious to the claims of merriment. And yet it is precisely this joyless condition of the natural world which drives us to take refuge in our moral resources, at the same time that it furnishes us with the leisure necessary for their successful development. The spirit of cheerfulness which, for the blessing of man, is implanted in his nature, deprived of the many issues by which, at other seasons, it walks abroad and breathes amid the sights and sounds of Nature, is driven to its own devices for modes of manifestation, and takes up its station by the blazing hearth. In rural districts, the varied occupations which call the sons of labour abroad into the fields are suspended by the austerities of the time; and to the cottage of the poor man has come a season of temporal repose, concurrently with the falling of that period which seals anew for him, as it were, the promises of an eternal rest. At no other portion of the year, could a feast of equal duration find so many classes of men at leisure for its reception.

> With his ice, and snow, and rime,
> Let bleak winter sternly come!
> There is not a sunnier clime
> Than the love-lit winter home.

Amid the comforts of the fireside, and all its sweet companionships and cheerful inspirations, there is something like the sense of a triumph obtained over the hostilities of the season. Nature, which at other times promotes the expansion of the feelings and contributes to the enjoyments of man, seems here to have promulgated her fiat against their indulgence; and there is a kind of consciousness of an inner world created, in evasion of her law – a tract won by the genius of the affections from the domain of desolation, spots of sunshine planted by the heart in the very bosom of shadow, a pillar of fire lit up in the darkness. And thus the sensation of a respite from toil, the charms of renewed companionship, the consciousness of a general sympathy of enjoyment running along all the links of the social chain, and the contrasts established within to the discomforts without, are all components of that propitious feeling to which the religious spirit of the season, and all its quaint and characteristic observances, make their appeal.

There is, too (connected with these latter feelings, and almost unacknowledged by the heart of man), another moral element of that cheerful sentiment which has sprung up within it. It consists in the prospect, even at this distant and gloomy period, of a coming spring. This is peculiarly the season of looking forward. Already, as it were, the infant face of the new year is perceived beneath the folds of the old one's garment. The business of the present year has terminated, and along the night which has succeeded to its season of labour have been set up a series of illuminations, which, we know, will be extinguished only that the business of another seed-time may begin.

Neither, amid all its dreary features, is the *natural* season without its own picturesque beauty, nor even entirely divested of all its summer indications of a living loveliness, or all suggestions of an eternal hope. Not only has it the peculiar beauties of old age, but it has besides lingering traces of that beauty which old age has not been able wholly to extinguish, and which come finely in aid of the moral hints and religious hopes of the season.

The former – the graces which are peculiar to the season itself – exist in many a natural aspect and grotesque effect, which is striking both for the variety it offers and for its own intrinsic loveliness.

> We may find it in the wintry boughs, as they cross the cold blue sky,
> While soft on icy pool and stream the pencilled shadows lie,
> When we look upon their tracery, by the fairy frost-work bound,
> Whence the flitting red-breast shakes a shower of blossoms
> to the ground.

The white mantle which the earth occasionally puts on with the rapidity of a spell, covering, in the course of a night and while we have slept, the familiar forms with a sort of strangeness that makes us feel as if we had awakened in some new and enchanted land; the fantastic forms assumed by the drifting snow; the wild and fanciful sketching of old winter upon the 'frosty pane'; the icicles that depend like stalactites from every projection, and sparkle in the sun like jewels of the most brilliant water; and, above all, the feathery investiture of the trees above alluded to, by which their minute tracery is brought out with a richness shaming the carving of the finest chisel – are amongst the features which exhibit the inexhaustible fertility of Nature in the production of striking and beautiful effects. Hear how one of our best poetesses, Mary Howitt, sings of these graces:

> One silent night hath passed, and lo,
> How beautiful the earth is now!
> All aspect of decay is gone,
> The hills have put their vesture on,
> And clothed is the forest bough.
>
> Say not 'tis an unlovely time!
> Turn to the wide, white waste thy view;
> Turn to the silent hills that rise
> In their cold beauty to the skies,
> And to those skies intensely blue.
>
> Walk now among the forest trees:
> Saidst thou that they were stripped and bare?
> Each heavy bough is bending down
> With snowy leaves and flowers – the crown
> Which Winter regally doth wear.

> 'Tis well; thy summer garden ne'er
> Was lovelier, with its birds and flowers,
> Than is this silent place of snow,
> With feathery branches drooping low,
> Wreathing around thee shadowy bowers!

While on the subject of the natural beauties of this season, we must introduce our readers to some admirable verses which have been furnished to us by our friend Mr Stoddart, the author of that fine poem the 'Death-Wake', and in which its peculiar aspects are described with a very graphic pen:

A Winter Landscape

The dew-lark sitteth on the ice, beside the reedless rill;
The leaf of the hawthorn flutters on the solitary hill;
The wild lake weareth on its heart a cold and changed look,
And meets, at the lip of its moon-lit marge, the spiritual brook.

Idly basks the silver swan, near to the isle of trees,
And to its proud breast come and kiss the billow and the breeze;
They wash the eider as they play about the bird of grace,
And boom, in the same slow mood, away, to the
                                            moveless mountain-base.

The chieftain-deer, amid the pines, his antlered forehead shows,
And scarcely are the mosses bent where that stately one arose;
His step is as the pressure of a light beloved hand,
And he looketh like a poet's dream in some enchanted land!

A voice of Winter, on the last wild gust of Autumn borne,
Is hurried from the hills afar, like the windings of a horn;
And solemnly and heavily the silver birches groan,
And the old ash waves his wizard hand to the dim, mysterious tone.

And noiselessly, across the heaven, a gray and vapory shred
Is wandering, fed by phantom clouds that one by one are led
Out of the wide North, where they grow within the aged sea,
And in their coils the yellow moon is labouring lazily!

She throws them from her mystic urn, as they were beckoned back
By some enchantress, working out her spells upon their track;
Or gathers up their fleecy folds, and shapes them, as they go,
To hang around her beautiful form a tracery of snow.

Lo, Winter cometh! – and his hoar is heavy on the hill,
And curiously the frostwork forms below the rimy rill;
The birth of morn is a gift of pearl to the heath and willow-tree,
And the green rush hangs o'er its water-bed, shining and silvery.

From the calm of the lake a vapour steals its restless wreath away,
And leaves not a crisp on the quiet tarn but the wake of the swan at play;
The deer holds up the glistening heath, where his hoof is lightly heard,
And the dew-lark circleth to his song – sun-lost and lonely bird!

But the season hath other striking aspects of its own. Pleasant, says
Southey:

> To the sobered soul,
> The silence of the wintry scene,
> When Nature shrouds her in her trance,
> In deep tranquillity.
>
> Not undelightful now to roam
> The wild heath sparkling on the sight;
> Not undelightful now to pace
> The forest's ample rounds,
>
> And see the spangled branches shine,
> And snatch the moss of many a hue,
> That varies the old tree's brown bark,
> Or o'er the gray-stone spreads.

Mr Southey might have mentioned, too – as belonging to the same class
of effects with those produced by the mosses 'of many a hue' that 'vary the
old tree's brown bark' – those members of the forest which retain their
dead and many tinted leaves till the ensuing spring, hanging occasional
wreaths of strange and fantastic beauty in the white tresses of winter,
together with the rich contrast presented by the red twigs of the dogwood
amid the dark colours of the surrounding boughs. The starry heavens, too,
at this period of the year, present an occasional aspect of extraordinary
brilliancy; and the long winter nights are illustrated by a pomp of
illumination, presenting magnificent contrasts to the cold and cheerless
earth, and offering unutterable revelations at once to the physical and
mental eye.

Amongst the traces of a *former* beauty not utterly extinguished, and the
suggestions of a summer feeling not wholly passed away, we have those
both of sight and scent and sound. The lark, 'all independent of the leafy
spring', as Wordsworth says, has not long ceased to pour his anthem
through the sky. In propitious seasons, such as we have enjoyed for some

years past, he is almost a Christmas-carol singer. The China-roses are with us still, and under proper management will stay with us till the snowdrops come. So will the anemones and the wallflowers; and the aconite may be won to come, long 'before the swallow dares, and take the winds of *January* with beauty'. The cold air may be kept fragrant with the breath of the scented coltsfoot, and the lingering perfume of the mignonette. Then we have rosemary, too, 'mocking the winter of the year with perfume' –

> Rosemary and rue, which keep
> Seeming and savour all the winter long.

'It looks,' says Leigh Hunt, pleasantly, 'as if we need have no winter, if we choose, as far as flowers are concerned.' 'There is a story,' he adds, 'in Boccaccio, of a magician who conjured up a garden in wintertime. His magic consisted in his having a knowledge beyond his time; and magic pleasures, so to speak, await on all who choose to exercise knowledge after his fashion.'

But what we would allude to more particularly here are the evergreens, which, with their rich and clustering berries, adorn the winter season, offering a provision for the few birds that still remain, and hanging a faint memory of summer about the hedges and the groves. The misletoe with its white berries, the holly (Virgil's acanthus) with its scarlet berries and pointed leaves, the ivy whose berries are green, the pyracanthus with its berries of deep orange, the arbutus exhibiting its flowers and fruit upon adjacent boughs, the glossy laurel and the pink-eyed laurestine (not to speak of the red berries of the May-bush, the purple sloes of the black-thorn, or others which show their clusters upon leafless boughs, nor of the evergreen trees – the pine, the fir, the cedar, or the cypress), are all so many pleasant remembrancers of the past, and so many types to man of that which is imperishable in his own nature. And it is probably both *because* they are such remembrancers of what the heart so much loves, and such types of what it so much desires, that they are gathered about our doors and within our homes at this period of natural decay and religious regeneration, and mingle their picturesque forms and hopeful morals with all the mysteries and ceremonies of the season.

Signs of the Season

We have said that the coming festivities of the season 'fling their shadows' long before: the *avant-couriers* of the old man are to be seen advancing in all directions. At home and abroad, in town and in country, in the remote farmstead and on the king's highway, we are met by the symptoms of his approach, and the arrangements making for his reception.

We will not dwell here on the domestic operations which are so familiar to all – the ample provision for good cheer, which has long been making in every man's home who can at any time afford to make good cheer at all. We need not remind our town readers of the increased activity visible in all the interior departments of each establishment, and the apparent extent and complication of its foreign relations; the councils held with the house-keeper and cook; the despatches to the butcher, baker, poulterer, and confectioner, which are their consequence; and the efficient state of preparation which is arising out of all these energetic movements. To our country readers we need not dwell upon the slaughter of fowls in the poultry yard, and game in the field, or the wholesale doings within doors for the manufacture of pastry of all conceivable kinds and in all its conceivable forms. And to neither the one nor the other is it necessary that we should speak of the packages, in every shape and size, which both are getting ready, for the interchange between friends of the commodities of their respective positions. Here, however, the town has clearly the advan-tage in point of gain, and the country in point of character – the former having little besides barrels of oysters and baskets of Billingsgate fish to furnish to the country larders in return for the entire range of the products of the dairy, farmyard, and gamefield.

But however lightly we may allude to the other articles which enter into the charge of the commissariat department, and have no distinctive character, at this particular season, beyond their unimaginable abun-dance, we are by no means at liberty, without a more special notice, to pass over the mystery of MINCE-PIE! We speak not here of the *merits* of that marvellous compound; because a dish which has maintained without impeachment, since long before the days of honest old Tusser (who calls these marvels shred-pies), the same supreme character which it holds amongst the men of these latter days, may very well dispense with our commendation; and every schoolboy knows, from his own repeated experience, the utter inadequacy of language to convey any notion of the ineffable flavour of this unapproachable viand. The poverty of speech is never so conspicuous as when even its richest forms are used for the purpose of describing that which is utterly beyond its resources; and we have witnessed most lamentable, although ludicrous, failures, on the part of eloquent but imprudent men, in their ambitious attempts to give expression to their sensations under the immediate influence of this unutterable combination. It is therefore to other properties than those which make their appeal to the palate that we must confine ourselves in our mention of mince-pie.

The origin of this famous dish, like that of the heroic in all kinds and classes, is involved in fable. By some it has been supposed, from the Oriental ingredients which enter into its composition, to have a reference (as probably had also the plum-porridge of those days) to the offerings made by the wise men of the East; and it was anciently the custom to make these pies of an oblong form, thereby representing the manger in which, on that occasion, those sages found the infant Jesus. Against this practice – which was of the same character with that of the little image called the Yule Dough, or Yule Cake, formerly presented by bakers to their customers at the anniversary of the Nativity – the Puritans made a vehement outcry, as idolatrous; and certainly it appears to us somewhat more objectionable than many of those which they denounced, in the same category. Of course, it was supported by the Catholics with a zeal the larger part of which (as in most cases of controversy where the passions are engaged) was derived from the opposition of their adversaries; and the latter having pronounced the mince-pie to be an abomination, the eating thereof was immediately established as a test of orthodoxy by the former. Sandys mentions that even when distressed for a comfortable meal, they would refuse to partake of this very tempting dish, when set before them, and mentions John Bunyan when in confinement as an example. He recommends that under such extreme circumstances they should be eaten with a protest, as might be done by a lawyer in a similar case.

In a struggle like this, however, it is clear that the advocates of mince-pie were likely to have the best of it, through the powerful auxiliary derived to their cause from the savouriness of the dish itself. The legend of the origin of eating roast pig, which we have on the authority of Charles Lamb, exhibits the rapid spread of that practice, against the sense of its abomination, on the strength of the irresistible appeals made to the palate by the *crackling*. And accordingly, in the case of mince-pie we find that the delicious compound has come down to our days, stripped of its objectionable forms and more

Country carol singers

mystic meanings, from the moment when they ceased to be topics of disputation, and is freely partaken of by the most rigid Presbyterian, who raises 'no question' thereon 'for conscience' sake'.

It may be observed, however, that relics of the more recondite virtues ascribed to this dish by the Catholics, in the days of its sectarian persecution, still exist in the superstitions which attach certain privileges and promises to its consumption. In some places, the form of this superstition, we believe, is, that for every house in which a mince-pie shall be eaten at the Christmas season, the eater shall enjoy a happy month in the coming year. As, however, this version would limit the consumption, as far as any *future* benefit is attached to it, to the insufficient number of twelve, we greatly prefer an edition of the same belief which we have met with elsewhere, and which promises a happy *day* for every individual pie eaten during the same period – thereby giving a man a direct and prospective interest in the consumption of as large a number out of three hundred and sixty-five as may happen to agree with his inclination.

Leaving, however, those proceedings which are going on within our homes, and of which the manufacture of mince-pies forms so important an article, we must turn to the symptoms of the approaching holiday that meet the eye at every turn which we make out of doors. He who will take the king's highway in his search after these, planting himself on the outside of a stagecoach, will have the greater number of such signs brought under his observation in the progress of a journey which whirls him through town and village, and by park and farmhouse.

The road is alive with travellers; and along its whole extent there is an air of aimless bustle, if we may so express ourselves – an appearance of active idleness. No doubt he who shall travel that same road in the days of hay-making or harvest will see as dense a population following their avocations in the open air and swarming in the fields. But then at those periods of labour the crowds are more widely scattered over the face of the country, and each individual is earnestly engaged in the prosecution of some positive pursuit, amid a silence scarcely broken by the distant whistle or occasional song that comes faintly to the ear through the rich sunny air. People are busier without being so bustling. But now all men are in action, though all men's business seems suspended. The population are gathered together in groups at the corners of streets or about the doors of ale-houses, and the mingling voices of the speakers and the sound of the merry laugh come sharp and ringing through the clear frosty air. There is the appearance, every way, of a season of transition. The only conspicuous evidence of the business of life going forward with a keen and steady view to its ordinary objects, exists in the abundant displays made at the windows of every shopkeeper, in every village along the road. Vehicles of all kinds are in motion; stagecoach, post chaise, and private carriage are alike filled with travellers passing in all directions to their several places of assembling, and give glimpses of faces bright with the reawakened affections that are radiating on all sides to common centres. Everywhere hearts are stirred and pulses quickened by pleasant anticipations; and many a current of feelings which for the rest of the year has wandered only in the direction of the world's miry ways and been darkened by its pollutions, met by the memories of the season and turned back from its unpleasing course, is flowing joyously back by every highway into the sweet regions of its pure and untainted spring.

But of all wayfarers who are journeying towards the haunts of Christmas, who so happy as the emancipated schoolboy? And of all vehicles that are carrying contributions of mirth to that general festival, what vehicle is so richly stored therewith as the post chaise that holds a group of these young travellers? The glad day which has been the subject of speculation so long before, and has been preceded by days which, in their imaginary calendar,

Coming home from school

are beyond any question the very longest days of all the year, has at length arrived, after seeming as if it never would arrive, and the long restrained and hourly increasing tide of expectation has at length burst its barriers, and is rushing forward with no little noise, into the sea of fruition. '*Eja! quid silemus?*' says the well-known breaking-up song of the Winchester boys; and the sentiment therein expressed is wideawake (as everything must be, on this morning, that lies within any reasonable distance of their voices) in the breast of every schoolboy, at all schools.

> Appropinquat ecce! felix
>   Hora gaudiorum,
> Post grave tedium,
> Advenit omnium
>   Meta petita laborum.
>   Domum, domum, dulce domum!
>   Domum, domum, dulce domum!
>   Dulce, dulce, dulce domum!
>   Dulce domum resonemus.
>
> Musa! libros mitte, fessa;
>   Mitte pensa dura,
> Mitte negotium,
> Jam datur otium,
>   Mea mittito cura!
>   Domum, domum, etc.

> Heus, Rogere, fer caballos;
>   Eja nunc eamus,
> Limen amabile,
> Matris et oscula,
>   Suaviter et repetamus.
>   Domum, domum, etc.
>
> Concinamus ad Penates,
>   Vox et audiatur;
> Phosphore! quid jubar,
>   Segnius emicans,
> Gaudia nostra moratur.
>   Domum, domum, etc.'

And away they go, well inclined to act up to the injunctions of the ancient song, '*Concinamus, O Sodales!*' Our readers will do well on the present occasion to translate the verb by its English equivalent – to shout. '*Vox et audiatur!*' – small doubt of that! That deaf-looking old woman by the way-side must be 'very deaf indeed' if the sounds of that merriment have failed at least to reach her ears – though they may get no further; for she looks like one of those in whom all the avenues by which mirth reaches the heart, where they have not been closed at their external outlets by the infirmities of age, are choked up within by the ruins of that heart itself. But the entire progress of these glad hearts today is in the nature of a triumph, and all objects in its course are ministers to their unreflecting mirth. Theirs is the blessed age, and this its most privileged day, when the spirit can extract from all things the chyle of cheerfulness. That urchin who is flinging alms (a most gracious act in childhood!) is doing so to the sound of his merry neighbour's trumpet; and yet the act performed and the duty remembered, amid all the heydey and effervescence of the spirits, has not lost its gracefulness for the frolicsome mood by which it is attended. There are men in this world who dispense their charities to the flourish of *their own* trumpets; and though they are practised performers on that instrument, and play with considerable skill, the effect is unpleasing and the act a mockery. Away go the light-hearted boys! Away past the aged and the poor – as happiness has long since done, and the happy have long continued to do! – awaking the shrill echoes of the road and all its adjacent fields with the sound of their revelry. Every schoolboy knows the programme. Flags flying, horns blowing, racing against rival chaises, taunts from the foremost, cheers from the hindmost, all sorts of practical jokes upon each other and upon all they meet and all they pass, and above all, the loud, ringing laugh – the laugh of boyhood, so unlike all other laughter, that comes out clear and distinct, direct from the heart, stopping nowhere on its way, not pausing to be questioned by the judgment nor restrained by the memory, presenting no hollowness nor flatness to the nicest attention, betraying no undertone to the finest ear, giving true and unbroken 'echoes to the seat where *mirth* is throned', born spontaneously of that spirit, and excited so often by causes too minute for older eyes to see. And it is in this very causelessness that consists the spell of childhood's laughter, and the secret of youth's unmingled joy. We seldom begin to seek *reasons* for being gay till we have had some for being grave; and the search after the former is very apt to bring us upon more of the latter. There are tares among that wheat. The moment we commence to distrust our light-heartedness, it begins to evade us. From the day when we think it necessary to reason upon our enjoyments, to philosophise upon our mirth, to analyse our gladness, their free and unmingled character is gone. The toy is taken to pieces to see of what it was composed, and can no more be put together in the same perfect form. They who have entered upon the paths of knowledge, or gone far into the recesses of experience, like the men of yore who ventured to explore the cave of Trophonius, may perhaps find something higher and better than the light-heartedness they lose, but they smile never more as they smiled of old. The fine, clear instrument of the spirit that we bring with us from heaven is liable to injury from all that acts upon it here; and the string that has once been broken or disordered, repair it as we may, *never* again gives out the precise tone which it did before. The old man – nay, even the young man – let him be as merry as he may, and laugh as long and loudly as he will, never laughs as the schoolboy laughs.

But of all this, and all the slumbering passions yet to be awakened in those young breasts, and of many a grief to come, there is no token to darken the joy of today. The mighty pleasures towards which they are hastening have as yet never 'broken the word of promise to their hope'. The postilions are of their party, and even he with the bottle-nose, who seems to be none of the youngest, is a boy for the nonce. The very horses appear to have caught the spirit of the occasion, and toss their heads and lay their haunches to the ground and fling out their forelegs as if they drew the car of Momus. The village boys return them shout for shout, fling up their hats as the triumph approaches, and follow it till their breath fails. The older passer-by returns their uproarious salute, taking no umbrage at their mischievous jokes and impish tricks, and turning, as the sounds of the merry voices die in the distance, to a vision of the days when he, too, was a boy, and an unconscious rehearsal of the half-forgotten song of 'Dulce, dulce domum!'

And then the *limen amabile*, and the *matris oscula*, and the *Penates*, towards which they are advancing; the yearning hearts that wait within those homes to clasp them; the bright eyes that are even now looking out from windows to catch the first token of 'their coming, and look brighter when they come'; the quiet halls that shall ring tonight to their young voices; and the lanes and alleys whose echoes they shall awaken tomorrow, and still more loudly when the ice comes; and, above all, the Christmas revelries themselves! The whole is one crowded scene of enjoyment, across whose long extent the happy schoolboy has as yet caught no glimpse of that *black Monday* which forms the opposite and distant portal of this haunted time.

Amongst the signs of the time that are conspicuous upon the roads, the traveller whose journeyings bring him towards those which lead into the metropolis will be struck by the droves of cattle that are making their painful way up to the great mart for this great festival. But a still more striking, though less noisy, Christmas symptom forms a very amusing object to him who leaves London by such of its highways as lead eastward. There is little exaggeration in the accompanying picture of a Lynn or Bury coach on its townward journey with its freight of turkeys at the Christmas season. Nay, as regards the freightage itself, the artist has kept himself within bounds. Many a time have we seen a Norfolk coach with its hampers piled on the roof and swung from beneath the body, and its birds depending, by every possible contrivance, from every part from which a bird could be made to hang. Nay, we believe it is not unusual with the proprietors, at this season, to refuse inside passengers of the human species, in favor of these Oriental gentry, who 'pay better'; and on such occasions, of course, they set at defiance the restriction which limits them to carrying 'four insides'. Within and without, the coaches are crammed with the bird of Turkey; and a gentleman townward bound, who presented himself at a Norwich coach-office at such a time, to inquire the 'fare to London', was pertly answered by the bookkeeper, 'Turkeys'. Our readers will acquit us of exaggeration when we tell them that Mr Hone, in his *Every-Day Book*, quotes from a historical account of Norwich an authentic statement of the number of turkeys which were transmitted from that city to London between a Saturday morning and the night of Sunday, in the December of 1793, which statement gives the number as one thousand seven hundred, the weight as nine tons, two hundredweight, and two pounds, and the value as £680. It is added that in the two following days these were followed by half as many more. We are unable to furnish the present statistics of the matter; but in forty years which have elapsed since that time, the demand, and of course the supply, must have greatly increased; and it is probable that the coach-proprietors find it convenient to put extra carriages on the road for these occasions.

In making the annexed sketch we presume that Mr Seymour must have

The Norfolk coach at Christmas

had in mind, and intended to illustrate by 'modern instances', that class of 'wise saws' such as 'Birds of a feather flock together', 'Tell me the company, and I will tell you the man', and others which tend generally to show that men are apt to catch the hues of surrounding objects, and take the features of their associates. If this was not his design, we have only the alternative conclusion, that he had drawn turkeys till he could draw nothing else, and till his best efforts at representing 'the human face divine' resulted in what the Scots call a 'bubbly-jock'. Some poet, in describing the perfections of his mistress's countenance, speaks of it as conveying the impression that she 'had looked on heaven, and caught its beauty'. Our friend the guard of this coach seems to have looked on those turkeys of which he has charge till he has 'caught their beauty'. It is impossible to conceive that the breath which he is pouring into that horn of his should issue in any other form of sound than that of a gobble. The coachman is clearly a turkey in disguise; and the old-looking figure that sits behind him, with something like a sausage round its neck, is probably his father. As for the swan with two necks that floats on the panel of the coach-door, it is a strange-looking bird at any time, but looks considerably more strange in its present situation. It is unquestionably out of place, and forms no fitting cognisance for a Norfolk coach at Christmas time.

Norfolk must be a noisy county. There must be a 'pretty considerable deal' of gabble towards the month of November in that English Turkistan. But what a silence must have fallen upon its farmyards since Christmas has come round! Turkeys are indisputably born to be killed. That is an axiom.

It is the end of their training, as it ought to be (and, in one sense, certainly *is*) of their desires. And such being the destiny of this bird, it may probably be an object of ambition with a respectable turkey to fulfil its fate at the period of this high festival. Certain it is that at no other time can it attain to such dignities as belong to the turkey who smokes on the well-stored table of a Christmas dinner – the most honoured dish of all the feast. Something like an anxiety for this promotion is to be inferred from the breathless haste of the turkey of which our artist has here given us a sketch, in its pursuit of the coach which has started for London without it. The picture is evidently a portrait. There is an air of verisimilitude in the eager features, and about the action altogether, of the bird, which stamps it genuine. In its anxiety it has come off without even waiting to be killed; and at the rate after which it appears to be travelling, is, we think, likely enough to come up with a heavily laden coach. We hope, however, that it is not in pursuit of the particular coach which we have seen on its way to the 'Swan with two Necks', because we verily believe there is no room on *that* conveyance for a single additional turkey, even if it should succeed in overtaking it.

One of the most striking signs of the season, and which meets the eye in all directions, is that which arises out of the ancient and still familiar practice of adorning our houses and churches with evergreens during the continuance of this festival. The decorations of our mantelpieces, and in many places of our windows, the wreaths which ornament our lamps and Christmas candles, the garniture of our tables, are alike gathered from the hedges and winter gardens; and in the neighbourhood of every town and village the traveller may meet with some such sylvan procession as is here represented, or some group of boys returning from the woods laden with their winter greenery, and like the sturdy ambassador in the plate, engaged

Too late for the coach

Bringing home Christmas

in what we have heard technically called 'bringing home Christmas'. This symptom of the approaching festivity is mentioned by Gay in his *Trivia*:

> When Rosemary and Bays, the poet's crown,
> Are bawl'd in frequent cries through all the town,
> Then judge the festival of Christmass near –
> Christmass, the joyous period of the year!
> Now with bright holly all the temples strow;
> With Lawrel green, and sacred Misletoe.

The practice of these decorations, which is recommended to modern times by its own pleasantness and natural beauty, is of very high antiquity, and has been ascribed by various writers to various sources. They who are desirous of tracing a Christian observance to a Christian cause remind us of those figurative expressions in the prophets which speak of the Messiah as the 'Branch of righteousness', etc., and describe by natural allusions the fertility which should attend his coming. 'The Lord shall comfort Zion,' says Isaiah: 'he will comfort all her waste places; and he will make her wilderness like Eden, and her desert like the garden of the Lord.' Again, 'The glory of Lebanon shall come unto thee, the fir tree, the pine tree, and the box together, to beautify the place of my sanctuary; and I will make the place of my feet glorious.' And Nehemiah, on an occasion of rejoicing, orders the people, after the law of Moses, to 'go forth unto the mount and fetch olive branches, and pine branches, and myrtle branches, and palm branches, and branches of thick trees', and to make booths thereof, 'every one upon the roof of his house, and in their courts, and in the courts of the house of God', and in the streets; 'and all the congregation of them that were come again out of the captivity' sat under these booths, 'and there was very great gladness.' A writer in the *Gentleman's Magazine* asks if this custom may not be referred, as well as that of the palms on Palm Sunday, to that passage in the Scripture account of Christ's entry into Jerusalem which states that the multitude 'cut down branches from the trees, and strawed them in the way'.

The practice, however, of introducing flowers and branches amongst the tokens of festivity seems, and very naturally, to have existed universally and at all times. It was, as we know, a pagan manifestation of rejoicing and worship, and is forbidden on that express ground in early councils of the Christian Church. Hone, in his *Every-Day Book*, quotes Polydore Virgil to the effect that 'trymming of the temples with hangynges, flowres, boughes, and garlondes, was taken of the heathen people, whiche decked their idols and houses with suche array'; and it came under the list of abominations denounced by the Puritans for the same reason. The practice was also in use amongst the nations both of Gothic and Celtic origin; and Brand quotes from Dr Chandler's *Travels in Greece* a very beautiful superstition, mentioned as the reason of this practice, amongst the votaries of Druidism. 'The houses,' he says, 'were decked with evergreens in December, that the sylvan spirits might repair to them and remain unnipped with frost and cold winds until a milder season had renewed the foliage of their darling abodes.'

In England, the practice, whencesoever derived, has existed from the very earliest days, and, in spite of outcry and prohibition, has come down in full vigour to our own. In former times, as we learn from Stow, in his *Survey of London*, not only were our houses and churches decorated with evergreens, but also the conduits, standards, and crosses in the streets; and in our own day they continue to form a garniture not only of our temples and our houses, but constitute a portion of the striking display made at this festive season in our markets and from the windows of our shops. Holly forms a decoration of the shambles, and every tub of butter has a sprig of rosemary in its breast.

The plants most commonly in use for this purpose appear to have generally been the holly, the ivy, the laurel, the rosemary, and the mistletoe; although the decorations were by no means limited to these materials. Brand expresses some surprise at finding cypress included in the list, as mentioned in the tract called *Round about our Coal-Fire*, and observes that he 'should as soon have expected to have seen the *yew* as the cypress used on this joyful occasion'. The fact, however, is that yew *is* frequently mentioned amongst the Christmas decorations, as well as box, pine, fir, and indeed the larger part of the Christmas plants which we have enumerated in a former chapter. The greater number of these appear to have been so used, not on account of any mystic meanings supposed to reside therein, but simply for the sake of their greenery or of their rich berries. Stow speaks of the houses being decked with 'whatsoever the year afforded to be green'; and Sandys observes that 'at present great variety is observed in decorating our houses and buildings, and many flowers are introduced that were unknown to our ancestors, but whose varied colours add to the cheerful effect; as the chrysanthemum, satin-flower, etc., mingling with the red berry of the holly and the mystic mistletoe. In the West of England,' he adds, 'the myrtle and laurustinum form a pleasing addition.' There is a very beautiful custom which we find mentioned in connection with the subject of evergreens as existing at this season of the year in some parts of Germany and Sicily. A large bough is set up in the principal room, the smaller branches of which are hung with little presents suitable to the different members of the household. 'A good deal of innocent mirth and spirit of courtesy,' it is observed, 'is produced by this custom.'

Herrick, however (a poet amid whose absurd conceits and intolerable affectation there are samples of the sweetest versification and touches of the deepest pathos, and who amongst a great deal that is liable to heavier objections still, has preserved many curious particulars of old ceremonies and obsolete superstitions), carries this custom of adorning our houses with evergreens over the entire year, and assigns to each plant its peculiar and appropriate season. To Christmas he appoints those which we have stated to be most commonly used on that occasion, but insists upon a change of decoration on the eve of Candlemas Day:

> Down with the rosemary, and so
> Down with the baies and misletoe;
> Down with the holly, ivie, all
> Wherewith you drest the Christmas hall;
> That so the superstitious find
> Not one least branch there left behind;

and he urges the maids to the careful performance of this charge by the following threat:

> For look! How many leaves there be
> Neglected there, maids, trust to me,
> So many goblins you shall see.

The plant by which he orders these to be replaced for Candlemas Day is box, whose turn is to continue –

> Until the dancing Easter Day
> Or Easter's Eve appeare.

Then the box is to make way for 'the crisped yew'; which is to be succeeded at Whitsuntide by birch and the flowers of the season; and these again are to yield to the –

> Green rushes, then, and sweetest bents,
> With cooler oken boughs;

whose reign continues till the period again comes round of preparation for Christmas. We believe that it is still usual in many parts of England to suffer the Christmas greens to remain in the windows of our churches, and sometimes of our houses, until Candlemas Eve.

Of those plants, then, which are considered as containing meanings that make them appropriate decorations for the Christmas-tide, or which have for any reason been peculiarly devoted to that season, the laurel, or bay, may be dismissed in a few words. Since the days of the ancient Romans, this tree has been at all times dedicated to all purposes of joyous commemoration, and its branches have been used as the emblems of peace and victory and joy. Of course, its application is obvious to a festival which includes them all, which celebrates 'peace on earth', 'glad tidings of great joy', and a triumph achieved over the powers of evil and the original curse by the coming of the Saviour.

We may add that, besides forming a portion of the household decorations, it is usual in some places to fling branches and sprigs of laurel on the Christmas fire, and seek for omens amid the curling and crackling of its leaves:

> When laurell spirts i' th' fire, and when the hearth
> Smiles to itselfe and guilds the roofe with mirth;
> When up the Thyrse is rais'd, and when the sound
> Of sacred orgies flyes around, around,

says Herrick. At the two English universities, the windows of the college chapels are still carefully decked with laurel at the season of Christmas.

The holly is a plant of peculiar veneration at this period of the year – so much so as to have acquired to itself by a popular metonymy the name of the season itself, being vulgarly called 'Christmas'. It is no doubt recommended to the general estimation in which it is held by the picturesque forms of its dark, glossy leaves and the brilliant clusters of its rich red berries. There is in the Harleian Manuscripts a very striking carol of so remote a date as the reign of Henry VI, which is quoted by most of the writers on this subject, and gives a very poetical statement of the respective claims of this plant and of the ivy to popular regard. The inference from the second and fourth verses (taken in connection with the authorities which place it amongst the plants used for the Christmas ornaments) would seem to be, that while the former was employed in the decorations within doors, the latter was confined to the exteriors of buildings. Mr Brand, however, considers those passages to allude to its being used as a vintner's sign and infers from others of the verses that it was also amongst the evergreens employed at funerals. It runs thus –

> Nay, Ivy! nay, it shall not be, I wys;
> Let Holy hafe the maystry, as the manner ys.
>
> Holy stond in the halle, fayre to behold;
> Ivy stond without the dore: she ys ful sore a cold.
> > Nay, Ivy! etc.
>
> Holy and hys mery men they dawnsyn and they syng.
> Ivy and hur maydenys they wepyn and they wryng.
> > Nay, Ivy! etc.
>
> Ivy hath a lyve; she laghtyt with the cold:
> So mot they all hafe that wyth Ivy hold.
> > Nay, Ivy! etc.
>
> Holy hat berys as rede as any rose,
> The foster the hunters kepe hem from the doos.
> > Nay, Ivy! etc.
>
> Ivy hath berys as blake as any slo;
> Ther com the oule and ete hym as she goo.
> > Nay, Ivy! etc.
>
> 'Holy hath byrdys a ful fayre flok,
> The Nyghtyngale, the Poppingy, the gayntyl Lavyrok.
> > Nay, Ivy! etc.
>
> Good Ivy, what byrdys ast thou?
> Non but the howlet that kreye 'How, how!'
> > Nay, Ivy! nay, hyt shal not, etc.'

We had some thoughts of modernising the orthography, and very slightly the diction, of this curious old ballad; but it reads best in its own quaint garb, and even those of our friends who are not in the habit of perusing ancient writings will find scarcely any difficulty in making it out.

The rosemary, besides its rich fragrance, and probably *because* thereof, was supposed to possess many occult virtues, and was used for the sake of one or other of them on occasions both of rejoicing and of mourning. It was believed to clear the head, to strengthen the memory, and to make touching appeals to the heart. For these reasons, it was borne both at weddings and at funerals. Herrick says –

> Grow for two ends, it matters not at all,
> Be't for my bridal or my burial.

'There's rosemary,' says Ophelia; 'that's for remembrance: pray you, love, remember;' and the custom of decking the corpse with this flower, as well as that of flinging its sprigs into the grave, would naturally spring out of this touching superstition. Its presence at bridals would seem to suggest that it was dedicated to hope as well as to memory. We have in Shakespeare's play of *Romeo and Juliet* allusions to the use of this herb on both of these important but very different occasions, which allusions are affecting from the application of both to the same young girl. The first, which refers to the joyous celebration, occurs in an interview between Romeo and the Nurse of Juliet, in which arrangements are making for the secret marriage, where the garrulous old woman observes, as hinting at Juliet's willingness, 'She hath the prettiest sententious of it, of you and rosemary, that it would do you good to hear it.' The second is in that scene in which Juliet is supposed to be dead:

> FRIAR   Come, is the bride ready to go to church?
> CAPULET Ready to go, but never to return!

And is inserted amongst the holy father's exhortations to resignation:

> Dry up your tears, and stick your rosemary
> On this fair corse; and, as the custom is,
> In all her best array bear her to church.

Independently of the beautiful suggestion to remembrance which is made by its enduring perfume, that precious perfume itself would recommend this herb, for reasons less fine, as 'strewings fitt'st for graves'. The fact of its being in bloom at this season would naturally introduce the rosemary, with all its fine morals, into the Christmas celebrations; and such customs as that which prescribed that the wassail bowl should be stirred with a sprig of this plant before it went round amongst friends, seem to have a very elegant reference to its secret virtues ('that's for remembrance', perhaps), and suggest that the revellings of the season in those old times were mingled with the best and most refined feelings of our nature.

But the mistletoe, the mystic mistletoe, where is the man whose school-boy days are gone by, in whom that word conjures up no merry memories?

'Oh, the mistletoe-bough!' Who has not, at the name, thronging visions of sweet faces that looked sweetest in those moments of their startled beauty beneath the pendent bough! If the old spells with which superstition has invested the mistletoe have lost some of their power over me, it has now another, which in earlier days I knew not of – the power to restore the distant and to raise the dead. I am to laugh no more as I have laughed of old beneath the influence of that mystic cognisance of the gay Christmas-tide; but even now as I write thereof, look in upon my heart bright portraits, traced with a skill which no mortal pencil shall achieve – faces on which the earth has long lain, and others from whom the wide spaces of the world have separated me for many a weary year; and, heavier far, some to whom *unkindness* has made me too long a stranger! There they rise and stand, one by one, beneath the merry snare, each with the heightened beauty on her cheek, which is the transient gift of the sacred bough!

O M—! How very fair is your image in the eye of memory, and how has your going away changed all things for me! The bright and the beautiful lie still about – still bright and beautiful even to me – but in another manner than when you were here. All things are tinged with your loss. All fair things have a look, and all sweet sounds a tone of mourning since you left me. How long it seems, as if ages, instead of years, of the grave had grown between us, as if, indeed, I had known you in some former and far-removed state of being! I do not love to think of you as dead. I strive to think of you rather as of one whom I have left behind in the quiet valley of our youth and our love – from whom I have wandered forth and lost my way amid the mazes of the world. But where is the clue that should lead me back to you? There may have been fairer (sweeter never) things than you in this fair world, but my heart could never be made to believe or understand it. Had I known you only in that world, I might not so have marked your beauty; but you were with me when the world left me. In the flood of the sunshine, when a thousand birds are about us, we go upon our way with a sense that there is melody around, but singling perhaps no one note to take home to the heart and make a worship of. But the one bird that sings to us in the dim and silent night – oh! none but they on whom the night has fallen can know how dear its song becomes, filling with its music all the deserted mansions of the lonely soul. But the bird is dead, the song is hushed, and the houses of my spirit are empty and silent and desolate!

And you whom the grave has not hidden, nor far distance removed, from whom I parted as if it were but yesterday, and yet of whom I have already learned to think as of one separated from me by long years of absence and death, as if it were very long since I had beheld you – as if I gazed upon you from a far distance across the lengthened and dreary alleys of the valley of the dead! Physically speaking, you are still within my reach; and yet are you to me as if the tomb or the cloister had received you, and made of you (what the world or the grave makes of all things we have loved) a dream of the night, a phantom of the imagination, an angel of the memory, a creation of the hour of shadows! Whatever may be your future fortunes, however your name may hereafter be borne to my mortal ear, my heart will ever refuse to picture *you* but as one who died in her youth!

And *you!* – you too are there, with your long fair hair and that harp of yours which was so long an ark of harmony for me. 'Alas! We had been friends in youth.' But *all* things bring *you* back, and I am haunted yet, and shall be through the world, by the airs which you were wont to sing me long ago. I remember that even in those days, at times, in the silent night, when broken snatches of melodies imperfectly remembered stole through the chambers of my heart – ever in the sweet tones in which it had learned to love them – I have asked myself if the ties that bound us might ever be like those passing and half-forgotten melodies; if the time could ever come when they should be like an old song learned in life's happier day, and whose memory has been treasured, to make us weep in the years when the heart has need to be soothed by weeping; if there would ever be a day when your name might be sounded in my ear as the name of a stranger! And that day has long since come –

For whispering tongues will poison truth.

How truly may we be said to live but in the past and in the future – to have our hearts made up of memory and of hope, for which the present becomes, hour after hour, more and more of a void! And alas! is it not true, as a consequence, that the more they are occupied with memory, the less room have they for hope? And thus the one is ever gaining upon the other, and the dark waters of memory are hourly spreading upon that shore where hope had room to build her edifices and to play about them, till at length they cover all, and hope, having 'no rest for the sole of her foot', flies forward to a higher and a better shore!

And such are my visions of the mistletoe; these are amongst the spirits that rise up to wait upon my memory – 'they and the other spirits' of the mystic bough! But brighter fancies has that charmed branch for many of our readers, and merrier spirits hide amid its leaves. Many a pleasant tale could we tell of the mistletoe bough which might amuse our readers more than the descriptions to which we are confined, if the limits of our volume would permit. But already our space is scarcely sufficient for our purpose. We think we can promise our readers in another volume a series of tales connected with the traditions and superstitions which are detailed in the present, and which may serve as illustrations of the customs of the Christmas-tide.

Some of the names by which this remarkable plant were formerly called are, 'misselden', 'misseldine' and, more commonly, 'missel'. Old Tusser tells us that:

> If snow do continue, sheep hardly that fare,
> Crave mistle and ivy;

and Archdeacon Nares says 'the missel-thrush' is so designated 'from feeding on its berries'. From the generality of the examples in which this plant is mentioned by the name of 'missel', it is suggested to us, by Mr Crofton Croker that the additional syllable given to the name now in common use is a corruption of the old *tod*, and that mistletoe, or mistletod, implies a *bush*, or bunch, of missel, such as is commonly hung up at Christmas. He quotes in support of this suggestion the corresponding phrase of 'ivy-tod', which occurs frequently in the writings of the Elizabethan age. If this be so, the expression 'the mistletoe bough' includes a tautology; but as it is popularly used, we retain it for the instruction of such antiquarians of remote future times as may consult our pages for some account of the good old customs which are disappearing so fast, and may fail to reach their day.

That this plant was held in veneration by the pagans, has been inferred from a passage in Virgil's description of the descent into the infernal regions. That passage is considered to have an allegorical reference to some of the religious ceremonies practised amongst the Greeks and Romans, and a comparison is therein drawn between the golden bough of the infernal regions, and what is obviously the misletoe:

> Quale solet silvis brumali frigore *viscum*
> Fronde virere nova, quod non sua seminat arbos,
> Et croceo fetu teretis circumdare truncos, etc.

The reference is given by Mr Christie in his 'Enquiry into the Ancient Greek Game' of Palamedes; and he mentions likewise the respect in which this plant was held by the Gothic as well as the Celtic nations. Sandys furnishes a legend from the Edda in proof of the extraordinary qualities ascribed to it by the former. Amongst the Celtic nations, it is well known to have been an object of great veneration, and the ceremony of collecting it by the Druids against the festival of the winter solstice was one of high solemnity. It was cut by the prince of the Druids himself, and with a golden sickle. It was said that those only of the oaks were sacred to the Druids which had the mistletoe upon them, and that the reverence of the people towards the priests, as well as their estimation of the mistletoe, proceeded in a great measure from the cures which the former effected by means of that plant. Medicinal properties, we believe, are still ascribed to it, and it was not very long ago deemed efficacious in the subduing of convulsive disorders. Sir John Colbatch, in his dissertation concerning it, observes that this beautiful plant must have been designed by the Almighty 'for further and more noble purposes than barely to feed thrushes, or to be hung up surreptitiously in houses to drive away evil spirits.' Against the latter it appears to have been used as a charm up to the last century.

Its introduction into the Christian festival might therefore be considered appropriate as emblematic of the conquest obtained over the spirits of darkness by the event of the Nativity; and perhaps its supposed healing properties might be deemed to recommend it further, as a symbol of the moral health to which man was restored from the original corruption of his nature, and a fitting demonstration of the joy which hailed the 'Sun of Righteousness' that had arisen, 'with *healing* in his wings'.

Notwithstanding all this, however, Brand is of opinion that its heathen origin should exclude it at all events from the decorations of our churches, and quotes a story told him by an old sexton at Teddington, in Middlesex, of the clergyman of that place having observed this profane plant intermingled with the holly and ivy which adorned the church, and ordered its immediate removal. Washington Irving, who has studied old English customs and manners with sincere regard, introduces a similar rebuke from the learned parson to his unlearned clerk, in his account of the Christmas spent by him at Bracebridge Hall.

The reverence of the mistletoe among the Ancient Britons appears, however, to have been limited to that which grew upon the oak; whereas the *Viscum album*, or common mistletoe – the sight of whose pearly berries brings the flush into the cheek of the maiden of modern days – may be gathered besides from the old apple-tree, the hawthorn, the lime-tree, and the Scotch or the silver fir. Whether there remain any traces of the old superstitions which elevated it into a moral or a medical amulet – beyond that which is connected with the custom alluded to in the opening of our remarks upon this plant, and represented by our artist here – we know not. We should, however, be very sorry to see any light let in amongst us which should fairly rout a belief connected with so agreeable a privilege as this. That privilege, as all our readers know, consists in the right to kiss any female who may be caught under the mistletoe bough – and, we may hope, will continue, for its own pleasantness, even if the superstition from which

The mistletoe bough

it springs should be finally lost. This superstition arose, clearly enough, out of the old mystic character of the plant in question, and erects it into a charm, the neglect of which exposes to the imminent danger of all the evils of old-maidenism. For, according to Archdeacon Nares, the tradition is, 'that the maid who was not kissed under it, at Christmas, would not be married in that year', – by which, we presume, the Archdeacon means in the following year. Accordingly, a branch of this parasitical plant was hung (formerly with great state, but now it is generally suspended with much secrecy) either from the centre of the roof, or over the door – and we recommend this latter situation to our readers, both as less exposed to untimely observation, and because every maiden who joins the party must of necessity do so by passing under it. We learn from Brand that the ceremony was not duly performed unless a berry was plucked off with each kiss. This berry, it is stated by other authorities, was to be presented for good luck to the maiden kissed; and Washington Irving adds that 'when the berries are all plucked, the privilege ceases'. If this be so, it behooves the maidens of a household to take good care that the branch provided for the occasion shall be as well furnished with these pearly tokens as the feast is likely to be with candidates for the holy state of matrimony. The practice is still of very common observance in kitchens and servants' halls, particularly in the country. But, as we have hinted, we have met with it (and so, we dare say, have most of our readers) in higher scenes; and many a merry laugh have we heard ring from beneath the mistletoe bough. There are lips in the world that we would gladly meet there in this coming season.

Another of the symptoms of the approaching season which has, at least to us, a very pleasing effect, consists in the bursts of solemn minstrelsy by which we are aroused from our slumbers in the still hour of the winter nights, or which, failing to break our sleep, mingle with our dreams, leading us into scenes of enchantment, and filling them with unearthly music. This midnight minstrelsy, whether it comes in the shape of human voices, hallowing the night by the chanting of the Christmas carol, or breaks upon the silence of the mid-watches from the mingling instruments of those wandering spirits of harmony, the waits, has in each case its origin in the *Gloria in Excelsis* – the song with which the angels hailed the birth of the Redeemer in the fields near Bethlehem. 'As soon,' says Jeremy Taylor, 'as these blessed choristers had sung their Christmas carol, and taught the Church a hymn to put into her offices forever on the anniversary of this festivity, the angels returned into heaven.' Accordingly, these nocturnal hymns, although they spread over the entire period of Advent, grow more and more fervent and frequent as the season approaches, and the night which ushers in the great day itself is filled throughout all its watches with the continued sounds of sacred harmony. How beautiful is the effect given to this music by this consideration of its meaning and its cause! Many and many a time have we been awakened by the melody of the waits when

> The floor of heaven
> *Was* thick inlaid with patines of bright gold –

and have lain and listened to their wild minstrelsy, its solemn swells and 'dying falls' kept musical by the distance and made holy by the time, till we have felt amid all those influences as if it were

> No mortal business, nor no sound
> That the earth owes,

and could have fancied that the 'morning stars' were again singing, as of old they 'sang together for joy', and that the sounds of their far anthem came floating to the earth. This sort of fancy has occurred over and over again to him who has looked out from his bed upon a sky full of stars, and listened at the same time to invisible and distant music, under the holy impressions of the season. Shakespeare has helped us to this feeling, perhaps, as we can trace his influence upon *all* our feelings, and upon none more than the most sacred or the most solemn:

> There's not the smallest orb which thou behold'st,
> But in his motion like an angel sings,
> Still quiring to the young-eyed cherubims;
> Such harmony is in immortal souls.

To the rudest carol that ever flung its notes upon the still air of these solemn hours we have hearkened with a hush of pleasure which recognised how well

> Soft stillness, and the night,
> Become the touches of sweet harmony!

And the wildest music that ever broke upon that solemn calm from the instruments of the most unskilful waits – if it were but remote enough to keep its asperities out of the ear, and send us only its floating tones – has brought Shakespeare into our hearts again:

PORTIA   Methinks it sounds much sweeter than by day.
NERISSA Silence bestows that virtue on it, madam.

The waits of today are the remote and degenerated successors of those ancient bards who filled an important place in the establishments of princes and nobles, as also of those wandering members of the fraternity who, having no fixed position, carried their gift of music from place to place as the tournament or the festival invited. Those of our readers who have much acquaintance with the old chroniclers have not to be told by us that these latter were frequently drawn together in considerable numbers by the Christmas celebrations. The name 'wait', or 'wayte', itself is of great antiquity amongst us, and appears to have been the title given to some member of the band of minstrels who either replaced the ancient minstrel-chronicler in the royal establishments, or was probably under his direction, the duty of which particular member it was to pass at night from door to door of the chambers and pipe the watches upon some species of instrument. As early as the reign of Edward III we have mention of this individual minstrel by his title of 'wayte', and in the subsequent ordinances for royal households the name frequently occurs. Dr Burney, in his *History of Music*, quotes from the *Liber niger domus regis*, of Edward IV's time, a full description of the duties, privileges, and perquisites of this ancient officer. It is probably from this member of the royal household and his office that the corporations for towns borrowed their earliest appointment of watchmen; and the ancestors of those ancient gentlemen whose most sweet voices are amongst the lost sounds of the metropolis, and whose mysterious cries will soon, we fear, be a dead language, were no doubt in their original institution minstrels or waits. The sworn waits are, we believe, still attached to many corporations (although some of their duties have been alienated, and some of their prerogatives usurped), and amongst others to that of the City of London. The bellman and those 'wandering voices', the watchmen, where they still exist, have, however, a title to the same high and far descent, and have succeeded to most of the offices of the ancient waits. It would seem, too, that both these latter important personages have at all times had it in view to assert their claim to a minstrel origin, their announcements being generally chanted in a species of music quite peculiar to themselves, and such as the world can never hope to hear again when these gentry shall be extinct. 'Oh, what a voice is silent!' wrote Barry Cornwall long before the introduction of the new police into our streets; and the passionate exclamation must surely have originated in a prophetic vision of the extinction of the Dogberry who piped the night-watches in Bedford Square. As for those wandering musicians who charm the long nights of the Christmas time with *unofficial* music, and are waits by courtesy, they bear the same relation to the corporation minstrels of modern times as did the travelling bards of former days to the ancient minstrels who were established in the households of nobles or of kings. The waits still on some occasions close their performance by calling the hour, and by certain other announcements descriptive of the weather or characteristic of the season.

The sacred origin and meaning of this practice have, however, in modern days been a good deal lost sight of by these uncertificated harmonists in their selection of tunes. In London, particularly, the appropriate music of religious celebration, which in awaking the sleeper should bring the lessons of the season directly to his heart, are (excepting perhaps on the eve of the Nativity itself) most frequently supplanted by the airs of the theatre; and the waits for the most part favour us by night with repetitions of the melodies with which the barrel-organists have laboured to make us familiarly acquainted during the day. It is with some such strain that the group of instrumentalists, by whom our artist has here represented these peripatetic musicians, appear to be regaling their neighbourhood, insofar as we may venture to judge of the character of the music, by the accompaniment which it is receiving from the lady in the distance. Not that we could by any means have conjectured from the appearance of the performers themselves that the air, however profane, had been at all of the lively, unless what poor

Waits

Matthews called the 'deadly lively', kind – and, in fact, the vicinity in which the lady appears may perhaps suggest that her joyous inspiration is not derived wholly from the music. She appears to be dancing 'unto her own heart's song'. If we may presume to argue from the aspects and attitudes of the gentlemen of the bass-viol and flute, he of the trombone (who is evidently performing with considerable energy) appears to have got a good way before his companions without being at all conscious of it; and, indeed, there is something about his accoutrements, if carefully inspected, which seems to hint that the source of his vigour, and perhaps of his unconsciousness, is of the same kind with that of the lady's liveliness. We have in the case of each a sort of insinuation as to the cause of the *spirited* character of the performances, and in that of our friend with the trombone it seems a good deal more clear that his pocket has contributed to the supply of his instrument than that his instrument will ever do much for the supply of his pocket. As for the violin, it is clearly in the enjoyment of a sinecure at this late hour, the sensitive performer having apparently lulled himself to sleep with his own music. 'Poor knave, I blame thee not; thou art o'er watched!'

> O murd'rous slumber,
> Lay'st thou thy leaden mace upon my boy
> That plays thee music? Gentle knave, good night;
> I will not do thee so much wrong to wake thee.

But we will not answer for the old gentleman with the water-jug, who looks down so benignantly from that window overhead. He seems about to furnish an illustration of the assertion that

> The heart that music cannot melt,
> Is fit for treasons, stratagems, and spoils;

and appears to have conceived a stratagem against the group below which, if carried into successful execution on this winter night, will probably *spoil* more than the music. It bids fair at once to waken the violin player and to silence the trombone.

The practice of hailing the Nativity with music, in commemoration of the song of the angels, is in full observance in Roman Catholic countries as well as in our own. There are, we fancy, few of our readers who have not had opportunities of listening to the divine strains which mingle in the Roman services that usher in the blessed morning itself. The *noëls* of France are of the same character as the Christmas carols of England; and the visits of our street musicians at this season are closely resembled by the wanderings of the Italian *pifferari*. These *pifferari* are Calabrian shepherds who come down from the mountains at the season of Advent, and enter the Italian cities, saluting with their hill music the shrines of the Virgin and

Child which adorn the streets. Of these rude minstrels Lady Morgan, in her 'Italy', gives some account, and states that having frequently observed them stopping to play before the shop of a carpenter in Rome, her inquiries on the subject were answered by the information that the intention of this part of their performance, was to give his due share of honour to Saint Joseph. Our friend Mr Hone, in his *Every-Day Book*, has given, from an old print in his possession, a representation of this practice, in which two of these mountaineers are playing before the shrine of the Virgin. The practice is continued till the anniversary day of the Nativity.

With modern carol-singing there are few of our readers, in town or in country (for the practice, like that of which we have just spoken, is still very general), who are not well acquainted. For some curious antiquarian information on the subject we must refer them to Mr Sandys's Introduction, and to a paper in Mr Hone's book of *Ancient Mysteries*. The word itself is derived by Brand, after Bourne, from *cantare*, to sing, and *rola*, an interjection of joy; and although in vulgar acceptance it has come to be understood as implying particularly those anthems by which the Christmas-tide is distinguished, it has at all times been properly applied to all songs which are sung upon any occasion of festival or rejoicing. In strictness, therefore, even in its application to the musical celebrations of Advent, a distinction should be drawn between those carols which are of a joyous or festive character, and those more solemn ones which would be better described by the title of Christmas hymns.

The practice itself, as applied to religious commemoration, is drawn from the very first ages of the Church. It is frequently referred to in the Apostolic writings, and the celebrated letter of the younger Pliny to the Emperor Trajan, in the seventh year of the second Christian century, mentions, amongst the habits of the primitive Christians, their assembling at stated times 'to sing among themselves alternately a hymn to Christ, as to God'. Such a practice, however, constitutes no peculiarity of the new worship, hymns of praise to their deities having made a portion of the rites of most religions. Indeed, in the more severe times of the Early Church, there are prohibitions against this form of worship, as against several other practices to which we have alluded, on the express ground of its resemblance to one of the customs of the pagan celebration.

The custom of celebrating the festivities of the season by the singing of carols in these islands, appears to have mingled with the Christmas observances from the earliest period. We have specimens of the carols themselves of a remote date, and have already given an extract from one, the manuscript of which, in the British Museum, is dated as far back as the thirteenth century. There are evidences of the universality of the practice in the fifteenth century; and the great popularity of these songs about this time is proved by the fact of a collection thereof having been printed in the early part of the following century by Wynkyn de Worde. It is to the Puritans that we appear to have been indebted for the introduction of the religious carol. Those enemies of all mirth, even in its most innocent or valuable forms, finding the practice of carol singing at this festive time too general and rooted to be dealt with by interdiction, appear to have endeavoured to effect their objects by directing it into a channel of their own, and probably retaining the ancient airs, to have adapted them to the strange religious ballads, of which we must give our readers a few specimens. The entire version of the Psalms of David made by Sternhold and Hopkins was published about the middle of the sixteenth century; and some time before the middle of the seventeenth a duodecimo volume appeared, under the title of *Psalmes or Songs of Zion*, 'turned into the language and set to the tunes of a strange land, by W. S. [William Slatyr], intended for Christmas Carols and fitted to divers of the most noted and common but solemne tunes everywhere in this land familiarly used and knowne.'

Of these old ballads of both kinds, many (and snatches of more) have survived to the present day, and may be heard, particularly in the Northern counties of England, ringing through the frosty air of the long winter nights, in the shrill voices of children, for several weeks before Christmas, probably, too, to the old traditional tunes. They are, however, as might be expected of compositions which have no more substantial depositary than the memories of the humble classes of the young, full of corruptions, which render some of them nearly unintelligible. The difficulty of restoring these old carols in their original forms is becoming yearly greater, in consequence of the modern carols, which are fast replacing them by a sort of authority. In country places many of the more polished carols, of modern composition, find their way into the Church services of this season; and amongst the singers who practise this manner of appealing to the charities of the season with most success are the children of the Sunday schools and the choristers of the village church. These, with their often sweet voices, bring to our doors the more select hymns and the musical training which they have gathered for more sacred places; and from a group like that which stands at the parsonage door in our plate, we are more likely to hear some carol of Heber's, some such beautiful anthem as that beginning, 'Hark! the herald angels sing', than the strange, rambling old Christmas songs which we well remember when we were boys. These latter, however, occasionally are not without a wild beauty of their own. We quote a fragment of one of them from memory. We think it begins:

> The moon shines bright, and the stars give light,
> A little before the day;

and wanders on somewhat after the following unconnected fashion:

> Awake, awake, good people all!
> Awake, and you shall hear
> How Christ our Lord died on the cross
> For those he loved so dear.
>
> O fair, O fair Jerusalem!
> When shall I come to thee?
> When shall my griefs be at an end,
> That I thy tents may see!
>
> The fields were green as green could be
> When, from his glorious seat,
> The Lord our God he watered us
> With his heavenly good and sweet.
>
> And for the saving of our souls
> Christ died upon the cross!
> We never shall do for Jesus Christ
> What he has done for us!
>
> The life of man is but a span,
> And cut down in its flower;
> We're here today, and gone tomorrow,
> We're all dead in an hour.
>
> Oh, teach well your children, men!
> The while that you are here,
> It will be better for your souls,
> When your corpse lies on the bier.
>
> Today you may be alive, dear man,
> With many a thousand pound;
> Tomorrow you may be a dead man,
> And your corpse laid under ground –
>
> With a turf at your head, dear man,
> And another at your feet.
> Your good deeds and your bad ones
> They will together meet.
>
> My song is done, and I must begone,
> I can stay no longer here;
> God bless you all, both great and small,
> And send you a happy new year.

Our Lancashire readers know that a similar wish to that expressed in the two last lines is generally delivered in recitative at the close of each carol, or before the singers abandon our doors – which wish, however, we have heard finally changed into a less quotable ejaculation in cases where the carolists had been allowed to sing unregarded.

The gradual decay into which these ancient religious ballads are rapidly falling was in some measure repaired by Mr Davies Gilbert in 1823, who published a collection containing upwards of twenty carols in a restored state, with the tunes to which it was usual to sing them in the West of England. Of Welsh carols, various collections are mentioned both by Hone and by Sandys, and in that country the practice is in better preservation than even in England. In Ireland, too, it exists to the present day, although we have not met with any collection of Irish carols; and in France, where there are numerous collections under the title of *noëls*, the custom is universal. In Scotland, however, it was extinguished, with the other Christmas practices, by the thunders of John Knox and his precisians, and we believe has never been in any degree restored. We should add that there are numerous carols for the Christmas season scattered through the writings of our old poets, amongst whom Herrick may be mentioned as conspicuous.

But the most ample and curious published collection of Christmas carols with which we have met is that by Mr Sandys to which we have so often alluded; and from the text of this collection we will give our readers one or two specimens of the quaint beauties which occasionally mingle in the curious texture of these old anthems. Mr Sandys's collection is divided into two parts, the first of which consists of ancient carols and Christmas songs from the early part of the fifteenth to the end of the seventeenth century. We wish that in cases where the authorship belongs to so conspicuous a name as Herrick – and indeed in all cases where it is ascertained – the names of the authors had been prefixed. The second part comprises a selection from carols which the editor states to be still used in the West of England. We can inform him that many of these we have ourselves heard, only some dozen years ago, screamed through the sharp evening air of Lancashire at the top pitch of voices that could clearly never have been given for any such purposes, 'making night hideous', or occasionally filling the calm watches with the farlulling sounds of wild, sweet harmony. The practice, however, is, under any circumstances, full of fine meanings that redeem the rudeness of performance; and for ourselves, we like the music at its best and worst.

Of the festive songs we have already given occasional examples in the progress of this work, and shall just now confine ourselves to extracts from those of a more religious character. From the old part of the collections before us we will give a verse of a short carol which, while it will exhibit in a very modified degree the familiar tone in which the writers of these ancient songs dealt with the incidents of the sacred story, is full of a tenderness arising out of that very manner of treatment. We give it in the literal form in which we find it in this collection, with the exception of extending an occasional cypher. It begins with a burden:

> A, my dere son, sayd mary, a, my dere,
> Kys thi moder, Jhesu, with a lawghyng chere;

and continues:

> This endnes nyght I sawe a syght all in my slepe,
> Mary that may she sang lullay and sore did wepe.
> To kepe she sawght full fast a bowte her son fro cold;
> Joseph seyd, wiff, my joy, my leff, say what ye wolde;
> No thyng my spouse is In this howse unto my pay;
> My son a kyng that made all thyng lyth in hay.
>
> 'A, my dere son.'

Some of these ancient carols run over the principal incidents in the scheme of man's fall and redemption; and we are sorry that our limits will not permit us to give such lengthened specimens as we should desire. We will, however, copy a few verses from one of a different kind, in which, beneath its ancient dress, our readers will see that there is much rude beauty. It begins –

> I come from heuin to tell
> The best nowellis that ever be fell.

But we must take it up further on:

> My saull and lyfe, stand up and see
> Quha lyes in ane cribe of tree;
> Quhat babe is that so gude and faire?
> It is Christ, God's Sonne and Aire.
>
> O God, that made all creature,
> How art thou becum so pure,
> That on the hay and straw will lye,
> Amang the asses, oxin, and kye?
>
> And were the world ten tymes so wide,
> Cled ouer with gold and stanes of pride,
> Unworthy zit it were to thee,
> Under thy feet ane stule to bee.

> The sylke and sandell, thee to eis,
> Are hay and sempill sweiling clais,
> Quhairin thow gloiris, greitest king,
> As thow in heuin were in thy ring.
>
> O my deir hert, zoung Jesus sweit,
> Prepare thy creddill in my spreit,
> And I sall rock thee in my hert,
> And neuer mair from thee depart.

The Star-song in this collection is, if our memory mislead us not, Herrick's, and taken from his *Noble Numbers*. It begins –

> Tell us, thou cleere and heavenly tongue,
> Where is the babe but lately sprung?
> Lies he the lillie-banks among?
>
> Or say if this new Birth of our's
> Sleep, laid within some ark of flowers,
> Spangled with deaw-light; thou canst cleere
> All doubts, and manifest the where.
>
> Declare to us, bright star, if we shall seek
> Him in the morning's blushing cheek,
> Or search the beds of spices through,
> To find him out?

The second part of Sandys's collection contains an imperfect version of a carol of which we find a full and corrected copy in Mr Hone's *Ancient Mysteries*, formed by that author's collation of various copies printed in different places. The beautiful verses which we quote are from Hone's version, and are wanting in that of Sandys. The ballad begins by elevating the Virgin Mary to a temporal rank which must rest upon that particular authority, and is probably a new fact for our readers:

> Joseph was an old man,
>   And an old man was he,
> And he married Mary,
>   Queen of Galilee –

which, for a carpenter, was certainly a distinguished alliance. It goes on to describe Joseph and his bride walking in a garden –

> Where the cherries they grew
>   Upon every tree;

and upon Joseph's refusal, in somewhat rude language, to pull some of these cherries for Mary, on the ground of her supposed misconduct:

> Oh! then bespoke Jesus,
>   All in his mother's womb,
> 'Go to the tree, Mary,
>   And it shall bow down;
>
> 'Go to the tree, Mary,
>   And it shall bow to thee,
> And the highest branch of all
>   Shall bow down to Mary's knee.'

And then, after describing Joseph's conviction and penitence at this testimony to Mary's truth, occur the beautiful verses to which we alluded:

> As Joseph was a walking,
>   He heard an angel sing:
> 'This night shall be born
>   Our heavenly king.
>
> 'He neither shall be born
>   In housen nor in hall,
> Nor in the place of Paradise,
>   But in an ox's stall.
>
> 'He neither shall be clothed
>   In purple nor in pall,
> But all in fair linen,
>   As were babies all.
>
> 'He neither shall be rock'd
>   In silver nor in gold,
> But in a wooden cradle,
>   That rocks on the mould.
>
> 'He neither shall be christen'd
>   In white wine nor in red,
> But with the spring water
>   With which we were christened.'

The strange, wild ballad beginning:

> I saw three ships come sailing in,
>   On Christmas day, on Christmas day;
> I saw three ships come sailing in,
>   On Christmas day in the morning –

and the still stranger one of 'The Holy Well', we would have copied at length, as examples of these curious relics, if we could have spared the space. Of the latter, however, we will give our readers some account, to show the singular liberties which were taken with sacred personages and things in these old carols. In the one in question, the boy Jesus, having asked his mother's permission to go and play, receives it, accompanied with the salutary injunction:

> 'And let me hear of no complaint
>   At night when you come home.'

> Sweet Jesus went down to yonder town,
>   As far as the Holy Well,
> And there did see as fine children
>   As any tongue can tell.

On preferring, however, his petition to these children –

> 'Little children, shall I play with you,
>   And you shall play with me?'

he is refused on the ground of his having been 'born in an ox's stall', they being 'lords' and ladies' sons'.

> Sweet Jesus turned him around,
> And he neither laugh'd nor smil'd,
> But the tears came trickling from his eye
> Like water from the skies.

Whereupon he returns home to report his grievance to his mother, who answers –

> 'Though you are but a maiden's child,
>   Born in an ox's stall,
> Thou art the Christ, the King of Heaven,
>   And the Saviour of them all.'

and then proceeds to give him advice neither consistent with the assertion in the last line, nor becoming her character –

> 'Sweet Jesus, go down to yonder town,
>   As far as the Holy Well,
> And take away those sinful souls,
>   And dip them deep in hell.'

> 'Nay, nay', sweet Jesus said,
>   'Nay, nay, that may not be;
> For there are too many sinful souls
>   Crying out for the help of me.'

Both these latter carols are given by Sandys as amongst those which are still popular in the West of England; and we remember to have ourselves heard them both many and many a time in its Northern counties.

We must give a single verse of one of the ancient French provincial *noëls*, for the purpose of introducing our readers to a strange species of chanted burden; and then we must stop. It is directed to be sung *sur un chant joyeux*, and begins thus:

> Quand Dieu naquit à Noël,
>   Dedans la Judée,
> On vit ce jour solemnel
>   La joie inondée;
> Il n'étoit ni petit ni grand
> Qui n'apportât son présent
> Et n'o, n'o, n'o, n'o,
> Et n'offrit, frit, frit,
> Et n'o, n'o, et n'offrit,
> Et n'offrit sans cesse Toute sa richesse.

Our readers are no doubt aware that the carol sheets still make their annual appearance at this season, not only in the metropolis, but also in Manchester, Birmingham, and perhaps other towns. In London, they pass into the hands of hawkers, who wander about our streets and suburbs enforcing the sale thereof by – in addition to the irresistible attraction of the woodcuts with which they are embellished – the further recommendation of their own versions and variations of the original tunes, yelled out in tones which could not be heard without alarm by any animals throughout the entire range of Nature, except the domesticated ones, who are 'broken' to it. For ourselves, we confess that we are not thoroughly broken yet, and experience very uneasy sensations at the approach of one of these alarming choirs.

> 'Tis said that the lion will turn and flee
> From a maid in the pride of her purity.

We would rather meet him under the protection of a group of London carol singers. We would undertake to explore the entire of central Africa, well provisioned and in such company, without the slightest apprehension, excepting such as was suggested by the music itself.

By these gentry a very spirited competition is kept up in the article of annoyance with the hurdy-gurdies, and other instruments of that class, which awaken the echoes of all our streets, and furnish a sufficient refutation of the assertion that we are not a musical nation. We have heard it said that the atmosphere of London is highly impregnated with coal-smoke and barrel-organs. The breath of ballad singers should enter into the account at this season. The sketch from life which we have given of one of these groups will convey to our readers a very lively notion of the carol singers of London, and supply them with a hint as to the condition in this flourishing metropolis of that branch of the fine arts. Our friends will perceive that this is a family of artists, from the oldest to the youngest. The children are born to an inheritance of song, and begin to enter upon its enjoyment in the cradle. That infant in arms made his *début* before the public a day or two after he was born, and is already an accomplished chorister; and the hopeful boy who is howling by his mother's side acquits himself as becomes the heir-at-law to parents who have sung through the world, and the next in reversion to his father's fiddle.

A very curious part of the business, however, is, that these people actually expect to get money for what they are doing! With the most perfect good faith, they really calculate upon making a profit by their outrages upon men's feelings! It is for the purpose of 'putting bread into their mouths' that those mouths are opened in that portentous manner. For ourselves, we have a strong conviction that the spread of the emigration mania has been greatly promoted by the increase of ballad singers in the land. We have frequently resolved to emigrate, on that account, ourselves; and if we could be perfectly certified of any desirable colony, to which no removals had taken place from the class in question, we believe we should no longer hesitate. The existence of that class is a grievous public wrong, and calls loudly for legislation. We have frequently thought that playing a hurdy-gurdy in the streets should be treated as a capital crime.

Of the annual sheets and of such other carols as may be recoverable from traditional or other sources, it is to be regretted that more copious collections are not made, by the lovers of old customs, ere it be too late. Brand speaks of a hereditary collection of ballads, almost as numerous as the Pepysian collection at Cambridge, which he saw, at Newcastle-upon-Tyne, in the printing-office of the late Mr Saint, amongst which were several carols for the Christmas season. Hone, in his *Ancient Mysteries*, gives a list of eighty-nine carols in his possession, all in present use (though likely soon to become obsolete), and exclusive of the modern compositions printed by religious societies, under the denomination of carols. He furnishes a curious proof of the attachment which the carol-buyers extend, from the old carols themselves, to the old rude cuts by which they are illustrated. 'Some of these,' he says, 'on a sheet of Christmas carols, in 1820, were so rude in execution that I requested the publisher, Mr T. Batchelar, of 115 Long Alley, Moorfields, to sell me the original blocks. I was a little surprised by his telling me that he was afraid it would be impossible to get any of the same kind cut again. When I

London carol singers

proffered to get much better engraved, and give them to him in exchange for his old ones, he said, "Yes, but better are not so good; I can get better myself. Now these are old favourites, and better cuts will not please my customers so well." ' We have before us several of the sheets for the present season, issued from the printing-office and toy warehouse of Mr Pitts, in the Seven Dials; and we grieve to say that, for the most part, they show a lamentable improvement in the embellishments, and an equally lamentable falling-off in the literary contents. One of these sheets, however, which bears the heading title of 'Divine Mirth', contains some of the *old* carols, and is adorned with impressions from cuts, rude enough, we should think, to please even the customers of Mr Batchelar.

Amongst the musical signs of the season we must not omit to place that once important gentleman, the bellman, who was anciently accustomed, as our excellent friend Mr Hone says, at this time, 'to make frequent nocturnal rambles, and proclaim all tidings which it seemed fitting to him that people should be awakened out of their sleep to hearken to.' From that ancient collection, *The Bellman's Treasury*, which was once this now decayed officer's vade-mecum, we shall have occasion to extract, here and there, in their proper places, the announcements by which, of old, he broke in upon the stillness of the several nights of this period. In the meantime our readers may take the following example of bellman verses, written by Herrick, and which we have extracted from his 'Hesperides':

From noise of scare-fires rest ye free,
From murders Benedicitie;
From all mischances that may fright
Your pleasing slumbers in the night.

'Mercie secure ye all, and keep
The goblin from ye while ye sleep.
Past one aclock, and almost two.
My masters all, good-day to you!

The bell of this ancient officer may still be heard, at the midnight hour of Christmas Eve (and perhaps on other nights), in the different parishes of London, performing the overture to a species of recitative, in which he sets forth (amongst other things) the virtues of his patrons (dwelling on their liberality), and offers them all the good wishes of the season. The printed papers containing the matter of these recitations he has been busy circulating amongst the parishioners for some time; and on the strength thereof, presents himself as a candidate for some expression of their good-will in return, which, however, he expects should be given in a more profitable form. These papers, like the carol sheets, have their margins adorned with woodcuts after Scriptural subjects. One of them now lies before us, and we grieve to say that the quaint ancient rhymes are therein substituted by meagre modern inventions, and the woodcuts exhibit a most ambitious pretension to be considered as specimens of improved art. There is a copy of Carlo Dolce's 'Last Supper' at the foot.

The beadle of today is in most respects changed, for the worse, from the bellman of old. Still, we are glad to hear his bell – which sounds much as it must have done of yore – lifting up its ancient voice amongst its fellows at this high and general season of bells and bob-majors.

The Second Part

The Christmas Days

The Lord of Misrule; the High and Mighty Prince Henry, Prince of Purpoole, Archduke of Stapulia and Bernardia, Duke of High and Nether Holborn, Marquis of St Giles and Tottenham Court, Count Palatine of Bloomsbury and Clerkenwell, Great Lord of the Cantons of Islington, Kentish Town, Paddington and Knightsbridge

GESTA GRAYORUM

The Christmas Days

Having given our readers a historical and general account of this ancient festival, and a particular explanation of some of the principal tokens which, in modern times as of old, bespeak the coming of its more high and ceremonious days, we must now proceed to furnish them with a more peculiar description of those individual days themselves; confining ourselves, as nearly as completeness of view will admit, within the limits which bound what is, in its most especial and emphatic sense, the Christmas season. In order, however, to attain this completeness of view, it has been necessary to allow ourselves certain points lying on both sides, *without* those strict boundaries; and the selection which we have made includes the two conditions of giving us latitude enough for our purpose, and keeping reasonably close to the heart of the subject at the same time. The reasons for this particular selection will more fully appear in the accounts which we have to give of the individual days on which that selection has fallen, and in the further remarks which we have to make, generally on that portion of the year which we place under the presidency of Our Lord of Misrule.

Christmas Presents

St Thomas's Day
21st December

This day, which is dedicated to the apostle St Thomas, we have chosen as the opening of the Christmas festivities; because it is that on which we first seem to get positive evidence of the presence of the old gentleman, and see the spirit of hospitality and benevolence which his coming creates brought into active operation. Of the manner in which this spirit exhibits itself in the metropolis, we are about presently to speak; but must previously notice that in many of the rural districts of England there are still lingering traces of ancient customs, which meet at this particular point of time and under the sanction of that same spirit. These practices, however various in their kinds, are for the most part relics in different shapes of the old mummeries, which we shall have to discuss at length in the course of the present chapter; and are but so many distinct forms in which the poor man's appeal is made to the rich man's charity, for a share in the good things of this merry festival.

Amongst these ancient customs may be mentioned the practice of 'going a gooding', which exists in some parts of Kent, and is performed by women, who present sprigs of evergreens and Christmas flowers, and beg for money in return. We believe the term 'going a gooding' scarcely requires illustration. It means, simply, going about to wish 'good even' – as, according to Nares, fully appears from this passage in Romeo and Juliet:

NURSE   God ye good morrow, gentlemen.
MERCUTIO   God ye *good den*, fair gentlewoman.

In this same county, St Thomas's Day is likewise known by the name of 'Doleing Day', on account of the distribution of the bounty of different charitable individuals. This word 'dole' is explained by Nares to mean 'a share or lot in any thing distributed', and to come from the verb *to deal*. He quotes Shakespeare for this also:

It was your presurmise
That in the *dole* of blows your son might drop.

The musical procession known in the Isle of Thanet and other parts of the same county by the name of 'hodening' (supposed, by some, to be an ancient relic of a festival ordained to commemorate the landing of our Saxon ancestors in that island, and which, in its form, is neither more nor less than a modification of the old practice of the 'hobby horse'), is to this day another of the customs of this particular period.

A custom analogous to these is still to be traced in Warwickshire; throughout which county it seems to have been the practice of the poor to go from door to door of every house 'with a bag to beg corn of the farmers, which they call going a-corning'. And in Herefordshire, a similar custom exists, where this day is called 'Mumping Day', that is, begging day.

To the same spirit we owe the Hagmena or Hogmanay practice, still in use in Scotland, as well as that of the Wren Boys in Ireland, both of which will be described hereafter, although their observance belongs to later days of the season, and probably many others which will variously suggest themselves to our various readers as existing in their several neighbourhoods.

In the great metropolis of England, where poverty and wretchedness exist in masses upon which private benevolence cannot efficiently act, and where imposture assumes their forms in a degree that baffles the charity of individuals, the bequests of our ancestors have been to a great extent placed for distribution in the hands of the various parish authorities. St Thomas's Day in London, therefore, is connected with these charities, by its being that on which some of the most important parochial proceedings take place; and amongst these are the wardmotes, held on this day for the election, by the freemen inhabitant householders, of the members of the Common Council, and other officers of the respective city wards.

The civil government of the City of London is said to bear a general resemblance to the legislative power of the empire; the Lord Mayor exercising the functions of monarchy, the Aldermen those of the peerage, and the Common Council those of the legislature. The principal difference is, that the Lord Mayor himself has no negative. The laws for the internal regulation of the city are wholly framed by these officers acting in common council. A Common-Councilman is, therefore, a personage of no mean importance.

Loving Christmas and its ceremonies with antiquarian veneration, we must profess likewise our profound respect for wards of such high sounding names as Dowgate, and Candlewick, and Cripplegate, and Vintry, and Portsoken; the last of which, be it spoken with due courtesy, has always reminded us of an alderman's nose; and for such distinguished callings as those of Cordwainers, and Lorimers, and Feltmakers, and Fishmongers, and Plasterers, and Vintners, and Barbers; each of whom we behold in perspective transformed into what Theodore Hook calls 'a splendid annual', or in less figurative language, Lord Mayor of London! There is a pantomimic magic in the word since the memorable days of Whittington. But to our theme.

Pepys, the gossiping secretary of the Admiralty, records in his curious diary his having gone on St Thomas's Day (21st December), 1663, 'to Shoe Lane to see a cocke-fighting at the new pit there, a spot,' he adds, 'I was never at in my life: but, Lord! to see the strange variety of people, from parliament-man (by name Wildes, that was deputy governor of the Tower when Robinson was Lord Mayor) to the poorest 'prentices, bakers, brewers, butchers, draymen, and what not; and all these fellows one with another cursing and betting. I soon had enough of it. It is strange to see how people of this poor rank, that look as if they had not bread to put into their mouths, shall bet three or four pounds at a time and lose it, and yet as much the next battle, so that one of them will lose £10 or £20 at a meeting.'

Now the cockfighting of our times, under the immediate patronage of St Thomas, and those of Pepys's differ little except in the character of the combatants. In his (comparatively speaking) barbarous days, it was sufficient to pit two birds, one against the other, to excite the public or amuse the spectators. But a purer taste prevails among the present citizens of London; for our modern 'fighting-cocks', as the candidates for civic honours are called, seem on this day to be fully occupied with the morning exhibition of their own foul tongues – and bets often run as high as parties, on these occasions.

'Saint Thomas's birds' – another name for these civic fighting-cocks – have been trained in various ale-house associations, such as the 'Ancient and honourable Lumber Troop', the venerable 'Society of Codgers', 'the free and easy Johns', the 'Councillors under the Cauliflower', and other well-known clubs – where politics, foreign and domestic, night after night are discussed, and mingle with the smoke of tobacco, inhaled through respectable clay pipes and washed down with nips of amber ale, or quarts of frothy-headed porter. Indeed, the qualification for admission into the Lumber Troop is, we have been told, the power of consuming a quart of porter at a draught, without once pausing to draw a breath – which feat must be performed before that august assembly. We once visited the headquarters of this porter-quaffing troop, and found the house, with some difficulty, near Gough Square – which lies in that intricate region between Holborn Hill and Fleet Street. It was a corner house, and an inscription upon the wall, in letters of gold, informed the passer-by that this was the place of meeting of the Lumber Troop. The room in which they met is small, dark, and ancient in appearance, with an old-fashioned chimney piece in the centre, and a dais or raised floor at one end, where, we presume, the officers of the troop take their seats. Above their heads, upon a shelf, some small brass cannon were placed as ornaments, and the walls of the room were decorated with the portraits of distinguished troopers – among whom Mr Alderman Wood, in a scarlet robe, and Mr Richard Taylor were pointed out to our notice. Over the fireplace hung the portrait of an old gentleman, in the warlike costume of Cromwell's time, who was, probably,

Some Fleet Street Hampden.

The obscurity which conceals the origin of many interesting and important institutions hangs over the early history of the Lumber Troop. Tradition asserts that, when Henry VIII went to the siege of Boulogne, he drained the country of all its soldiers; and the citizens of London who remained behind, inspired with martial ardour, formed themselves into a troop for the protection of old England. In the grotesque and gouty appearance of these troopers, their name of the Lumber Troop is said to have originated. Their field days, as may be expected, were exhibitions of merriment; and their guards and midnight watches scenes of feasting and revelry. The 'Lumber-pye' was formerly a dish in much repute, being composed of high-seasoned meats and savoury ingredients, for the preparation of which receipts may be found in the old cookery books. Recently, it has been corrupted into Lombard Pie, on account, as is said, of its Italian origin – but we profess allegiance to the more ancient name.

Let those who hold lightly the dignity of a Lumber Trooper, and who perhaps have smiled at the details here given, inquire of the representatives of the city of London in the parliament of England, their opinion of the matter. We have been assured that these jolly troopers influence every city election to such an extent that, without an understanding with these worthies, no candidate can have a chance of success. In the same way, the codgers, in Codger's Hall, Bride Lane (said to have been instituted in 1756, by some of the people of the Inner Temple, who imagined their free thoughts and profound cogitations worthy of attention, and charged half-a-crown for the *entrée*), and other ale-house clubs, exert their more limited power. Hone, in his *Every-Day Book*, observes that 'these societies are undercurrents that set in strong, and often turn the tide of an election in favour of some "good fellow", who is good nowhere but in "sot's-hole".' And he adds, commenting upon St Thomas's Day, 'Now the "gentlemen of the inquest", chosen "at the church" in the morning, dine together, as the first important duty of their office; and the re-elected ward beadles are busy with the fresh chosen constables; and the watchmen [this was before the days of the police] are particularly civil to every "drunken gentleman" who happens to look like one of the new authorities. And now the bellman, who revives the history and poetry of his predecessors, will vociferate –

'My masters all, this is St Thomas'-day,
And Christmas now can't be far off, you'll say.
And when you to the Ward-motes do repair,
I hope such good men will be chosen there,
As constables for the ensuing year,
As will not grudge the watchmen good strong beer.'

The illustration of this part of our subject, which our artist has given, exhibits the scene of one of these parish elections; and includes, in the distance, a vision of those good things to which all business matters in England – and above all, in its eastern metropolitan city – are but prefaces.

We may observe, here, that St Thomas's Day is commonly called the shortest of the year, although the difference between its length and that of the twenty-second is not perceptible. The hours of the sun's rising and setting, on each of those days, are marked as the same in our calendars, and the latter is sometimes spoken of as the shortest day.

Sports of this Season

As the days which intervene between this and the Eve of Christmas are distinguished by no special ceremonial of their own, and as the numerous observances attached to several of the particular days which follow will sufficiently prolong those parts of our subject, we will take this opportunity of alluding to some of the sports and festivities not peculiar to any one day, but extending more or less generally over the entire season.

Burton in his *Anatomy of Melancholy* mentions, as the winter amusements of his day, 'Cardes, tables and dice, shovelboard, chesse-play, the philosopher's game, small trunkes, shuttlecocke, billiards, musicke, masks, singing, dancing, ule-games, frolicks, jests, riddles, catches, purposes, questions and commands, merry tales of errant knights, queenes, lovers, lords, ladies, giants, dwarfes, theeves, cheaters, witches, fayries, goblins, friers,' etc. Amongst the list of Christmas sports, we elsewhere find mention of 'jugglers, and jack-puddings, scrambling for nuts and apples, dancing the hobby-horse, hunting owls and squirrels, the fool-plough, hot-cockles, a stick moving on a pivot with an apple at one end and a candle at the other, so that he who missed his bite burned his nose, blindman's buff, forfeits, interludes and mock plays': also of 'thread my needle, Nan', 'he can do little that can't do this', feed the dove, hunt the slipper, shoeing the wild mare, post and pair, snap-dragon, the gathering of omens, and a great variety of others. In this long enumeration, our readers will recognise many which have come down to the present day, and form still the amusement of

St Thomas's Day

their winter evenings at the Christmas-tide, or on the merry night of Halloween. For an account of many of those which are no longer to be found in the list of holiday games, we must refer such of our readers as it may interest to Brand's *Popular Antiquities*, and Strutt's *English Sports*. A description of them would be out of place in this volume; and we have mentioned them only as confirming a remark which we have elsewhere made; viz., that in addition to such recreations as arise out of the season or belong to it in a special sense, whatever other games or amusements have at any time been of popular use, have generally inserted themselves into this lengthened and joyous festival; and that all the forms in which mirth or happiness habitually sought expression congregated from all quarters at the ringing of the Christmas bells.

To the Tregetours, or jugglers, who anciently made mirth at the Christmas fireside, there are several allusions in Chaucer's tales; and Aubrey, in reference thereto, mentions some of the tricks by which they contributed to the entertainments of the season. The exhibitions of such gentry in modern times are generally of a more public kind, and it is rarely that they find their way to our firesides. But we have still the galantee-showman wandering up and down

Galantee show

our streets and squares, with his musical prelude and tempting anouncement sounding through the sharp evening air, and summoned into our warm rooms to display the shadowy marvels of his mysterious box to the young group, who gaze in great wonder and some awe from their inspiring places by the cheerful hearth.

Not that our firesides are altogether without domestic fortune-tellers or amateur practitioners in the art of sleight-of-hand. But the prophecies of the former are drawn from, and the feats of the other performed with the cards. Indeed, we must not omit to particularise cards as furnishing in all their uses one of the great resources at this season of long evenings and indoor amusements, as they appear also to have formed an express feature of the Christmas entertainments of all ranks of people in old times. We are told that the squire of three hundred a year in Queen Anne's time 'never played at cards but at Christmas, when the family pack was produced from the mantelpiece'; and Stevenson, an old writer of Charles the Second's time, in an enumeration of the preparations making for the mirth of the season, tells us that 'the country-maid leaves half her market and must be sent again, if she forgets a pack of cards on Christmas Eve'. And who of us all has not shared in the uproarious mirth which young and unclouded spirits find, amid the intrigues and speculations of a round game! To the overscrupulous on religious grounds, who, looking upon cards as the 'devil's books', and to the moral alarmist who, considering card-playing to be in itself gaming, would each object to this species of recreation for the young and innocent, it may be interesting to know that the practice has been defended by that bishop of bishops, Jeremy Taylor himself, and that he insists upon no argument against the innocence of a practice being inferred from its abuse.

We have before alluded to the bards and harpers who assembled in ancient days at this time of wassail, making the old halls to echo to the voice of music, and stirring the blood with the legends of chivalry or chilling it with the wizard tale. And the tale and the song are amongst the spirits that wait on Christmas still, and charm the long winter evenings with their yet undiminished spells. Many a Christmas evening has flown over our heads on the wings of music, sweeter, far sweeter, dearer, a thousand times dearer, than ever was played by wandering minstrel or uttered by stipendiary bard; and we have formed a portion of happy groups, when some thrilling story has sent a chain of sympathetic feeling through hearts that shall beat in unison no more, and tales of the grave and its tenants have sent a paleness into cheeks that the grave itself has since made paler still.

The winter hearth is the very land of gossip-red. There it is that superstition loves to tell her marvels, and curiosity to gather them. The gloom and desolation without, with the wild, unearthly voice of the blast, as it sweeps over a waste of snows and cuts sharp against the leafless branches, or the wan sepulchral light that shows the dreary earth as it were covered with a pall, and the trees like spectres rising from beneath it, alike send men huddling round the blazing fire, and awaken those impressions of the wild and shadowy and unsubstantial, to which tales of marvel or of terror are such welcome food. But other inspirations are born of the blaze itself; and the jest and the laugh and the merry narration are of the spirits that are raised within the magic circles that surround it.

> They should have drawn thee by the high heap't hearth,
>> Old Winter! seated in thy great armed-chair,
> Watching the children at their Christmas mirth;
>> Or circled by them, as thy lips declare
> Some merry jest, or tale of murder dire,
>> Or troubled spirit that disturbs the night;
> Pausing at times to move the languid fire,
>> Or taste the old October, brown and bright.

The song and the story, the recitation and the book read aloud are, in town and in village, mansion and farmhouse, amongst the universal resources of the winter nights now, as they or their equivalents have at all times been. The narratives of 'old adventures, and valiaunces of noble knights, in times past', the stories of Sir Bevys of Southampton and Sir Guy of Warwick, of Adam Bell, Clymme of the Clough, and William of Cloudesley, with other ancient romances or historical rhymes, which formed the recreation of the common people at their Christmas dinners and bride-ales long ago, may have made way for the wild legend of the sea, or fearful anecdote:

> Of horrid apparition, tall and ghastly,
> That walks at dead of night, or takes its stand
> O'er some new opened grave, and, strange to tell,
> Evanishes at crowing of the cock;

and for the more touching ballads which sing of the late repentance of the cruel Barbara Allan:

> O mither, mither, mak my bed,
>> O mak it saft and narrow;
> Since my love died for me today,
>> I'll die for him to morrow;

or how the

> Pretty babes, with hand in hand,
>   Went wandering up and down;
> But never more could see the man
>   Returning from the town;

or how 'there came a ghost to Margaret's door', and chilled the life-blood in her veins, by his awful announcement:

> My bones are buried in a kirk-yard,
>   Afar beyond the sea;
> And it is but my sprite, Marg'ret,
>   That's speaking now to thee;

or may have been replaced, in higher quarters, by the improved narrative literature of the present day, and the traditions or memories which haunt all homes. But the spirit of the entertainment itself is still the same, varied only by circumstances in its forms.

It is apparently by a group of the latter kind that this branch of the Christmas amusements is illustrated in the plate. The youthful members of a family are listening, in all probability, to some tale of their sires, related by the withered crone, who, grown old in that service, links those young beings with a generation gone by, and stands, as it were, prophesying 'betwixt the living and the dead'. If we may judge from the aspect of the aged sybil herself, and the pale and earnest faces that surround her, the narrative which she is imparting is one of the fearful class, and not to be listened to beyond the cheering inspirations of that bright fire; although the moving shadows which it flings upon the old walls are amongst the terrors which are born of her story. For the scene of these emotions, the artist has chosen, as artists still love to do, the chamber of an ancient mansion, with its huge chimney and oriel-window. And it may be that for picturesque effects which are to address themselves to the eye, artists are right in so doing. No doubt, the high chronicles of chivalry, and the mysterious traditions of the past, comport well with the gloom of the gothic gallery – and, certainly, the long rambling passages of an old house afford at once room for the wandering of ghosts, and that dim, shadowy light by which imagination sees them best. But the true poetry of life is not confined to ancient dwellings; and every house, in every crowded thoroughfare of every city, has its own tales to tell around the Christmas fire. The most pert-looking dwelling of them all, that may seem as if it were forever staring out of its sash windows into the street, has its own mysteries, and is, if it have been tenanted sufficiently long, as closely haunted by recollections as the baron's castle, or the squire's old manorhouse. Like them –

Story Telling

Its stones have voices, and *its* walls do live;
It is the house of memory!

Within its neat parlours and light saloons, the lyre of human passions
has been struck on all its chords. Birth and death, marriage and separation,
joy and grief, in all their familiar forms, have knocked at its painted door,
and crossed its narrow threshold; and the hearts within have their own
traditions of the past, and their own reckonings to take, and their own
anecdotes to revise, and their own ghosts to bring back, amid the
commemorations of this festal time.

And – whatever may be said for the ancient ghost stories, which are fast
losing ground – fitting it is that, amid the mirth of this pleasant time, such
thoughts should be occasionally stirred, and those phantoms of the heart
brought back. Not that the joy of the young and hopeful should be thereby
darkened, but that they may be duly warned that 'youth's a stuff will not
endure', and taught in time the tenure upon which hope is held. That was
a beautiful custom of the Jews which led them, when they built houses, to
leave ever some part unfinished, as a memento of the ruin and desolation
of their city. Not that they, therefore, built the less, or the less cheerfully;
but that in the very midst of their amplest accommodations they preserved
a perpetual and salutary reference to the evil of their condition – a useful
check upon their worldly thoughts. And thus should mirth be welcomed
and hopes built up, wherever the materials present themselves; but a mark
should, notwithstanding, be placed upon the brightest of them all,
remembrances ever let in, which may recall to us the imperfect condition

of our nature here, and speak of the certain decay which must attend all hopes erected for mere earthly dwellings.

But *you* should speak of this, you for whom the following lines were written long ago, though they have not yet met your eye, you who have learnt this lesson more sternly than even I, and speak so well of *all* things! Many a 'Winter's Tale' have we two read together (Shakespeare's among the rest – and how often!), and many a written lay has linked our thoughts in a sympathy of sentiment, on many an evening of Christmas. It may be that on some night of that which is approaching, these lines may meet your notice, and through them, *one more* winter's eve may yet be spent by you and me, in a communion of thought and feeling. No fear that joy should carry it all, with us! No danger that the ghosts of the past should fail to mingle with our Christmas feelings, in that hour! There can be no future hope built up for you or me, or for most others who have passed the first season of youth, to which something shall not be wanting; which shall not, like the houses of the Jews, be left imperfect in some part; and for the same reason – even for the memories of the ruined past!

> Farewell! I do not bid thee weep;
> The hoarded love of many years,
> The visions hearts like thine must keep,
> May not be told by tears!
> No! tears are but the spirit's showers,
> To wash its *lighter* clouds away,
> In breasts where sun-bows, like the flowers,
> Are born of rain and ray;
> But gone from thine is all the glow
> That helped to form life's promise-bow!
>
> Farewell! I know that never more
> Thy spirit, like the bird of day,
> Upon its own sweet song shall soar
> Along a sunny way!
> The hour that wakes the waterfall
> To music, in its far-off flight,
> And hears the silver fountains call,
> Like angels through the night,
> Shall bring thee songs whose tones are sighs
> From harps whose chords are memories!
>
> Night! when, like perfumes that have slept,
> All day, within the wild-flower's heart,
> Steal out the thoughts the soul has kept

In silence and apart;
And voices we have pined to hear,
Through many a long and lonely day,
Come back upon the dreaming ear,
From grave-lands, far away;
And gleams look forth, of spirit-eyes,
Like stars along the darkening skies!

When fancy and the lark are still –
Those riders of the morning gale!
And walks the moon o'er vale and hill
With memory and the nightingale;
The moon that is the daylight's ghost
(As memory is the ghost of hope),
And holds a lamp to all things lost
Beneath night's solemn cope,
Pale as the light by memory led
Along the cities of the dead!

Alas, for thee! alas for thine!
Thy youth that is no longer young!
Whose heart, like Delphi's ruined shrine,
Gives oracles – oh! still divine! –
But never more in song!
Whose breast, like Echo's haunted hall,
Is filled with murmurs of *the past*,
Ere yet its 'gold was dim', and all
Its 'pleasant things' laid waste!
From whose sweet windows never more
Shall look the sunny soul of yore!

Farewell! I do not bid thee weep,
The smile and tear are past for thee;
The river of thy thoughts must keep
Its solemn course, too still and deep
For idle eyes to see!
Oh! earthly things are all too far
To throw their shadows o'er its stream!
But, now and then, a silver star,
And, now and then, a gleam
Of glory from the skies be given,
To light its waves with dreams of heaven!

To the outdoor sports of this merry time which arise out of the natural phenomena of the season itself, we need do no more than allude here, because every schoolboy knows far more about them than we are now able to tell him, though we, too, reckoned them all amidst the delights of our boyhood. The rapid motions and graceful manœuvres of the skilful amongst the skaters, the active games connected with this exercise (such as the golf of our northern neighbours, not very commonly practised in England), the merry accidents of the sliders, and the loud and mischievous laugh of the joyous groups of snowballers – are all amongst the picturesque features by which the Christmas time is commonly marked in these islands. To be sure, the kind of seasons seems altogether to have abandoned us in which the ice furnished a field for those diversions during a period of six weeks; and the days are gone when fairs were held on the broad Thames, and books were printed and medals struck on the very pathway of his fierce and daily tides. Even now as we write, however, in this present year of grace, old Winter stands without the door in something like the garb in which as boys we loved him best, and that old aspect of which we have such pleasant memories, and which Cowper has so well described:

> O Winter! ruler of the inverted year!
> Thy scattered hair with sleet-like ashes filled;
> Thy breath congealed upon thy lips; thy cheeks
> Fringed with a beard made white with other snows
> Than those of age; thy forehead wrapt in clouds;
> A leafless branch thy sceptre; and thy throne
> A sliding car indebted to no wheels,
> But urged by storms along thy slippery way!

In looking over a description of London we have met with a quotation of a passage from FitzStephen, an old historian of that city, in which he gives a quaint description of these familiar sports, as they were practised in King Henry the Second's day on the large pond or marsh which then occupied the site of what is now Moorfields. The passage is short and we will quote it.

'When that vast lake,' he says, 'which waters the walls of the city towards the north is hard frozen, the youth in great numbers go and divert themselves on the ice. Some, taking a small run for increment of velocity, place their feet at a proper distance and are carried sliding sideways a great way. Others will make a large cake of ice, and seating one of their companions upon it, they take hold of one another's hands and draw him along; when it happens that, moving so swiftly on so slippery a place, they all fall headlong. Others there are who are still more expert in these amusements on the ice; they place certain bones, the leg bones of animals, under the soles of their feet by tying them round their ankles, and then, taking a pole shod with iron into their hands, they push themselves forward by striking it against the ice, and are carried on with a velocity equal to the flight of a bird or a bolt discharged from a cross-bow.'

But amongst all the amusements which in cities contribute to make the Christmas time a period of enchantments for the young and happy, there is another, which must not be passed over without a word of special notice; and that one is the theatre – a world of enchantment in itself. We verily believe that no man ever forgets the night on which, as a boy, he first witnessed the representation of a play. All sights and sounds that reached his senses before the withdrawing of the mysterious curtain, all things which preceded his introduction to that land of marvels which lies beyond, are mingled inextricably with the memories of that night, and haunt him through many an after year. The very smell of the lamps and orange-peel, the discordant cries, the ringing of the prompter's bell, and above all the heavy dark green curtain itself, become essential parts of the charm in which his spirit is long after held. It was so with ourselves; and though many a year is gone by since that happy hour of our lives, and most of the spells which were then cast have been long since broken, yet we felt another taken from us when at Drury Lane an attempt was made to substitute a rich curtain of crimson and gold for the plain dark fall of green. And then the overture, the enchanting prelude to all the wonders that await us, the unearthly music leading us into fairyland, the incantation at whose voice, apparently, the mysterious veil on which our eyes have been so long and so earnestly rivetted rises, as if by its own act, and reveals to us the mysteries of an enchanted world! From that moment, all things that lie on this side the charmed boundary are lost sight of, and all the wonders that are going on beyond it are looked on with the most undoubting faith. It is not for a moment suspected that the actors therein are beings of natures like ourselves, nor is there any questioning but that we are gazing upon scenes and doings separated from the realities of life. Verily do we believe that never again in this life are so many new and bewildering and bewitching feelings awakened in his breast, as on the first night in which the boy is spectator of a theatrical performance, if he be old enough to enjoy and not quite old enough clearly to understand what is going on.

At this holiday period of the year, the boxes of our theatres are filled with the happy faces, and their walls ring with the sweet laughter of children. All things are matters of amazement and subjects of exclamation. But in London above all things – far, far beyond all other things (though it does not begin for some days later than this) is the pantomime with its gorgeous scenery and incomprehensible transformations and ineffable fun. 'Ready to leap out of the box,' says Leigh Hunt, 'they joy in the mischief of the clown, laugh at the thwacks he gets for his meddling, and feel no small portion of contempt for his ignorance in not knowing that hot water will scald, and gunpowder explode; while with head aside to give fresh energy to the strokes, they ring their little palms against each other in testimony of exuberant delight.' The winter pantomimes are introduced on the evening next after Christmas night; and some account of this entertainment seems, as a feature of the season, due to our Christmas readers.

From Italy, then, we appear to have derived our pantomime – the legitimate drama of Christmas, and to pagan times and deities the origin of our pantomimical characters may be directly referred. The nimble harlequin of our stage is the Mercury of the ancients and in his magic wand and charmed cap may be recognised that god's caduceus and petasus. Our columbine is Psyche, our clown Momus, and our pantaloon is conjectured to be the modern representative of Charon – variously habited, indeed, according to Venetian fancy and feelings. Even Punch, the friend of our childhood, the great-headed, long-nosed, hump-backed 'Mister Punch', it seems, was known to the Romans, under the name of Maccus.

Our pantomime, however, is an inferior translation, rather than a good copy, from its Italian original. The rich humour, the ready wit, the exquisite raciness of the Italian performance have all evaporated, and with us are burlesqued by the vapid joke, the stale trick, and acts of low buffoonery. We read of the pantomimic actors, Constantini and Cecchini, being ennobled; of Louis XIII patronising the merits of Nicholas Barbieri, and raising him to fortune; that Tiberio Fiurilli, the inventor of the character of Scaramouch, was the early companion of Louis XIV, and that the wit of the harlequin Dominic made him a favoured guest at the same monarch's table. These instances of distinction are alone sufficient proof of the superior refinement of the actors of Italian pantomime, above our vulgar tribe of tumblers. The Italian artists were fellows 'of infinite jest', whose ready wit enabled them to support extempore dialogue, suiting 'the action to the word, and the word to the action'; for the Arlequino of Italy was not a mute like his English representative. Many of the Italian harlequins were authors of considerable reputation; Ruzzante, who flourished about 1530, may be regarded as the Shakespeare of pantomime. 'Till his time,' says D'Israeli, 'they had servilely copied the duped fathers, the wild sons, and the tricking valets of Plautus and Terence; and perhaps, not being writers of sufficient skill but of some invention, were satisfied to sketch the plots of dramas, boldly trusting to extempore acting and dialogue. Ruzzante peopled the Italian stage with a fresh, enlivening crowd of pantomimic characters. The insipid dotards of the ancient comedy were transformed into the Venetian Pantaloon, and the Bolognese Doctor; while

Christmas Pantomime

the hare-brained fellow, the arch knave, and the booby, were furnished from Milan, Bergamo, and Calabria. He gave his newly created beings new language and a new dress. From Plautus, he appears to have taken the hint of introducing all the Italian dialects into one comedy, by making each character use his own – and even the modern Greek, which, it seems, afforded many an unexpected play on words for the Italian. This new kind of pleasure, like the language of Babel, charmed the national ear; every province would have its dialect introduced on the scene, which often served the purpose both of recreation and a little innocent malice. Their masks and dresses were furnished by the grotesque masqueraders of the Carnival, which, doubtless, often contributed many scenes and humours to the quick and fanciful genius of Ruzzante.'

To the interesting essay, by the author of the 'Curiosities of Literature', from whence this extract is derived, we beg leave to refer the reader for an anecdotical history of pantomime. Mr D'Israeli in conclusion observes, that 'in gesticulation and humour our Rich appears to have been a complete mime; his genius was entirely confined to pantomime, and he had the glory of introducing Harlequin on the English stage, which he played under the feigned name of Lun. He could describe to the audience by his signs and gestures, as intelligibly as others could express by words. There is a large caricature print of the triumph which Rich had obtained over the severe muses of tragedy and comedy, which lasted too long not to excite jealousy and opposition from the *corps dramatique*.

'Garrick, who once introduced a speaking Harlequin, has celebrated the silent but powerful language of Rich –

"When LUN appeared, with matchless art and whim,
He gave the power of speech to every limb,
Tho' mask'd and mute, convey'd his quick intent,
And told in frolic gestures what he meant;
But now the motley coat and sword of wood
Require a tongue to make them understood." '

Foote, it was, we think, who attempted to get a standing for a Harlequin with a wooden leg upon the English stage; and though he was supported by a clown upon crutches, these and other efforts to effect a witty reform in the mechanism of an English pantomime proved unsuccessful. 'Why is this burlesque race here,' inquires Mr D'Israeli, 'privileged to cost so much, to do so little and repeat that little so often?' In 1827, according to a statement which we believe to be tolerably correct, the 'getting up', as it is termed, of the pantomimes produced on the 26th of December, in London, cost at –

Covent Garden	£1,000
Drury Lane	1,000
Surrey	500
Adelphi	200
Olympic	150
Sadler's Wells	100
West London	100
Making the total of	£3,050

and in other years, we believe the cost has been considerably more; and yet this enormous expenditure left no impression on the popular memory, mere stage-trick being far below the exhibition of a juggler. True it is, that clever artists have been for many years employed to design and paint the scenery of the pantomimes, and consequently admirable pictures have been exhibited, especially at the national theatres, where this feature, indeed, constitutes the main attraction of the evening's performance. The stupid tragedy of 'George Barn-well,' produced for the sake of the city apprentices, was formerly the usual prelude to the Christmas pantomime on the night of St Stephen's Day. Hone, in his *Every-Day Book*, has chronicled that 'the representation of this tragedy was omitted in the Christmas holidays of 1819, at both theatres, for the first time'. To be sure, this dull affair answered the purpose as well as any other, it being an established rule with the tenants of the theatrical Olympus that nothing shall be heard save their own thunders, previously to the pantomime on St Stephen's night. The most famous pantomime which has been played in our times is unquestionably Mother Goose. When it was produced, or to whom the authorship is ascribed, we know not; but in 1808 it was revived and played at the Haymarket, with an additional scene representing the burning of Covent Garden Theatre. The pantomimes of the last thirty years have failed to effect a total eclipse of the brilliancy of 'Harlequin and Mother Goose, or the Golden Egg'; which found its way into the list of provincial stock pieces.

Connected with this golden age of English pantomime, the recollection of Grimaldi, Joey Grimaldi, as the gallery folk delighted to call him, is an obvious association. His acting, like that of Liston, must have been seen to be understood or appreciated; for no description can convey an adequate idea of the power of expression and gesture. They who have not seen Joey may never hope to look upon his like; and they who have seen him must never expect to see his like again. On the English stage never was clown like Grimaldi! He was far more than a clown, he was a great comic actor. But his constitution soon gave way under the trials to which it was exposed. In the depth of winter, after performing at Sadler's Wells, he was brought down night after night wrapped in blankets to Covent Garden; and there had, for the second time in the course of the same evening, to go through the allotted series of grimaces, leaps, and tumbles. Poor Grimaldi, sunk by these exertions into a premature old age, was finally obliged to retire from the stage on 27 June, 1828; and the *Literary Gazette* thus pleasantly, but feelingly, announced his intention:

Our immense favourite, Grimaldi, under the severe pressure of years and infirmities, is enabled through the good feeling and prompt liberality of Mr Price, to take a benefit at Drury Lane on Friday next; the last of Joseph Grimaldi! Drury's, Covent Garden's, Sadler's, everybody's Joe! The friend of Harlequin and Farley-kin! the town clown! greatest of fools! daintiest of motleys! the true ami des enfans! The tricks and changes of life, sadder, alas! than those of pantomime, have made a dismal difference between the former flapping, filching, laughing, bounding antic and the present Grimaldi. He has no spring in his foot, no mirth in his eye! The corners of his mouth droop mournfully earthward; and he stoops in the back, like the weariest of Time's porters! L'Allegro has done with him, and Il Penseroso claims him for its own! It is said, besides, that his pockets are neither so large nor so well stuffed as they used to be on the stage: and it is hard to suppose fun without funds, or broad grins in narrow circumstances.

The mummers, who still go about at this season of the year in some parts of England, are the last descendants of those maskers, who in former times, as we have shown at length, contributed to the celebrations of the season, at once amongst the highest and lowest classes of the land; as their performances present, also, the last semblances of those ancient Mysteries and Moralities, by which the splendid pageants of the court were preceded. Sir Walter Scott, in a note to *Marmion*, seems to intimate that these mummeries are, in fact, the offspring and relics of the old Mysteries themselves. The fact, however, seems rather to be, that these exhibitions existed before the introduction of the Scripture plays; and that the one and the other are separate forms of a practice copied directly from the festival observances of the pagans. Accordingly, Brand speaks of a species of mumming which 'consists in changing clothes between men and women who, when dressed in each other's habits go from one neighbour's house to another, partaking of Christmas cheer and making merry with them in disguise'; and which practice he traces directly to the Roman Sigillaria. In various parts of the Continent also, as in France and Germany, certain forms of mumming long existed, which appear to have been originally borrowed from the rites of idolatry: and the Scottish Guisars, or Guisarts, if the very ingenious explanation of their hogmanay cry given by Mr Repp (and for which we refer our readers to vol. iv., part I, of the *Archæologia Scotica*) be correct, connect themselves with the superstitions of the northern nations.

Amongst the forms of ancient mumming which have come down to the present or recent times, we may observe that the hobby-horse formed as late as the seventeenth century a prominent character, and that something of this kind seems still to exist. Dr Plot, in his *History of Staffordshire* mentions a performance called the 'Hobbyhorse Dance', as having taken place at Abbot's Bromley during the Christmas season, within the memory of man; and we have already shown that a modification of the same practice continues to the present day, or did to within a few years back, in the Isle of Thanet. This dance is described by Dr Plot as being composed of 'a person who carried the image of a horse between his legs, made of thin boards, and in his hand a bow and arrow. The latter, passing through a hole in the bow and stopping on a shoulder, made a snapping noise when drawn to and fro, keeping time with the music. With this man danced six others, carrying on their shoulders as many reindeer heads with the arms of the chief families to whom the revenues of the town belonged. They danced the heys, and other country dances. To the above Hobbyhorse there belonged a pot, which was kept by turns by the reeves of the town, who provided cakes and ale to put into this pot – all people who had any kindness for the good intent of the institution of the sport, giving pence a-piece for themselves and families. Foreigners also that came to see it contributed; and the money, after defraying the expense of the cakes and ale, went to repair the church and support the poor.' A reason given by some as the origin of this practice, we have already stated in our mention of 'hodening'; and our readers will see that its object, like that of the other similar observances of this season, was charity.

In some parts of the north of England, a custom exists to the present time which appears to be composed of the ancient Roman sword-dance, or, perhaps, the sword-dance of the northern nations, and lingering traces of the obsolete 'Festival of Fools'. This practice, which is called the 'Fool Plough', consists in a pageant composed of 'a number of sword-dancers dragging a plough, with music, and one, sometimes two, in very strange attire; the Bessy in the grotesque habit of an old woman, and the fool almost covered with skins, a hairy cap on, and the tail of some animal hanging from his back. The office of one of these characters, in which he is very assiduous, is to go about rattling a box amongst the spectators of the dance, in which he receives their little donations.' Our readers will probably remember that a set of these mummers are introduced by Washington Irving, in his account of a Christmas spent in Yorkshire.

The old Christmas play of 'Saint George and the Dragon' is still amongst the most popular amusements of this season in many parts of England. Whether this particular kind of performance is to be considered as dating from the return of the Crusaders, or that similar representations had existed previously, the characters of which alone were changed by that event, does not appear from any other remains that have reached us. There is evidence, however, that plays founded upon the legend of Saint George are of a very remote date; and, in all probability, they were introduced not long after the age of the Crusades. From various contributors to Mr Hone's *Every-Day Book*, we learn that versions of these plays are still performed amongst the lower orders at the Christmas-tide, in the extreme western counties of England, as also in Cumberland, and some others of the more northern ones; and one of those correspondents, dating from Falkirk, gives an account of a play still performed by the Guisars, in some parts of Scotland, which is of similar construction and evidently borrowed from the same source, but in which one Galgacus is substituted for Saint George, as the hero of the piece; and the drama is made by that substitution to commemorate the successful battle of the Grampians, by the Scots under that leader, against the invader, Agricola. If Mr Reddock be right in this opinion, Agricola is for the nonce elevated to the title of king of Macedon. The party who carries the bag for these mummers is a very questionable trustee, being no other than Judas Iscariot. Sir Walter Scott, in his notes to *Marmion*, speaks of the same play as one in which he and his companions were in the habit of taking parts, when boys; and mentions the characters of the old Scripture plays having got mixed up with it in the version familiar to him. He enumerates Saint

Peter, who carried the keys; Saint Paul, who was armed with a sword; and Judas, who had the bag for contributions; and says that he believes there was also a Saint George. It is not unlikely there might, though he is not mentioned by Mr Reddock, for the confusion of characters in all these versions is very great. In the Whitehaven edition, Saint George is son to the king of Egypt, and the hero who carries all before him is Alexander. He conquers Saint George and kills the king of Egypt. In fact the legend, as it exists in the old romance of 'Sir Bevys of Hampton', has everywhere been mixed up with extraneous matter, and scarcely any two sets of performers render it alike. The plot seems, in all, to be pretty nearly the same; and the doctor, with his marvellous cures and empirical gibberish, seems to be common to them all. 'But so little,' says Sandys, 'do the actors know the history of their own drama, that sometimes General Wolfe is introduced, who first fights Saint George, and then sings a song about his own death. I have also seen the Duke of Wellington represented.' Mr Reddock mentions that, during the war with France, one of the characters in his version 'was made to say that he had been "fighting the French", and that the *loon* who took leg bail was no less a personage than' the great Napoleon. Mr Sandys mentions that occasionally there is a sort of anti-masque, or burlesque (if the burlesque itself *can* be burlesqued) at the end of the performance; when some comic characters enter, called Hub Bub, Old Squire, etc., and the piece concludes with a dance. At other times, the performances are wound up by a song.

We may mention that we have in our possession an Irish version of the same play, as it is still played by the boys in that country; in which version, as might be expected, the championship is given to Saint Patrick, who asserts that Saint George was nothing more than 'Saint Patrick's boy', and fed his horses. Another of the characters in this edition of the story is Oliver Cromwell, who, after certain grandiloquent boastings (amongst others, that he had 'conquered many nations with his copper nose'), calls upon no less personage than Beelzebub to step in and confirm his assertions.

The costume and accoutrements of these mummers (of whom we have given a representation at page 49) appear to be pretty generally of the same kind, and, for the most part, to resemble those of morris-dancers. They are thus correctly described by Mr Sandys. Saint George and the other tragic performers wear 'white trousers and waistcoats, showing their shirt-sleeves, and are much decorated with ribbons and handkerchiefs, each carrying a drawn sword in his hand, if they can be procured, otherwise a cudgel. They wear high caps of pasteboard covered with fancy paper, adorned with beads, small pieces of looking-glass, bugles, etc., several long strips of pith generally hanging down from the top, with shreds of different coloured cloth strung on them, the whole having a fanciful and smart effect. The Turk sometimes has a turban. Father Christmas is personified as a grotesque old man, wearing a large mask and wig, with a huge club in his hand. The doctor, who is sort of merry-andrew to the piece, is dressed in some ridiculous way, with a three-cornered hat and painted face. The female, when there is one, is in the costume of her great-grandmother. The hobby-horse, when introduced, has a sort of representation of a horse's hide; but the dragon and the giant, when there is one, frequently appear with the same style of dress as the knights.'

We will present our readers with the version of this old drama given by Mr Sandys, as still performed in Cornwall. Elsewhere, we have met with some slight variations upon even this Cornwall piece, but will be content to print it as we find it in the collection in question. Our Lancashire readers will at once recognise its close resemblance to the play performed in that county, about the time of Easter, by the Peace-eggers, or Paste-eggers, of whom we shall speak, in their proper place, in a future volume.

Enter the Turkish Knight

KNIGHT   Open your doors and let me in,
I hope your favours I shall win;
Whether I rise or whether I fall
I'll do my best to please you all.
Saint George is here, and swears he will come in,
And if he does, I know he'll pierce my skin.
If you will not believe what I do say,
Let Father Christmas come in – clear the way!

[*Retires*

Enter Father Christmas

FATHER C.   Here come I, old Father Christmas,
Welcome, or welcome not,
I hope old Father Christmas
Will never be forgot.
I am not come here to laugh or to jeer,
But for a pocketful of money and a skinful of beer.
If you will not believe what I do say,
Come in the King of Egypt – clear the way!

Enter the King of Egypt

KING OF E.   Here I, the King of Egypt, boldly do appear,
Saint George! Saint George! walk in, my only son and heir,
Walk in, my son, Saint George! and boldly act thy part,
That all the people here may see thy wond'rous art.

Enter Saint George

ST GEORGE   Here come I, Saint George, from Britain did I spring,
             I'll fight the Dragon bold, my wonders to begin,
             I'll clip his wings, he shall not fly;
             I'll cut him down, or else I die.

Enter the Dragon

DRAGON   Who's he that seeks the Dragon's blood,
             And calls so angry, and so loud?
             That English dog, will he before me stand?
             I'll cut him down with my courageous hand.
             With my long teeth and scurvy jaw,
             Of such I'd break up half a score,
             And stay my stomach, till I'd more.

                              [*Saint George and the Dragon fight –
                                        the latter is killed*

FATHER C.   Is there a doctor to be found
             All ready, near at hand,
             To cure a deep and deadly wound,
             And make the champion stand?

Enter Doctor

DOCTOR   Oh! yes, there is a doctor to be found
             All ready, near at hand,
             To cure a deep and deadly wound,
             And make the champion stand.

FATHER C.   What can you cure?

DOCTOR   All sorts of diseases,
             Whatever you pleases,
             The phthisic, the palsy, and the gout;
             If the devil's in, I'll blow him out.

FATHER C.   What is your fee?

DOCTOR   Fifteen pound, it is my fee,
             The money to lay down;
             But, as 'tis such a rogue as thee,
             I cure for ten pound.
             I carry a little bottle of alicumpane,
             Here Jack, take a little of my flip flop,
             Pour it down thy tip top,
             Rise up and fight again.

                              [*The Doctor performs his cure, the fight is
                                  renewed, and the Dragon again killed*

ST GEORGE   Here am I, Saint George,
            That worthy champion bold!
            And with my sword and spear
            I won three crowns of gold!
            I fought the fiery dragon,
            And brought him to the slaughter;
            By that I won fair Sabra,
            The King of Egypt's daughter.
            Where is the man, that now me will defy?
            I'll cut his giblets full of holes, and make his buttons fly.

The Turkish Knight advances

KNIGHT   Here come I, the Turkish knight,
            Come from the Turkish land to fight!
            I'll fight Saint George, who is my foe,
            I'll make him yield, before I go;
            He brags to such a high degree,
            He thinks there's none can do the like of he.

ST GOERGE   Where is the Turk, that will before me stand?
            I'll cut him down with my courageous hand.

                          [*They fight, the Knight is overcome,*
                                    and falls on one knee

KNIGHT   Oh! pardon me, Saint George! pardon of thee I crave,
            Oh! pardon me, this night, and I will be thy slave.

ST GEORGE   No pardon shalt thou have, while I have foot to stand.
            So rise thee up again, and fight out sword in hand.

                          [*They fight again, and the Knight is killed;*
                          Father Christmas calls for the Doctor, with whom the same
                          dialogue occurs as before, and the cure is performed.

Enter the Giant Turpin

GIANT   Here come I, the Giant! bold Turpin is my name,
            And all the nations round do tremble at my fame.
            Where'er I go, they tremble at my sight,
            No lord or champion long with me would fight.

ST GEORGE   Here's one that dares to look thee in the face,
            And soon will send thee to another place.

                          [*They fight, and the Giant is killed; medical aid is called*
                          in, as before, and the cure performed by the
                          Doctor, who then, according to the stage
                          direction, is given a basin of girdy
                          grout, and a kick, and driven out.

FATHER C.   Now, ladies and gentlemen, your sport is most ended.
So prepare for the hat, which is highly commended.
The hat it would speak, if it had but a tongue.
Come throw in your money, and think it no wrong.

And these, with the dance filling up the intervals and enlivening the winter nights, are amongst the sports and amusements which extend themselves over the Christmas season and connect together its more special and characteristic observances.

Christmas Eve
24th December

Some say, that ever 'gainst that season comes
Wherein our Saviour's birth is celebrated,
This bird of dawning singeth all night long:
And then, they say, no spirit dares stir abroad;
The nights are wholesome; then no planets strike.
No fairy takes, nor witch hath power to charm,
So hallow'd and so gracious is the time.

HAMLET

The progress of the Christmas celebrations has at length brought us up to the immediate threshold of that high day in honour of which they are all instituted; and amid the crowd of festivities by which it is on all sides surrounded, the Christian heart makes a pause tonight. Not that the Eve of Christmas is marked by an entire abstinence from that spirit of festival by which the rest of this season is distinguished, nor that the joyous character of the event on whose immediate verge it stands requires that it should. No part of that season is more generally dedicated to the assembling of friends than are the great day itself and the eve which ushers it in. Still, however, the feelings of rejoicing which properly belong to the blessed occasion are chastened by the immediate presence of the occasion itself; and touching traditions and beautiful superstitions have given an air of solemnity to the night, beneath whose influence the spirit of commemoration assumes a religious character, and takes a softened tone.

Before, however, touching upon the customs and ceremonies of the night, or upon those natural superstitions which have hung themselves around its sacred watches, we must take a glimpse at an out-of-door scene which forms a curious enough feature of Christmas Eve, and is rather connected with the great festival of tomorrow than with the hushed and expectant feelings which are the fitting moral condition of tonight.

Everywhere throughout the British isles, Christmas Eve is marked by an increased activity about the good things of this life. 'Now,' says Stevenson, an old writer whom we have already quoted for the customs of Charles the Second's time, 'capons and hens, besides turkeys, geese, ducks, with beef and mutton, must all die; for in twelve days a multitude of people will not be fed with a little'; and the preparations in this respect of this present period of grace, are made much after the ancient prescription of Stevenson. The abundant displays of every kind of edible in the London markets on Christmas Eve, with a view to the twelve days' festival of which it is the overture, the blaze of lights amid which they are exhibited and the evergreen decorations by which they are embowered, together with the crowds of idlers or of purchasers that wander through these well-stored magazines, present a picture of abundance and a congress of faces well worthy of a single visit from the stranger, to whom a London market on the eve of Christmas is as yet a novelty.

The approach of Christmas Eve in the metropolis is marked by the Smithfield show of overfed cattle; by the enormous beasts and birds, for the fattening of which medals and cups and prizes have been awarded by committees of amateur graziers and feeders; in honour of which monstrosities, dinners have been eaten, toasts drunk, and speeches made. These prodigious specimens of corpulency we behold, after being thus glorified, led like victims of antiquity decked with ribbons and other tokens of triumph, or perhaps instead of led, we should, as the animals are scarcely able to waddle, have used the word goaded, to be immolated at the altar of gluttony in celebration of Christmas! To admiring crowds, on the eve itself, are the results of oil-cake and turnip-feeding displayed in the various butcher's shops of the metropolis and its vicinity; and the efficacy of walnut-cramming is illustrated in Leadenhall market, where Norfolk turkeys and Dorking fowls appear in numbers and magnitude unrivalled. The average weight given for each turkey, by the statement heretofore quoted by us of the number and gravity of those birds sent up to London from Norfolk during two days of a Christmas some years ago, is nearly twelve pounds; but what is called a fine bird in Leadenhall Market weighs, when trussed, from eighteen to one or two-and-twenty pounds – the average price of which may be stated at twenty shillings; and prize turkeys have been known to weigh more than a quarter of a hundred weight.

Brawn is another dish of this season, and is sold by the poulterers, fishmongers, and pastrycooks. The supply for the consumption of London is chiefly derived from Canterbury, Oxfordshire, and Hampshire. 'It is manufactured from the flesh of large boars, which are suffered to live in a half-wild state, and, when put up to fatten, are strapped and belted tight round the principal parts of the carcass, in order to make the flesh become dense and brawny. This article comes to market in rolls about two feet long and ten inches in diameter, packed in wicker baskets.'

Sandys observes that 'Brawn is a dish of great antiquity, and may be found in most of the old bills of fare for coronation and other great feasts'.

The market on Christmas Eve

'Brawn, mustard, and malmsey were directed for breakfast at Christmas, during Queen Elizabeth's reign; and Dugdale, in his account of the Inner Temple Revels, of the same age, states the same directions for that society. The French,' continues Sandys, 'do not appear to have been so well acquainted with it; for, on the capture of Calais by them, they found a large quantity, which they guessed to be some dainty, and tried every means of preparing it; in vain did they roast it, bake it, and boil it; it was impracticable and impenetrable to their culinary arts. Its merits, however, being at length discovered, "Ha!" said the monks, "what delightful fish!" – and immediately added it to their fast-day viands. The Jews, again, could not believe it was procured from that impure beast, the hog, and included it in their list of clean animals.'

Amid the interior forms to be observed, on this evening, by those who would keep their Christmas after the old orthodox fashion, the first to be noticed is that of the Yule Clog. This huge block, which, in ancient times, and consistently with the capacity of its vast receptacle, was frequently the root of a large tree, it was the practice to introduce into the house with great ceremony, and to the sound of music. Herrick's direction is:

> Come, bring with a noise
> My merrie, merrie boys,
>   The Christmas log to the firing;
> While my good dame she
> Bids you all be free,
>   And drink to your heart's desiring.

In Drake's 'Winter Nights' mention is made of the Yule Clog, as lying, 'in ponderous majesty, on the kitchen floor', until 'each had sung his Yule song, standing on its centre', – ere it was consigned to the flames that

> Went roaring up the chimney wide.

This Yule Clog, according to Herrick, was to be lighted with the brand of the last year's log, which had been carefully laid aside for the purpose, and music was to be played during the ceremony of lighting:

> With the last yeere's brand
> Light the new block, and
>   For good successe in his spending,
> On your psaltries play,
> That sweet luck may
>   Come while the log is a teending.

This log appears to have been considered as sanctifying the rooftree, and was probably deemed a protection against those evil spirits over whom this season was in every way a triumph. Accordingly, various superstitions mingled with the prescribed ceremonials in respect of it. From the authority already quoted on this subject, we learn that its virtues were not to be extracted, unless it were lighted with clean hands – a direction, probably, including both a useful household hint to the domestics, and, it may be, a moral of a higher kind:

> Wash your hands or else the fire
> Will not tend to your desire;
> Unwash'd hands, ye maidens, know,
> Dead the fire though ye blow.

Around this fire, when duly lighted, the hospitalities of the evening were dispensed; and as the flames played about it and above it, with a pleasant song of their own, the song and the tale and the jest went cheerily round. In different districts, different omens attached themselves to circumstances connected with this observance, but generally it was deemed an evil one if the log went out during the night or, we suppose, during the symposium. The extinguished brand was, of course, to be preserved, to furnish its ministry to the ceremonial of the ensuing year.

The Yule Clog is still lighted up, on Christmas Eve, in various parts of England, and particularly in the north. In some places, where a block of sufficient dimensions is not readily come by, it is usual to lay aside a large coal for the purpose, which, if not quite orthodox, is an exceedingly good succedaneum, and a very rich source of cheerful inspirations.

Another feature of this evening, in the houses of the more wealthy, was the tall Christmas candles, with their wreaths of evergreens, which were lighted up, along with the Yule log, and placed on the upper table, or dais, of ancient days. Those of our readers who desire to light the Christmas candles this year, may place them on the sideboard, or in any other conspicuous situation. Brand, however, considers the Yule log and the Christmas candle to be but one observance, and that the former is only a substitute for the latter. By our ancestors, of the Latin church, Christmas was formerly called the 'Feast of Lights', and numbers of lights were displayed on the occasion. The lights and the title were both typical of the religious light dawning upon the world at that sacred period – of the advent, in fact, of the 'Light of lights', and the conquest over moral darkness. Hence, it is thought, arose the *domestic* ceremony of the Christmas candle, and that the Yule block was but another form of the same – the poor man's Christmas candle.

Occasionally, the Catholics appear to have made these Christmas candles (as also the candles exhibited by them, on other occasions of the commemorations connected with their religion) in a triangular form, as typical of the Trinity. Mr Hone, in his volume on the subject of 'Ancient Mysteries', gives a representation of one of these candles; and Mr Crofton Croker, in a letter to us, speaking of the huge dip candles called Christmas candles, exhibited at this season in the chandlers' shops in Ireland, and presented by them to their customers, says, 'It was the custom, I have been told (for the mystery of such matters was confined to the kitchen), to burn the three branches down to the point in which they united, and the remainder was reserved to "see in", as it was termed, the new year by.' 'There is,' says Mr Croker, 'always considerable ceremony observed in lighting these great candles on Christmas Eve. It is thought unlucky to snuff one; and certain auguries are drawn from the manner and duration of their burning.'

The customs peculiar to Christmas Eve are numerous, and various in different parts of the British isles; the peculiarities, in most cases, arising from local circumstances or traditions, and determining the *particular* forms of a celebration which is *universal*. To enter upon anything like an enumeration of these, it would be necessary to allow ourselves another volume. We must, therefore, confine ourselves to the general observances by which the Christmas spirit works, and each of our readers will have no difficulty in connecting the several local customs which come under his own notice with the particular feature of common celebration to which they belong.

But all men, in all places, who would keep Christmas Eve as Christmas Eve should be kept, must set the wassail bowl a-flowing for the occasion. 'Fill me a mighty bowl!' says Herrick, 'up to the brim!' and though this fountain of 'quips and cranks and wreathed smiles', belongs, in an especial sense, to Twelfth Night (Twelfth Night not being Twelfth Night without it), yet it should be compounded for every one of the festival nights, and invoked to spread its inspirations over the entire season.

> Honour to you who sit
> Near to the well of wit,
> And drink your fill of it!

again says our friend Herrick (what could we do without him, in this Christmas book of ours?). And surely, judging by such effects as we have witnessed, Herrick must have meant the wassail bowl. We are perfectly aware that there are certain other dwellers in that same bowl. Truth has been said to lie at the bottom of a well; and we have certainly seen him unseasonably brought up out of the very well in question, by those who have gone farther into its depths than was necessary for reaching the abode of wit. No doubt, truth is at all times a very respectable personage; but there are certain times when he and wit do not meet on the best of terms, and he is apt, occasionally, to be somewhat of a revel-marrer. The garb and temper in which he often follows wit out of that bowl are not those in which he appears to the most advantage. We know, also, that there is yet a deeper deep, in which worse things still reside; and although there be pearls there, too – and the skilful diver may bring treasures up out of that bowl, and escape all its evil spirits, besides – yet it is, at any rate, not on this night of subdued mirth that we intend to recommend an exploration of these farther depths. But still the bowl should be produced, and go round. A cheerful sporting with the light bubbles that wit flings up to its surface are perfectly consistent with the sacred character of the night, and, for ourselves, *we* will have a wassail bowl this Christmas Eve.

The word 'wassail' is derived from the Saxon *was haile*; which word, and *drinc-heil* (*heil*, health) were, as appears from old authors quoted by Brand, the usual ancient phrases of quaffing among the English and equivalent to the 'Here's to you', and 'I pledge you', of the present day. 'The wassail bowl,' says Warton, 'is Shakspeare's gossip's bowl, in the *Midsummer Night's Dream*.' It should be composed, by those who can afford it, of some rich wine highly spiced and sweetened, with roasted apples floating on its surface. But ale was more commonly substituted for the wine, mingled with nutmeg, ginger, sugar, toast, and roasted crabs. 'It is,' says Leigh Hunt, 'a good-natured bowl, and accommodates itself to the means of all classes, rich and poor. You may have it of the costliest wine or the humblest malt liquor. But in no case must the roasted apples be forgotten. They are the *sine qua non* of the wassail bowl, as the wassail bowl is of the day (*he* is speaking of New Year's Day); and very pleasant they are,

Wassail bowl

provided they are not mixed up too much with the beverage, balmy, comfortable, and different, a sort of meat in the drink, but innocent withal and reminding you of the orchards. They mix their flavour with the beverage, and the beverage with them, giving a new meaning to the line of the poet:

> The gentler apple's winy juice;

for both winy and gentler have they become by this process. Our ancestors gave them the affectionate name of "lamb's wool"; for we cannot help thinking, in spite of what is intimated by one of our authorities, that this term applied more particularly to the apples and not so much to the bowl altogether; though if it did, it shows how indispensably necessary to it they were considered.' With all deference to Mr Leigh Hunt's pleasant and graceful trifling, lamb's wool was the title given to the composition itself, no doubt on account of the delicate and harmonious qualities to which the apples contribute their share. Our readers will find an account of the alleged origin of this annual practice in a curious description of an old wassail bowl, carved upon the oaken beam that supported a chimney piece in an old mansion in Kent, which description is copied by Hone into his *Every-Day Book*, from the 'Antiquarian Repertory'. In the halls of our ancestors, this bowl was introduced with the inspiring cry of 'wassail', three times repeated, and immediately answered by a song from the chaplain. We hope our readers will sing to the wassail bowl this Christmas-tide.

We find that in some parts of Ireland and in Germany, and probably in districts of England, too, Christmas Eve is treated as a night of omens, and that practices exist for gathering its auguries having a resemblance to those of our northern neighbours at Halloween. Many beautiful, and some solemn superstitions belong to this night and the following morning. It is stated by Sir Walter Scott, in one of his notes to *Marmion*, to be an article of popular faith, 'that they who are born on Christmas or Good Friday have the power of seeing spirits, and even of commanding them'; and he adds that 'the Spaniards imputed the haggard and downcast looks of their Philip II to the disagreeable visions to which this privilege subjected him'.

Among the finest superstitions of the night may be mentioned that which is alluded to by Shakespeare in the lines which we have placed as the epigraph to the present chapter. It is a consequence or application of that very ancient and popular belief which assigns the night for the wanderings of spirits, and supposes them, at the crowing of 'the cock, that is the trumpet to the morn', to start 'like a guilty thing upon a fearful summons', and betake themselves to flight. Here again, as in so many cases of vulgar superstition, a sort of mental metonymy has taken place; and the crowing of the cock, which in the early stage of the belief was imagined to be the signal for the departure of evil spirits, only *because* it announced the morning, is, in the further stage which we are examining, held to be a sound *in itself* intolerable to these shadowy beings. Accordingly it is supposed that on the eve of Christmas 'the bird of dawning singeth all night long', to scare away all evil things from infesting the hallowed hours:

> And then, they say, no spirit dares stir abroad;
> The nights are wholesome; then no planets strike,
> No fairy takes, nor witch hath power to charm,
> So hallow'd and so gracious is the time.

In the south-west of England there exists a superstitious notion that the oxen are to be found kneeling in their stalls at midnight of this vigil, as if in adoration of the Nativity – an idea which Brand, no doubt correctly, supposes to have originated from the representations by early painters of the event itself. That writer mentions a Cornish peasant who told him (1790) of his having with some others watched several oxen in their stalls, on the eve of old Christmas Day. 'At twelve o'clock at night, they observed the two oldest oxen fall upon their knees, and, as he expressed it in the idiom of the country, make "a cruel moan like Christian creatures".' To those who regard the analogies of the human mind, who mark the progress of tradition, who study the diffusion of certain fancies, and their influence upon mankind, an anecdote related by Mr Howison in his *Sketches of*

Upper Canada, is full of comparative interest. He mentions meeting an Indian at midnight, creeping cautiously along in the stillness of a beautiful moonlight Christmas Eve. The Indian made signals to him to be silent; and when questioned as to his reason replied – 'Me watch to see the deer kneel; this is Christmas night, and all the deer fall upon their knees to the Great Spirit, and look up.'

In various parts of England, bees are popularly said to express their veneration for the Nativity by 'singing', as it is called, in their hives at midnight, upon Christmas Eve: and in some places, particularly in Derbyshire, it is asserted that the watcher may hear the ringing of subterranean bells. In the mining districts again, the workmen declare that:

> Ever 'gainst that season comes
> Wherein our Saviour's birth is celebrated,

high mass is solemnly performed in that cavern which contains the richest lode of ore, that it is brilliantly lighted up with candles, and that the service is chanted by unseen choristers.

Superstitions of this kind seem to be embodied in the carol commencing with 'I saw three ships come sailing in', to which we have before alluded; the rhythm of which old song is to our ear singularly melodious:

> And all the bells on earth shall ring
> On Christmas-day, on Christmas-day,
> And all the bells on earth shall ring
> On Christmas-day in the morning.
>
> And all the angels in heaven shall sing
> On Christmas-day, on Christmas-day,
> And all the angels in heaven shall sing
> On Christmas-day in the morning.
>
> And all the souls on earth shall sing
> On Christmas-day, on Christmas-day,
> And all the souls on earth shall sing,
> On Christmas-day in the morning.

Such fancies are but the natural echoes in the popular mind of ancient songs and customs; and so strongly is that mind impressed with the feeling of a triumph pervading the entire natural economy on

> the happy night
> That to the cottage as the crown,
> Brought tidings of salvation down,

that even the torpid bees are figured in its superstitions to utter a voice of gladness, the music of sweet chimes to issue from the bosom of the earth, and rich harmonies to echo and high ceremonies to be gorgeously performed, amid the hush and mystery of buried cells.

We must not omit to mention that these supposed natural testimonies to the triumph of the time have been in some places used as means of divination on a very curious question. The change of style introduced into our calendars nearly a century ago, and by which Christmas Day was displaced from its ancient position therein, gave great dissatisfaction on many accounts, and on none more than that of its interference with this ancient festival. The fifth and sixth of January continued long to be observed as the true anniversary of the Nativity and its vigil; and the kneeling of the cattle, the humming of the bees, and the ringing of subterranean bells, were anxiously watched for authentications on this subject. The singular fact of the budding about the period of old Christmas Day of the Cadenham oak, in the New Forest of Hampshire, and the same remarkable feature of the Glastonbury thorn (explained in various ways, but probably nowhere more satisfactorily than in the number for 31 December, 1833, of the *Saturday Magazine*), were of course used by the vulgar as confirmation of their own tradition; and the putting forth of their leaves was earnestly waited for as an unquestionable homage to the joyous spirit of the true period.

We have already alluded to the high ceremonies with which the great day is ushered in amongst the Catholics, and to the beautiful music of the midnight mass:

> That only night of all the year
> Saw the stoled priest his chalice rear.

The reader who would have a very graphic and striking account of the Christmas Eve mass, as performed by torchlight amid the hills in certain districts of Ireland, will find one in Mr Carleton's 'Traits and Stories of the Irish Peasantry'.

We have also mentioned that all the watches of this hallowed night shall ring to the sounds of earthly minstrelsy, intimating, as best they may, the heavenly choirs that hailed its rising over Judea nearly two centuries ago. Not for the shepherds alone, was that song! Its music was for us, as for them; and all minstrelsy, however rude, is welcome on this night that gives us any echoes of it, however wild. For us too, on the blessed day of which this vigil keeps the door, 'is born in the city of David, a Saviour, which is Christ the Lord'; and we, too, amid the sacred services of tomorrow will 'go even unto Bethlehem, and see this thing which is come to pass, which the Lord hath made known to us'.

Christmas Day
25th December

And now has arrived the great and important day itself which gives its title to the whole of this happy season, and the high and blessed work of man's redemption is begun. The pæean of universal rejoicing swells up on every side; and after those religious exercises which are the language that man's joy should take first, the day is one of brightened spirits and general congratulation. In no way can man better express his sense of its inestimable gift than by the condition of mind that receives gladly, and gives freely; than by mustering his worldly affections, that he may renew them in the spirit of the time. This is not the proper place to speak more minutely of the *religious* sentiments and services which belong to the season than we have already done. We may merely remark that the streets of the city and the thousand pathways of the country are crowded on this morning by rich and poor, young and old, coming in on all sides, gathering from all quarters, to hear the particulars of the 'glad tidings' proclaimed; and each lofty cathedral and lowly village church sends up a voice to join the mighty chorus whose glad burden is – 'Glory to God in the highest; and on earth peace, good will toward men.'

From the religious duties of the day, we must turn at once to its secular observances; and these we will take in the order, with reference to the progress of its hours, in which they come, mingling the customs of modern times with those of the past in our pages, as, in many respects, we wish our readers would do in practice.

The sketch represents the earliest, and not the least important, of the worldly ceremonies of the day, the due observance thereof being essential to the due observance of that later ceremony which no man holds to be unimportant, least of all on Christmas Day, the dinner. But, 'Oh! Molly Dumpling! Oh, thou cook!' if that clock of yours be right, you are far behindhand with your work! You should have risen when you were disturbed by the waits at three o'clock this morning! To have discharged your duty faithfully, you should have consigned that huge pudding at least two hours earlier to the reeking caldron! We are informed by those who understand such matters, that a plum pudding of the ordinary size requires from ten to twelve hours boiling; so that a pudding calculated for the appetites of such a party as our artist has assembled further on for its consumption, and due regard being had to the somewhat earlier hour than on days in general at which a Christmas dinner is commonly discussed, should have found its way into the boiler certainly before six o'clock. Molly evidently wants a word of advice from the ancient bellman:

> Up, Doll, Peg, Susan! You all spoke to me
> Betimes to call you, and 'tis now past three,
> Get up on your but-ends, and rub your eyes,
> For shame, no longer lye abed, but rise;
> The pewter still to scow'r and house to clean,
> And you abed! good girls, what is 't you mean?

On the subject of the identity of the modern plum pudding with the ancient *hackin*, we are furnished with the following curious remarks by Mr Crofton Croker, which we think well worth submitting for the consideration of the curious in such matters.

'The "hackin",' says that amusing old tract, entitled "Round about our Coal Fire", ' "must be boiled by daybreak, or else two young men must take the maiden [i.e., the cook] by the arms, and run her round the marketplace, till she is ashamed of her laziness." Brand, whose explanation Hone in his *Every-Day Book* has adopted, renders "hackin" by "the great sausage"; and Nares tells us, that the word means "a large sort of sausage, being a part of the cheer provided for Christmas festivities" – deriving the word from *hack*, to cut or chop. Agreeing in this derivation, we do not admit Nares's explanation. "Hackin", literally taken, is mince-meat of any kind; but Christmas mince-meat, everybody knows, means a composition of meat and suet (hacked small) seasoned with fruit and spices. And from the passage above quoted, that "the hackin must be boiled, i.e., boiling, by daybreak,' it is obvious the worthy archdeacon who, as well as Brand and Hone, has explained it as a great sausage, did not see that "hackin" is neither more nor less than the old name for the national English dish of plum pudding.

'We have heard first-rate authorities upon this subject assert, the late Dr Kitchener and Mr Douce were amongst the number, that plum pudding, the renowned English plum pudding, was a dish comparatively speaking of modern invention; and that plum porridge was its ancient representative. But this, for the honour of England, we never would allow, and always fought a hard battle upon the point. Brand indeed devotes a section of his observations on popular antiquities to "Yule-doughs, mince-pies, Christmas-pies, and plum porridge", omitting plum pudding, which new Christmas dish, or rather new name for an old Christmas dish,

Christmas pudding

appears to have been introduced with the reign of the "merry monarch", Charles II. A revolution always creates a change in manners, fashions, tastes, and names; and our theory is that, among other changes, the "hackin" of our ancestors was then baptised plum pudding. In *Poor Robin's Almanack* for 1676, it is observed of Christmas – "Good cheer doth so abound as if all the world were made of minced-pies, plum pudding, and furmity." And we might produce other quotations to show that, as the name "hackin" fell into disuse about this period, it was generally supplanted by that of plum pudding.'

Plum pudding is a truly national dish, and refuses to flourish out of England. It can obtain no footing in France. A Frenchman will dress like an Englishman, swear like an Englishman, and get drunk like an Englishman; but if you would offend him forever, compel him to eat plum pudding. A few of the leading restaurateurs, wishing to appear extraordinary, have *plomb-pooding* upon their cartes; but in no instance is it ever ordered by a Frenchman. Everybody has heard the story of Saint Louis – Henri Quatre – or whoever else it might be – who, wishing to regale the English ambassador on Christmas Day with a plum pudding, procured an excellent receipt for making one, which he gave to his cook with strict injunctions that it should be prepared with due attention to all particulars. The weight of the ingredients, the size of the copper, the quantity of water, the duration of time – everything was attended to, except one trifle; the king forgot the cloth; and the pudding was served up like so much soup, in immense tureens, to the surprise of the ambassador, who was, however, too well-bred to express his astonishment.

Amongst our ancestors, the duties of the day which followed first after those of religion were the duties which immediately spring out of a religion like ours – those of charity.

> When
> Among their children, comfortable men
> Gather about great fires, and yet feel cold,
> Alas! then for the houseless beggar old!

was a sentiment of which they never allowed themselves to lose sight. Amid the preparations making for his own enjoyment, and the comforts by which he set at defiance the austerities of the season, the old English gentleman did not forget the affecting truths so beautifully embodied in words by Mary Howitt:

> In rich men's halls, the fire is piled,
> And ermine robes keep out the weather;
> In poor men's huts, the fire is low,
> Through broken panes the keen winds blow,
> And old and young are cold together.
>
> Oh! poverty is disconsolate!
> Its pains are many, its foes are strong!
> The rich man, in his jovial cheer,
> Wishes 't was winter through the year;
> The poor man, 'mid his wants profound,
> With all his little children round,
> Prays God that winter be not long!

Immediately after the services of the day, the country gentleman stood of old, at his own gate (as we have represented him at page 73), and superintended the distribution of alms to the aged and the destitute. The hall, prepared for the festival of himself and his friends, was previously

A country church on Christmas morning

opened to his tenants and retainers; and the good things of the season were freely dispensed to all. 'There was once,' says the writer of 'Round about our Coal Fire', 'hospitality in the land. An English gentleman at the opening of the great day had all his tenants and neighbours enter his hall by daybreak; the strong beer was broached, and the black-jacks went plentifully about, with toast, sugar, nutmeg, and good Cheshire cheese. . . The servants were then running here and there with merry hearts and jolly countenances. Every one was busy in welcoming of guests, and looked as snug as new-licked puppies. The lasses were as blithe and buxom as the maids in good Queen Bess's days, when they ate sirloins of roast-beef for breakfast. Peg would scuttle about to make a toast for John, while Tom run *harum-scarum* to draw a jug of ale for Margery.'

Of this scene we have given a representation at page 37; and much of this ancient spirit, we hope and believe, still survives in this Christian country. The solemn festivals of ancient superstition were marked either by bloody sacrifice, secret revelling, or open licentiousness. There was no celebration of rites, real or symbolical, which might become a religion of cheerfulness, decency, and mercy. There was no medium between a mysteriousness dark and gloomy as the grave, and a wild and savage enthusiasm or riotous frenzy, which mingled with the worship of the gods the impassioned depravity of human nature. From Moloch, upon whose dreadful altar children were offered, to Bacchus, at whose shrine reason and virtue were prostrated, there were none of the fabled deities of antiquity whose service united the spirit of devotion with innocent

Old Christmas

> *In furry pall yclad,*
> *His brows enwreathed with holly never sere.*
> *Old Christmas comes to close the wained year.*
>
> BAMPFYLDE

pleasures and the exercise of the domestic charities. This was reserved for the Christian religion, one of the marks of whose divinity it is that it can mingle with many of the pleasures, and all the virtues of the world, without sullying the purity of its glory – without depressing the sublime elevation of its character. The rites of Ceres were thought profaned if the most virtuous believer of the divinity of that goddess beheld them without having undergone the ceremonies of special initiation. The worship of Saturn gave rise to a liberty inconsistent with the ordinary government of states. At the altar of Diana, on certain days, the Spartans flogged children to death. And the offerings which on state occasions the Romans made to Jupiter, were such as feudal vassals might offer to their warlike lord. But now, thank God! – to use the words of Milton's Hymn on the Nativity:

Peor and Baalim
Forsake their temples dim,
   With that twice-batter'd God of Palestine;
And mooned Ashtaroth
Heaven's queen and mother both,
   Now sits not girt with tapers' holy shine;
The Lybick Hammon shrinks his horn;
In vain the Tyrian maids their wounded Thammuz mourn.

And sullen Moloch, fled,
Has left in shadows dread
   His burning idol all of blackest hue;
In vain with cymbals' ring,
They call the grisly king,
   In dismal dance about the furnace blue:
The brutish Gods of Nile as fast,
Iris, and Orus, and the dog Anubis haste.

Nor is Osiris seen
In Memphian grove or green,
   Trampling the unshowered grass with lowings loud;
Nor can he be at rest,
Within his sacred chest;
   Nought but profoundest hell can be his shroud.
In vain, with timbrelled anthems dark,
The sable-stoled sorcerers bear his worshipp'd ark.

He feels from Judah's land
The dreaded Infant's hand;
   The rays of Bethlehem blind his dusky eyne;
Nor all the gods beside
Longer dare abide;
   Not Typhon huge, ending in snaky twine:
Our Babe, to show his God-head true,
Can in his swaddling bands control the damned crew.

Oh! how different were those religions of the passions and the senses from that of the sentiments and pure affections of the Christian heart; which, as it rises to heaven in sublime devotion, expands in charity towards its kind, until it comprehends all humanity in the bond of universal benevolence. To ameliorate the temporal, as well as elevate the spiritual state of man, is its distinguishing excellence, the sublime peculiarity of its character as a religious dispensation. All the systems of superstition were external and gross, or mysterious and occult. They either encouraged the follies and the passions of men, or by a vain and fruitless knowledge flattered their vanity. But Christianity came to repress the one and to dissipate the other; to make the exercise of the virtues the result and the proof of mental attachment to the doctrines which, while they afford grand subjects of eternal interest, contain the principles of all true civilisation. It is in this religion alone that faith is the sister of charity; that the former brightens with the beams of another world the institutions by which the latter blesses this – those institutions of mercy and of instruction which cover the land with monuments of humanity that are nowhere to be found but among the temples of our faith.

And now, when silent and desolate are even the high places over which Augustus ruled, fallen majestic Rome with all her gods, the religion proclaimed to the humble shepherds, whose sound was first heard by the moonlight streams and under the green boughs, has erected on the ruins of ancient grandeur a sublimer dominion than all those principalities of the earth which refused its hospitality. It came in gentleness and lowliness and the spirit of peace; and now it grasps the power of the universe, and wields the civilised energies of the greatest of all the nations to the beneficent extension of its authority – imperishable in its glory, and bloodless in its triumphs!

On the opposite side, our artist has given a lively and correct representation of the high festival anciently celebrated on Christmas Day in the old baronial hall; and has presented it at that important moment when the procession of the boar's head is making its way, with the customary ceremonies, to the upper table. Our account of Christmas would not be complete without some notice of this grand dish at the feasts of our ancestors, and some description of the forms which attended its introduction.

The boar's head soused, then, was carried into the great hall with much state, preceded by the Master of the Revels, and followed by choristers and minstrels, singing and playing compositions in its honour. Dugdale relates that at the Inner Temple, for the first course of the Christmas dinner, was 'served in, a fair and large bore's head upon a silver platter, with minstrelsye'. And here we would observe, what we do not think has been before remarked, that the boar's head carols appear to have systematically consisted of three verses. A manuscript, indeed, which we once met with, stated that the 'caroll, upon the bringynge in of the bore's head, was sung to the glorie of the blessed Trinytie'; and the three subsequent illustrative specimens – in which the peculiarity mentioned may be observed – tend to confirm this notion. At St John's, Oxford, in 1607, before the bearer of the boar's head – who was selected for his height and lustiness, and wore a green silk scarf, with an empty sword-scabbard dangling at his side – went

Bringing in the boar's head

a runner dressed in a horseman's coat, having a boar's spear in his hand, a huntsman in green carrying the naked and bloody sword belonging to the head-bearer's scabbard, and 'two pages in tafatye sarcenet', each with a 'mess of mustard'. Upon which occasion these verses were sung:

> The boare is dead,
> Loe, heare is his head,
>   What man could have done more
> Then his head of to strike,
> Meleager like,
>   And bringe it as I doe before?

> 'He livinge spoyled
> Where good men toyled,
>   Which made kinde Ceres sorrye;
> But now, dead and drawne,
> Is very good brawne,
>   And wee have brought it for ye.

> 'Then sett downe the swineyard,
> The foe to the vineyard,
>   Lett Bacchus crowne his fall;
> Lett this boare's head and mustard
> Stand for pigg, goose, and custard,
>   And so you are welcome all.

So important was the office of boar's-head bearer considered to be, that, in 1170, Holinshed has chronicled the circumstance of England's king, Henry II, bringing up to the table of his son, the young prince, a boar's head, with trumpeters going before him. From this species of service it is probable that many of our heraldic bearings have originated. 'The ancient crest of the family of Edgecumbe,' observes Ritson, 'was the boar's head crowned with bays upon a charger; which,' he adds, 'has been very injudiciously changed into the entire animal.'

This same diligent arranger and illustrator of our old ballads gives us, in his collection of ancient songs, a Boar's-head Carol, which probably belongs to the fourteenth century, from a manuscript in his possession — now, we believe, in the British Museum.

In die nativitatis

> Nowell, nowell, nowell, nowell,
> Tydyngs gode y thyngke to telle.
> The borys hede that we bryng here,
> Be tokeneth a prince with owte pere,
> Ys born this day to bye vs dere,
> > Nowell.
>
> 'A bore ys a souerayn beste,
> And acceptable in every feste,
> So mote thys lorde be to moste & leste,
> > Nowell.
>
> 'This borys hede we bryng with song,
> In worchyp of hym that thus sprang
> Of a virgyne to redresse all wrong,
> > Nowell.'

The printing-press of Wynkyn de Worde has preserved to us the carol believed to have been generally used, prior to 1521, upon these occasions; a modernised version of which continues to be sung in Queen's College, Oxford. It is entitled 'A Caroll bringyne in the Bores heed'; and runs thus:

> *Caput apri defero*
> *Reddens laudes Domino,*
> The bore's heade in hande bring I
> With garlandes gay and rosemary,
> I pray you all synge merely,
> > *Qui estis in convivio.*

Christmas dinner

The bore's head I understande
Is the chefe servyce in this lande,
Loke wherever it be fande,
  Servite cum cantico.

Be gladde, lordes both more and lasse,
For this hath ordayned our stewarde,
To chere you all this Christmasse,
The bore's head with mustarde.

A tradition of the same college states the introduction there of the boar's head (which according to Ritson, is now a mere representation 'neatly carved in wood') to be contrived 'as a commemoration of an act of valour performed by a student of the college, who while walking in the neighbouring forest of Shotover, and reading Aristotle, was suddenly attacked by a wild boar. The furious beast came open-mouthed upon the youth; who, however, very courageously, and with a happy presence of mind, is said to have rammed in the volume, and cried *græocum est*, fairly choking the savage with the sage.' To this legend a humorous 'song in honour of the Boar's head at Queen's College, Oxford', refers, having for its motto, *Tam Marti quam Mercurio*, but for which we cannot afford space.

The ancient mode of garnishing the boar's head was with sprigs of sweet-scented herbs. Dekker, than whom we could not name a more appropriate authority on this subject, speaking of persons apprehensive of catching the plague, says, 'They went (most bitterly) miching and muffled up and down, with rue and wormwood stuft into their eares and nostrils, looking like so many bore's heads, stuck with branches of rosemary, to be served in for brawne at Christmas.' The following lines describe the manner of serving up this famous dish:

> . . . if you would send up the brawner's head,
> Sweet rosemary and bays around it spread;
> His foaming tusks let some large pippin grace,
> Or 'midst these thundering spears an orange place;
> Sauce like himself, offensive to its foes,
> The roguish mustard, dangerous to the nose;
> Sack, and the well spiced hippocras, the wine
> Wassail, the bowl with ancient ribands fine,
> Porridge with plums, and Turkeys, with the chine.

Sack and hippocras are no longer to be found in our cellars; but, as we have shown, we still compound the wassail bowl.

The Christmas dinner of modern days is, as most of our readers know, a gathering together of generations, an assembling of Israel by its tribes. In the one before us, the artist has given a pretty extensive muster. We have them of the seven ages and the several professions. Contrast with this modern Christmas dinner, as well as with the high festival of yore, the dreary picture of a Christmas Day and dinner, under the stern prescription of the Puritans, as given in his Diary, by Pepys, the chatty secretary to the Admiralty. '1668, Christmas-day. To dinner,' thus he writes, 'alone with my wife; who, poor wretch! sat undressed all day till ten at night, altering and lacing of a noble petticoat; while I, by her, making the boy read to me the life of Julius Cæsar and Des Cartes' book of Music.'

To the heads of the very respectable family before us, we have already been introduced, in an earlier part of this volume, and are glad to meet with them again, under circumstances so auspicious, and supported by their junior branches. In a family so flourishing, we might have expected to escape the exhibition of antiquated celibacy. But, no! that is clearly an old maid, who is hobnobbing with the gentleman in the foreground, and, we must say, there is something about *him* which carries a strong suspicion of old-bachelorship. We suppose the one and the other are to be found in most families. However, they are not the parties who least enjoy this sort of *reunions*. We fancy, it is known to most people that meetings of this description are very happy ones amongst the members of a family, and remarkably uninteresting to third parties. We should certainly prefer reading Descartes, with Pepys and his wife, to finding ourselves a 'foreigner' in such a group as the present.

But the best of the day is yet to come! and we should have no objection to join the younger members of that group in the merry sports that await the evening. We need not give the programme. It is like that of all the other Christmas nights. The blazing fire, the song, the dance, the riddle, the jest, and many another merry sport, are of its spirits. Mischief will be committed under the mistletoe bough, and all the good wishes of the season sent round under the sanction of the wassail bowl.

St Stephen's Day
26th December

This day, which, in our calendar, is still dedicated to the first Christian martyr, St Stephen (for John the Baptist perished in the same cause before the consummation of the old law and the full introduction of the Christian dispensation), is more popularly known by the title of Boxing Day; and its importance amongst the Christmas festivities is derived from the practice whence that title comes.

We have already mentioned that the custom of bestowing gifts at seasons of joyous commemoration has been a form of thankfulness at most periods; and that it may have been directly borrowed, by the Christian worshippers, from the polytheists of Rome, along with those other modes of celebration which descended to the Christmas festival from that source – introduced, however, amongst our own observances, under Scripture sanctions, drawn both from the Old and New Testaments. The particular form of that practice whose donations are known by the title of Christmas-boxes (and which appear to differ from New-year's gifts in this, that the former, passing from the rich to the poor and from the master to his dependants, are not reciprocal in their distribution, whereas the latter are those gifts, for the mutual expression of goodwill and congratulation, which are exchanged between friends and acquaintances), was, perhaps, originally one of the observances of Christmas Day, and made a portion of its charities. The multiplied business of that festival, however, probably caused it to be postponed till the day following, and thereby placed the Christmas-boxes under the patronage of St Stephen. The title itself has been derived by some, from the box which was kept on board of every vessel that sailed upon a distant voyage, for the reception of donations to the priest – who, in return, was expected to offer masses for the safety of the expedition, to the particular saint having charge of the ship – and above all, of the box. This box was not to be opened till the return of the vessel; and we can conceive that, in cases where the mariners had had a perilous time of it, this casket would be found to enclose a tolerable offering. Probably the state of the box might be as good an evidence as the logbook, of the character of the voyage

Boxing Day

which had been achieved. The mass was at that time called Christmass, and the boxes kept to pay for it were, of course, called Christmass-boxes. The poor, amongst those who had an interest in the fate of these ships, or of those who sailed in them, were in the habit of begging money from the rich, that they might contribute to the mass boxes; and hence the title which has descended to our day, giving to the anniversary of St Stephen's martyrdom the title of Christmas-boxing day, and, by corruption, its present popular one of Boxing Day.

A relic of these ancient boxes yet exists in the earthen or wooden box, with a slit in it, which still bears the same name, and is carried by servants and children for the purpose of gathering money, at this season, being broken only when the period of collection is supposed to be over.

Most of our readers know that it was the practice, not many years ago (and in some places is so still), for families to keep lists of the servants, of tradesmen and others, who were considered to have a claim upon them for a Christmas-box, at this time. The practice, besides opening a door to great extortion, is one in every way of considerable annoyance, and is on the decline. There is, however, as they who are exposed to it know, some danger in setting it at defiance, where it is yet in force. One of the most amusing circumstances arising out of this determination to evade the annoyances of Boxing Day, is related by Sandys. A person in trade had imprudently given directions that he should be denied, on this day, to all applicants for money; and amongst those who presented themselves at his door, on this errand, was unfortunately a rather importunate creditor.

In the height of his indignation at being somewhat uncourteously repulsed, he immediately consulted his lawyer, and, having done *that*, we need scarcely relate the catastrophe. It follows as a matter of course. A docket was struck against the unsuspecting victim of Christmas-boxophobia.

Boxing Day, however, is still a great day in London. Upon this anniversary, every street resounds with the clang of hall-door knockers. Rap follows rap, in *rap*id succession, the harsh and discordant tones of iron mingling with those of rich and sonorous brass, and giving a degenerate imitation of the brazen clangour of the trumpet, which formed the summons to the gate in days of old, and which, together with the martial music of the drum, appears to have been adopted, at a later period, by the Christmas-boxers, on St Stephen's Day. Pepys, in his Diary (1668), records his having been 'called up by drums and trumpets; these things and boxes,' he adds, 'have cost me much money this Christmas, and will do more.' Which passage seems to have been in the memory of our facetious publisher, when he made the following entry in his journal of last year, from whence we have taken the liberty of transcribing it. 'Called out,' says Spooner (1834), 'by the parish beadle, dustmen, and charity-boys. The postman, street-sweepers, chimney-sweepers, lamp-lighters, and waits will all be sure to wait upon me. These fellows have cost me much money this Christmas, and will do more, the next.'

There is an amusing account, given by a writer of the querulous class, of a Boxing Day in London, a century ago. 'By the time I was up,' says he, 'my servants could do nothing but run to the door. Inquiring the meaning, I was answered, the people were come for their Christmas-box: this was logic to me; but I found at last that, because I had laid out a great deal of ready-money with my brewer, baker, and other tradesmen, they kindly thought it my duty to present their servants with some money, for the favour of having their goods. This provoked me a little, but being told it was the "custom", I complied. These were followed by the watch, beadles, dustmen, and an innumerable tribe; but what vexed me the most was the clerk, who has an extraordinary place, and makes as good an appearance as most tradesmen in the parish; to see him come a-boxing, *alias*, a-begging, I thought was intolerable; however I found it was "the custom", too; so I gave him half-a-crown, as I was likewise obliged to do to the bellman, for breaking my rest for many nights together.'

The manner in which the beadle approaches his 'good masters and mistresses', for a Christmas-box, particularly in the villages near the British metropolis, is, as we have before said, by the presentation of a copy of printed verses, ornamented with wood engravings. These broadsides are usually termed 'Bellman's verses'; and we quite agree with Mr Leigh Hunt in his opinion, that 'good bellman's verses will not do at all. There have been,' he remarks, 'some such things of late "most tolerable and not to be endured"'. We have seen them witty, which is a great mistake. Warton and Cowper unthinkingly set the way.' 'The very absurdity of the bellman's verses is only pleasant, nay, only bearable, when we suppose them written by some actual doggrel-poet, in good faith. Mere mediocrity hardly allows us to give our Christmas-box, or to believe it now-a-days in earnest; and the smartness of your cleverest wordly-wise men is felt to be wholly out of place. No, no! give us the good old decrepit bellman's verses, hobbling as their bringer, and taking themselves for something respectable, like his cocked-hat – or give us none at all.'

Upon the bellman's verses which were last year circulated by the beadles of Putney, Chiswick, and other parishes on the west side of London, it was recorded, that they were 'first printed in the year 1735', and our curiosity induced us to inquire of the printer the number annually consumed. 'We used, sir,' said he, 'not many years ago, to print ten thousand copies, and even more, but now I suppose we don't print above three thousand.' Whether the trade of this particular dealer in bellman's verses has passed into other hands, or whether the encouragement given to the circulation of these broadsides has declined, the statement of an individual will not, of course, enable us to determine. But we are inclined to think that, like other old Christmas customs, the popularity of bellman's verses is passing away, and that, before many years have elapsed, penny magazines and unstamped newspapers will have completely superseded these relics of the rude, but sincere, piety of our ancestors.

The claims of dustmen to be remembered upon 'Boxing-day' were formerly urged, without literary pretensions; but now 'the march of intellect' has rendered it necessary for them to issue their addresses in print. One of these, which lies before us, represents that 'the United Association of Dustmen and Scavengers, of the Parish of — have the honour to pay their humble duty and respects to the good [*Master* or *Mistress*] of this house, and to solicit a Christmas mark of approbation of their unwearied exertions, which they flatter themselves conduce so eminently to the comfort and salubrity of the greatest metropolitan city of civilised Europe.' Here, however, is another, in which the spirit of St Stephen's Day is embittered by the rivalries of business; and the harmony of those two respectable bodies, the scavengers and dustmen, appears to have been disturbed. The dustmen, it will be seen, repudiate the scavengers, and appeal to Saint Stephen on a separate interest.

To the Worthy Inhabitants of the Southampton Estate

LADIES AND GENTLEMEN – At this season, when you are pleased to give to labouring men, employed in collecting your dust, a donation called Christmas-box, advantage of which is often taken by persons assuming the name of Dustmen, obtaining under false pretences your bounty, we humbly submit to your consideration, to prevent such imposition, to bestow no gift on any not producing a brass figure of the following description – A Scotch Fifer, French horn, etc., between his legs; James Dee and Jerry Cane; Southampton Paving Act, on the bell; Contractor, Thomas Salisbury.

No connection with scavengers. Please not to return this bill to any one.

The principal wait also leaves a notice of a more imposing description, stating a regular appointment to the office by warrant and admission, with all the ancient forms of the City and Liberty of Westminster; and bears a silver badge and chain, with the arms of that city.

We cannot dismiss the various modes of collecting Christmas-boxes, without a few words upon the pieces of writing carried about by parish boys, and which once presented the only evidence that the schoolmaster was abroad. It appears formerly to have been the practice at this season to hang up in our churches the work of the most skilful penman in the parish, after it had been generally exhibited; the subject of which was the life of some saint, or other religious legend. Pepys thus mentions the custom: '26 December, 1665. Saw some fine writing work and flourishing of Mr Hore, with one that I knew long ago, an acquaintance of Mr Tomson's at Westminster, that is this man's clerk. It is the story of the several Archbishops of Canterbury, engrossed on vellum, to hang up in Canterbury cathedral in tables in lieu of the old ones, which are almost worn out.'

To this usage, which was no doubt of monkish origin, we are inclined to refer the specimens of calligraphy upon gaudily ornamented sheets of paper, brought round on St Stephen's Day by parish boys and charity-school children, and displayed for admiration and reward. The walls of schoolrooms, and the houses of the children's parents are afterwards decorated with these 'Christmas pieces', in the same manner as were anciently the walls of churches.

There are in the different Christian countries of Europe a variety of popular practices connected with St Stephen's Day; such as that of bleeding horses, which is mentioned by old Tusser in his *December's Abstract*:

> At Christmas is good
> To let thy horse blood;

and more particularly in his *December's Husbandry*:

> Ere Christmas be passed, let horse be let blood
> For many a purpose, it doth them much good,
> The *day of St Stephen* old fathers did use.

These various popular observances, however, are generally of that local and peculiar kind which we are compelled to omit in our enumeration, for reasons already given. But there is one of so striking a character, that we must pause to give some account of it.

This custom, which is called 'hunting the wren', is generally practised by the peasantry of the south of Ireland on St Stephen's Day. It bears a close resemblance to the Manx proceedings described by Waldron – as taking place however on a different day. 'On the 24th of December,' says that writer, in his account of the Isle of Man, 'towards evening the servants in general have a holiday: they go not to bed all night, but ramble about till the bells ring in all the churches, which is at twelve o'clock. Prayers being over, they go to hunt the wren; and after having found one of these poor birds they kill her and lay her on a bier with the utmost solemnity, bringing her to the parish church and burying her with a whimsical kind of solemnity, Singing dirges over her in the Manx language, which they call her knell; after which Christmas begins.'

The Wren-boys in Ireland, who are also called Droleens, go from house to house for the purpose of levying contributions, carrying one or more of these birds in the midst of a bush of holly, gaily decorated with coloured ribbons; which birds they have, like the Manx mummers, employed their morning in killing. The following is their song; of which they deliver themselves in most monotonous music:

> The wren, the wren, the king of all birds,
> St Stephen's day was caught in the furze,
> Although he is little, his family's great,
> I pray you, good landlady, give us a treat.

> My box would speak, if it had but a tongue,
> And two or three shillings would do it no wrong;
> Sing holly, sing ivy – sing ivy, sing holly,
> A drop just to drink, it would drown melancholy.

> And if you draw it of the best,
> I hope, in heaven your soul will rest;
> But if you draw it of the small,
> It won't agree with these Wren-boys at all.

If an immediate acknowledgment, either in money or drink, is not made in return for the civility of their visit, some such nonsensical verses as the following are added:

> Last Christmas-day, I turned the spit,
> I burned my fingers (I feel it yet),
> A cock sparrow flew over the table,
> The dish began to fight with the ladle.
>
> The spit got up like a naked man,
> And swore he'd fight with the dripping pan;
> The pan got up and cocked his tail,
> And swore he'd send them all to jail.

The story told to account for the title of 'king of all birds', here given to the wren, is a curious sample of Irish ingenuity, and is thus stated in the clever *Tales of the Munster Festivals*, by an Irish servant in answer to his master's inquiry:

'Saint Stephen! why what the mischief, I ask you again, have I to do with Saint Stephen?'

'Nothen, sure, sir, only this being his day, when all the boys o' the place go about that way with the wran, the king of all birds, sir, as they say (bekays wanst when all the birds wanted to choose a king, and they said they'd have the bird that would fly highest, the aigle flew higher than any of 'em, till at last when he could n't fly an inch higher, a little rogue of a wran that was a-hide under his wing took a fly above him a piece, and was crowned king, of the aigle an' all, sir), tied in the middle o' the holly that way you see, sir, by the leg, that is. An old custom, sir.'

Vainly have we endeavoured to arrive at the probable origin of hunting and killing these little birds upon this day. The tradition commonly related is by no means satisfactory. It is said that a Danish army would have been surprised and destroyed by some Irish troops, had not a wren given the alarm by pecking at some crumbs upon a drumhead – the remains of the sleeping drummer's supper; which roused him, when he instantly beat to arms. And that from this circumstance the wren became an object of hatred to the Irish.

Songs similar in spirit to that of the Irish Droleen boys were popularly sung by the Greeks. In D'Israeli's *Curiosities of Literature*, may be found translations of 'the crow song', and 'the swallow song'; between which and the Irish wren song the resemblance is very striking. 'Swallow-singing or chelidonising, as the Greek term is', was, it appears, a method of collecting eleemosynary gifts in the month of Boedromion or August. We think

D'Israeli is right in his opinion that there is probably a closer connection between the custom which produced the songs of the crow and the swallow and that of our northern mummeries, than may be at first sight suspected. The subject of mumming we have elsewhere treated at some length; but this curious variety of the practice, and the manner in which it seems to connect the subject with the ceremonies of the Greeks, we could not allow ourselves wholly to omit.

New Year's Eve
31st December

This is the last day of the year, and the feelings which belong to it are of a tangled yarn. Regrets for the past are mingled with hopes of the future; and the heart of man, between the meeting years, stands like the head of Janus looking two ways.

The day and eve which precede the New Year are marked, in England, by few outward observances, save such as are common to the season; and it is in the peculiar trains of thought to which they give rise that they have a character of their own.

In Scotland, on the other hand, the festival of this season is, since the Reformation, nearly limited to these two days; and the last day of the year is distinguished both by omens and by customs peculiar to itself. In Mr Stewart's *Popular Superstitions of the Highlands*, there is an account of some of these omens, as they were gathered, at no distant period, in that land of mist and mystery; and a singular example may be mentioned in the auguries drawn from what was called the Candlemas bull. The term Candlemas, which has been given to this season, in Scotland and elsewhere, is supposed to have had its origin in some old religious ceremonies which were performed by candlelight; and the bull was a passing cloud, which in Highland imagination assumed the form of that animal, and from whose rise or fall, or motions generally on this night, the seer prognosticated good or bad weather. Something of the same kind is mentioned in Sir John Sinclair's *Statistical Account of Scotland*, who explains more particularly the auguries gathered from the state of the atmosphere on New Year's Eve. The superstition in question, however, is not peculiar to the Highlands of Scotland, but shared with the northern European nations in general, most of whom assigned portentous qualities to the winds of New Year's Eve.

It is on this night that those Scottish mummers, the Guisars, to whom we have already more than once alluded, still go about the streets, habited in antic dresses, having their faces covered with vizards and carrying cudgels in their hands. The doggerel lines repeated by these masquers, as given by Mr Callender, in a paper contributed by him to the Transactions of the Antiquarian Society of Scotland, are as follows:

Hogmanay,
Trollolay,
Gie me o' your white bread,
I'll hae nane o' your grey;

and much learning has been exhausted, and ingenuity exercised in their explanation. The admirable paper of Mr Repp, in the same Transactions (to which we have already alluded, and which we recommend to the notice of our antiquarian readers), connects them, as we have before hinted, with another superstition common to many of the northern nations; and which may be compared with one of the articles of popular belief before described as prevailing in England, on Christmas Eve; that, viz., which seems to imply that the spirits of evil are at this time in peculiar activity, unless kept down by holier and more powerful influences. According to this able investigator, the moment of midnight, on New Year's Eve, was considered to be a general removing term for the races of genii, whether good or bad; and the first two lines of the cry in question, which as he explains them, after the Anglo-Saxon and Icelandic dialects, were words of appeal to the good genii (the hoghmen or hillmen), and of execration against the evil ones (the trolles), were so used, in consequence of such belief (that these different spirits were, at that hour, in motion), and of the further one that the words of men had power to determine that motion to their own advantage. It is well known that, in some countries, and we may mention Germany, great importance is attached to words involuntarily uttered at certain seasons, and under certain circumstances, and they are supposed to be either words of betrayal, leaving the speaker open to the machinations of evil spirits, who may apply them in a strained and fatal sense, if at all ambiguous; or words of power, controlling the designs of demons, and compelling them to work out the good of the utterer, against their will. Now a superstition of this kind, Mr Repp says, attaches *generally* to the doctrines of demonology; and he states that he could prove his position by many instances from Arabic and Persian fairy lore. We may observe that some of the Highland superstitions mentioned by Mr Stewart, such as that of sprinkling the household with water drawn from *the dead and living ford*, and that of fumigating the apartments and half smothering their tenants with the smoke from burning piles of the juniper-bush (both considered to operate as charms against the spells of witchcraft and the malignity of evil eyes), have, evidently, their origin in that same belief, that the powers of evil are on the wing at this mysterious and solemn time of natural transition.

Some ancient superstitions are likewise alluded to in the old dialogue of Dives and Pauper, as being in force at the beginning of the year, and which appear to have had a like origin with the Highland ones above described.

As an example, mention may be made of the practice of 'setting of mete or drynke by nighte on the benche, to fede Alholde or Gobelyn'.

We must not forget to observe that Brand speaks of an ancient custom, which he says is still retained in some parts of England, in which young women go about on this eve carrying a wassail bowl, and singing certain verses from door to door, which custom has certainly some analogy with the hogmanay practice in Scotland. And we may further state, while we are in the way of tracing resemblances, that the *het pint*, which, in Scotland, was formerly carried about the streets at the midnight of the New Year's coming in, and which was composed of ale, spirits, sugar, and nutmeg or cinnamon, is neither more nor less, though it was borne about in a kettle, than a Scottish version of the wassail bowl.

In Ritson's collection of ancient songs, there is a very spirited carol given at length, which appears to have been sung by these English wassail mummers, in honour of their bowl; but which some of its verses prove to be a Twelfth Night song, and show, therefore, that a similar practice marked the night of the Epiphany. It begins right heartily:

> A jolly wassel-bowl,
> 　A wassel of good ale,
> Well fare the butler's soul
> 　That setteth this to sale;
> 　　　　Our jolly wassel;

but is too long for insertion in our pages. We should mention here, however, that ale in all its forms, whether in that of wassail composition or in its own simple dignity, 'prince of liquors, old or new!' was ever the most cherished beverage of our ancestors, and many and enthusiastic are the songs in its praise. Our readers may take the following verse from a very pleasant example of these carols:

> I love no rost, but a nut brown toste,
> 　And a crab layde in the fyre,
> A little bread shall do me stead,
> 　Much breade I not desyre:
> No froste nor snow, no winde, I trowe,
> 　Can hurt mee if I wolde;
> I am so wrapt, and throwly lapt
> 　Of jolly good ale and olde.
> 　　Back and syde go bare, go bare,
> 　　　Both foote and hand, go colde;
> 　　But belly God send thee good ale inoughe,
> 　　　Whether it be new or olde.

We believe that most of the customs which, up to a recent period, filled the streets of Edinburgh with mirth and bustle, on the eve of the New Year, have met with discouragement, and of late fallen into disuse, in consequence of some outrages which were committed under their shelter, in the year 1811. We presume, however, that there are still many places of the northern kingdom, in which the youth waits impatiently for the striking of the midnight hour, that he may be the earliest to cross the threshold of his mistress, and the lassie listens eagerly, from the moment when its chiming has ceased, to catch the sound of the *first-foot* on the floor:

> The *first foot's* entering step,
> That sudden on the floor is welcome heard,
> Ere blushing maids have braided up their hair;
> The laugh, the *hearty kiss*, the good New Year,
> Pronounced with honest warmth.

Considerable importance was formerly, and probably is still, attached to this custom. The welfare of a family, particularly of the fairer portion of its members, was supposed to depend much on the character of the person who might first cross the threshold, after the mid-hour of this night had sounded. Great care was therefore taken to exclude all improper persons; and when the privilege of the season is taken into consideration (that viz., of the hearty kiss above mentioned), it is probable that the maidens themselves might consider it desirable to interfere after their own fashion in the previous arrangements which were to secure the priority of admission to an unobjectionable guest.

But our space does not permit us to inquire at length in the present volume into any other customs than those which belong to an *English* Christmas season. We have only been able occasionally to advert to others, even amongst our own sister nations, when they helped to throw light upon those which on this occasion are our immediate subject. We must therefore return at once to the only general and conspicuous observance of this eve in England, viz., that which is commonly called 'seeing the New Year in'.

It is almost impossible for man on this day to be insensible to the 'still small voices' that call upon him for a gathering up of his thoughts. In the very midst of the house of mirth, a shadow passes through the heart and summons it to a solemn conference. The skeleton who sits at all feasts, though overlooked at most from long habit, gets power on this day to wave his hand, and points emphatically, with his 'slow-moving finger', to the long record whose burden is 'passing away!' The handwriting of Time comes visibly out upon the wall; and the spirit pauses to read its lessons, and take an account of the wrecks which it registers and the changes which it announces. Properly speaking, every day is the commencement of a new year, and the termination of an old one; but it is only, as we have said at the beginning of this book, by these emphatic markings that man is attracted to a consideration of a fact, whose daily recurrence at once makes its weighty importance and causes it to be forgotten, as if it were of none!

But on this particular day, no man fails to remember that –

> Again the silent wheels of time
> Their annual round have driven;

and how solemn are the reflections which suggest themselves to him who casts his eye over the space of a year, in a spirit which can look beyond his own personal share in its doings, and embrace the wide human interests that such a retrospect includes! 'What a mighty sum of events,' says that excellent writer, William Howitt, 'has been consummated; what a tide of passions and affections has flowed; what lives and deaths have alternately arrived; what destinies have been fixed forever! . . . Once more our planet has completed one of those journeys in the heavens which perfect all the fruitful changes of its peopled surface, and mete out the few stages of our existence; and every day, every hour of that progress has in all her wide lands, in all her million hearts, left traces that eternity shall behold.' Oh! blessed they and rich, beyond all other blessedness and all other wealth which 'Time's effacing fingers' may have left them, who, on the last night of the year, can turn from reviews like these to sleep upon the pillow of a good conscience, though that pillow should be moistened, aye, steeped in their tears!

No doubt it is in the name of his own private affections that man is first summoned to that review, which the wise will end by thus extending; and the first reckoning which each will naturally take is that of the treasures which may have been lost or gained to himself in the year which is about to close. Through many, many a heart, that summons rings in the low, sweet, mournful voice of some beloved one, whom in that bereaving space we have laid in the 'narrow house': and then it will happen (for man is covetous of his griefs, when his attention is once called to them) that the ghost which took him out into the churchyard to visit its own tomb, will end by carrying him round its dreary precincts and showing him all the graves that he has planted from his childhood. There will be hours on a day like this to many, and in some year or another to most, when the cheerful hopes which are also of the natural spirit of the season would contend in vain with the memories which it conjures up, but for that furthest and brightest hope which lies beyond the rest, and which is at this moment typified and shadowed forth by the returning sun and the renewing year.

We cannot refrain from pausing here, to quote for our readers a few exquisite and affecting lines written in the seventeenth century by Henry King, Bishop of Chichester, to one such beloved remembrancer, and in the cheering spirit of that same precious hope. We fancy they are very little known.

> Sleep on, my love! in thy cold bed,
> Never to be disquieted!
> My last 'good-night!' – thou wilt not wake
> Till I thy fate shall overtake;
> Till age, or grief, or sickness must
> Marry my body to that dust
> It so much loves – and fill the room
> My heart keeps empty in thy tomb.
> Stay for me there! – I will not faile
> To meet thee in that hollow vale –
> And think not much of my delay,
> I am already on the way,
> And follow thee with all the speed
> Desire can make, or sorrows breed.
> Each minute is a short degree.
> And every houre a step tow'rds thee –
> At night, when I betake to rest,
> Next morn I rise nearer my West
> Of life, almost by eight houres' sail,
> Than when sleep breathed his drowsy gale!

There are in the last volume of poems published by Mr Tennyson, some beautiful verses, in which the natural thoughts that inevitably haunt this season of change are touchingly expressed, as they arise even in the young breast of one for whom 'seasons and their change' are immediately about to be no more. We are in a mood which tempts us to extract them.

> If you're waking, call me early, call me early, mother dear,
> For I would see the sun rise upon the glad New-year –
> It is the last New-year that I shall ever see,
> Then ye may lay me low i' the mould, and think no more of me.
>
> Tonight I saw the sun set: he set and left behind
> The good old year, the dear old time, and all my peace of mind;
> And the New-year's coming up, mother, but I shall never see
> The may upon the blackthorn, the leaf upon the tree.
>
> Last May we made a crown of flowers: we had a merry day:
> Beneath the hawthorn on the green they made me Queen of May;

And we danced about the maypole, and in the hazel-copse,
Till Charles's wain came out above the tall white chimney-tops.

There's not a flower on all the hills: the frost is on the pane:
I only wish to live till the snowdrops come again:
I wish the snow would melt and the sun come out on high –
I long to see a flower so before the day I die.

The building rook'll caw from the windy tall elm-tree,
And the tufted plover pipe along the fallow lea,
And the swallow'll come back again with summer o'er the wave,
But I shall lie alone, mother, within the moulde ring grave.

Upon the chancel casement, and upon that grave of mine,
In the early, early morning the summer sun'll shine,
Before the red cock crows from the farm upon the hill,
When you are warm asleep, mother, and all the world is still.

When the flowers come again, mother, beneath the waning light,
Ye'll never see me more in the long gray fields at night;
When from the dry dark wold the summer airs blow cool,
On the oat-grass and the sword-grass, and the bulrush in the pool.

Ye'll bury me, my mother, just beneath the hawthorn shade,
And ye'll come sometimes and see me where I am lowly laid,
I shall not forget ye, mother, I shall hear ye when ye pass,
With your feet above my head in the long and pleasant grass.

I have been wild and wayward, but ye'll forgive me now:
Ye'll kiss me, my own mother, upon my cheek and brow;
Nay – nay, ye must not weep, nor let your grief be wild,
Ye should not fret for me, mother, ye have another child.

If I can, I'll come again, mother, from out my resting-place
Tho' ye'll not see me, mother, I shall look upon your face;
Tho' I cannot speak a word, I shall hearken what ye say,
And be often – often with ye when ye think I'm far away.

Good-night! good-night! when I have said good-night for evermore,
And ye see me carried out from the threshold of the door,
Don't let Effie come to see me till my grave be growing green;
She'll be a better child to you than ever I have been.

She'll find my garden tools upon the granary floor;
Let her take 'em – they are hers – I shall never garden more:

But tell her, when I'm gone, to train the rosebush that I set,
About the parlour window, and the box of mignonette.

Good-night, sweet mother! call me when it begins to dawn:
All night I lie awake, but I fall asleep at morn:
But I would see the sun rise upon the glad New year,
So, if you're waking, call me, call me early, mother dear!

And it is wholesome that the mournful reflections which the period suggests *should* be indulged, but not to the neglect of its more cheerful influences. The New Year's Eve is in all quarters looked upon as a time of rejoicing; and perhaps no night of this merry season is more universally dedicated to festivity. Men are for the most part met in groups to hail the coming year with propitiatory honours; and copious libations are poured to its honour, as if to determine it to look upon us with a benignant aspect. We generally spend *our* New Year's Eve in some such group; but, we confess, it is not every class of wassailers that will suit us for the occasion. The fact is, after all our resolves to work up our minds to the pitch of gladness, aye, and notwithstanding our *success*, too, there are *other* feelings that *will* intrude in spite of us; and we like to find ourselves in a party where their presence is not looked upon as a marrer of the revels. When fitly associated for such a night, we find the very feelings in question for the most part to harmonise very delightfully with the predominant spirit of the time, producing a sort of mixed sensation which is full of luxury and tenderness. Bye the by, we have no great wish to have for our companions at any time those precisians who insist greatly on the *external* solemnities. 'Ye are sae grave, nae doubt ye're wise,' says Burns. But for ourselves, gentlemen, our sympathies lie with those who can be made to understand that the garb of even folly may by possibility be at times worn by those who conceal beneath it more sickness of the heart, as well as more wisdom, than shall ever be dreamt of in *your* philosophy – who know, in fact, that that same folly is sometimes the very saddest thing in the world; that the jingle of the cap and bells is too often but a vain device, like that of the ancient Corybantes, to drown the 'still small' sounds whose wailing is yet heard over all.

And on the night before us, of all nights in the year, the smile and the laugh go freely round, but ever and anon there is, as it were, the echo of a far sigh. A birth in which we have a mighty interest is about to take place, but every now and then comes to the heart the impression of low whispering and soft treading in the background, as of those who wait about a death-bed. We are in a state of divided feelings, somewhat resembling his whose joy at the falling of a rich inheritance is dashed by tender recollections of the friend by whose departure it came. Let Mr Tennyson explain for us why this is so:

Full knee-deep lies the winter snow,
And the winter winds are wearily sighing:
Toll ye the church-bell sad and slow,
And tread softly and speak low,
For the old year lies a-dying.
    Old year, you must not die.
    You came to us so readily,
    You lived with us so steadily,
    Old year, you shall not die.

He lieth still: he doth not move:
He will not see the dawn of day.
He hath no other life above.
He gave me a friend, and a true true-love,
And the New-year will take 'em away.
    Old year, you must not go.
    So long as you have been with us,
    Such joy as you have seen with us,
    Old year, you shall not go!

He frothed his bumpers to the brim;
A jollier year we shall not see.
But tho' his eyes are waxing dim,
And tho' his foes speak ill of him,
He was a friend to me!
    Old year, you shall not die.
    We did so laugh and cry with you,
    I've half a mind to die with you,
    Old year, if you *must* die.

He was full of joke and jest,
But all his merry quips are o'er.
To see him die, across the waste
His son and heir doth ride post-haste,
But he'll be dead before!
    Every one for his own!
    The night is starry and cold, my friend,
    And the New-year, blithe and bold, my friend,
    Comes up to take his own.

How hard he breathes! – over the snow,
I heard just now the crowing cock.
The shadows flicker to and fro;
The cricket chirps: the light burns low:

Seeing-in the New Year

'Tis nearly one [twelve?] o'clock.
   Shake hands before you die.
   Old year, we'll dearly rue for you.
   What is it we can do for you?
   Speak out before you die!

His face is growing sharp and thin.
Alack! our friend is gone!
Close up his eyes: tie up his chin:
Step from the corpse, and let *him* in
That standeth there alone,
   And waiteth at the door.
   There's a new foot on the floor, my friend,
   And a new face at the door, my friend,
   A new face at the door!

Occasionally, too, there will come a thought across us, in these hours, which *cannot* be made to harmonise with the feelings we are seeking to encourage, and has the unpleasing effect of a discord.

It is felt at times, for instance, to be a sort of indecency that we should be looking out merrily for the New Year, when the old one is perishing by our side, and, for an instant, the heart's joyous issues are thrown back upon it. And then, again, the looker forward to hail the 'coming guest' will suddenly fix his eyes upon the veil which shrouds that face; and the chill of a moment will creep over his heart, as he speculates on what it may conceal, or, gazing on the sealed book which the New Year carries in his hand, asks himself how many of those who sit with him on this night about the social table, may have their names written in its last page! Thoughts like these, however, are instantly treated like informers, and ducked, as they deserve to be, in the wassail bowl.

But, in any case, we have never failed to observe that, as the midnight hour draws near, a hush falls upon these assemblies; and when men rise to usher in the newcomer, it is for the most part in silence. We do not believe *that* moment is ever a merry one. The blithe spirits of the night stand still. The glasses are full – but so is the heart, and the eye is strained upon the finger of the dial whose notes are to sound the arrival, as if held there by a spell. We do not think that any man, of all that group whom our artist has represented, could turn his face away from the dial, even by an effort; and he who could, would be out of place in any assembly of which we made one, unless we were out of place ourselves. The instant the solemn sounds of the midnight chime have ceased, the bells from a thousand steeples lift up their merry voices, but they never, at that moment, found a true echo in *our* hearts; and the shout which rises from the wassail table, in answer, has ever seemed to us to want much of the mirth to which it makes such boisterous pretension.

But this oppressive sensation soon passes away; and the glad bells of the spirit, like those of the steeples, ring freely out. When the old year is fairly withdrawn, when we have ceased to hear the sound of the falling earth upon its coffin-lid, when the heir stands absolutely in our presence, and the curtain which hides his features has begun slowly to rise (while the gazer on that curtain can discover, as yet, nothing of the dark things that lie behind, and the hopes which the New Year brings are seen through it, by their own light) – then does the heart shake off all that interfered with its hearty enjoyment, and then 'comes in the sweet o' the night!' We are, ourselves, of that party in the plate; and it will be late, we promise you, before we separate. One song to the past! and then, 'shall we set about some revels?' – as our old friend, Sir Andrew, has it.

> Here's to the year that's awa!
> We'll drink it, in strong and in sma';
> And to each bonny lassie that we dearly loo'd,
> In the days o' the year that's awa!
>
> Here's to the soldier who bled!
> To the sailor who bravely did fa'!
> Oh, their fame shall remain, though their spirits are fled,
> On the wings o' the year that's awa!

> Here's to the friend we can trust,
> When the storms of adversity blaw;
> Who can join in our song, and be nearest our heart,
> Nor depart – like the year that's awa!

And now are we in the humour, this New Year's morning, for keeping such vigils as they did in Illyria; for 'were we', too, 'not born under Taurus?' No advocates do we mean to be for those whose zeal in symposiac matters, like that of Bardolph, 'burns in their noses'; but occasions there are, and this is one, when we hold it lawful to sound the wassail bowl to some considerable depth. Like honest Isaak Walton, we love to keep within the bounds of 'such mirth as does not make friends ashamed to look on one another, next morning'; but we feel that we may venture to be a little intemperate, in the present instance, and yet hold our heads up, even if we should chance to meet one of those gentry whom Burns presumes to be wise, because they 'are sae grave'. What says Innocentius? – and he was a Father of the Church; *Fecundi calices, quem non fecere disertum?*' 'Carry Master Silence to bed!' therefore, for we are about to be talkative, and expect to be answered. No man need sit with us longer than he likes: but it is the opening of another year, and *we* must see more of it. We find much virtue in Sir Toby's excellent reasoning, that 'not to be abed after midnight is to be up betimes'; and have no sympathy for those who would insist, today, with the stolid Sir Andrew, that 'to be up late is to be up late'. 'A false conclusion!' says Sir Toby; and so say we. So fill the glasses, once more, from the wassail bowl, and let us 'rouse the night-owl' in another 'catch'!

But alas! it is later than we thought, and the owl is gone to bed; for we hear the cry of that other bird whom Herrick calls 'the Bellman of the night':

> Hark! the cock crows, and yon bright star
> Tells us the day himself's not far;
> And see! where, breaking from the night,
> He gilds the eastern hills with light!

Honest Master Cotton had evidently been sitting up all night, himself, when he wrote these lines; and being therefore a boon companion, and a true observer of Christmas proprieties, we will take his warning, and to bed ourselves. So 'a good New Year to you, my masters! and many of them!' as the bellman (not Herrick's) says, on this morning.

New Year's Day
1st January

The first of January, forming the accomplishment of the eight days after the birth of Christ, has been sometimes called the octave of Christmas; and is celebrated in our church services as the day of the Circumcision.

Of this day we have little left to say; almost all that belongs to it having been of necessity anticipated in the progress of those remarks which have brought us up to it. It is a day of universal congratulation; and one on which, so far as we may judge from external signs, a general expansion of the heart takes place. Even they who have no hearts to open, or hearts which are not opened by such ordinary occasions, adopt the phraseology of those whom *all* genial hints call into sympathy with their fellow-creatures; and the gracious compliments of the season may be heard falling from lips on which they must surely wither in the very act of passing. To have your morning's salutation from a worthy like our friend with the umbrella in the plate, must be much the same thing as riding out into the highway, and getting your New Year's greeting from a raven by the roadside. Mathews's undertaker, who used to sing the song of 'Merry I have been, and merry could I be', at his club, to a tune considerably below a dirge in point of liveliness, was a brother of the same family.

Of New Year's gifts, which are the distinguishing feature of this day, we have already said enough, in pointing out the distinction betwixt them and Christmas-boxes. They still pass generally from friend to friend, and between the different members of a family; and are in such cases, very pleasant remembrancers; but the practice in ancient times had some very objectionable features. It was formerly customary for the nobles and those about the court to make presents on this day to the sovereign; who, if he were a prince with anything like a princely mind, took care that the returns which he made in kind should at least balance the cost to the subject. The custom, however, became a serious tax when the nobles had to do with a sovereign of another character; and in Elizabeth's day it was an affair of no trifling expense to maintain ground as a courtier. The lists of the *kind* of gifts which she exacted from all who approached her (for the necessity of giving, the consequences of not giving, amounted to an exaction), and the

accounts of the childish eagerness with which she turned over the
wardrobe finery, furnished in great abundance as the sort of gift most
suited to her capacity of appreciation, furnish admirable illustrations of
her mind. She is said to have taken good care that her returns should leave
a very substantial balance in her own favour. The practice is stated to have
been extinguished in the reign of George III.

A worse custom still, however, was that of presenting gifts to the
Chancellor by suitors in his court, for the purpose of influencing his
judgments. The abuses of the New-Year's-gift practice have, however, been
cleared away, and have left it what it now is – a beautiful form for the
interchanges of affection and the expression of friendship.

In Paris, where this day is called the 'Jour d'Etrennes', the practice is of
still more universal observance than with us, and the streets are brilliant
with the displays made in every window of the articles which are to furnish
these tokens of kindness, and with the gay equipages and well-dressed
pedestrians passing in all directions, to be the bearers of them, and offer
the compliments which are appropriate to the season. The thousand bells
of the city are pealing from its hundred belfries, filling the air with an
indescribable sense of festival, and would alone set the whole capital in
motion if they were a people that ever sat still. This singing of a thousand
bells is likewise a striking feature of the day in London; and no one who
has not heard the mingling voices of these high choristers in a metropolis,
can form any notion of the wild and stirring effects produced by the racing
and crossing and mingling of their myriad notes. It is as if the glad voices of
the earth had a chorus of echoes in the sky; as if the spirit of its rejoicing
were caught up by 'airy tongues', and flung in a cloud of incense-like
music to the gates of heaven.

We need scarcely mention that most of the other forms in which the
mirth of the season exhibits itself, are in demand for this occasion; and
that among the merry evenings of the Christmas-tide, not the least merry is
that which closes New Year's Day. To the youngsters of society, that day
and eve have probably been the most trying of all; and the strong
excitements of a happy spirit drive the weary head to an earlier pillow than
the young heart of this season at all approves. But his is the weariness that
the sweet sleep of youth so surely recruits; and tomorrow shall see him
early afoot, once more engaged in those winter amusements which are to
form his resource till the novelties of Twelfth Day arrive.

> There will come an eve to a longer day,
> That will find thee tired – but not of play;
> And thou wilt lean as thou leanest now,
> With drooping limbs and an aching brow;

And wish the shadows would faster creep,
And long to go to thy quiet sleep! –
Well were it then if thine aching brow
Were as free from sin and shame as now!

Twelfth Day and Twelfth Night
6th January

Twelfth Day (so called from its being the twelfth after Christmas Day) is that on which the festival of the Epiphany is held. This feast of the Christian Church was instituted, according to Picart, in the fourth century, to commemorate the manifestation of our Saviour to the Gentiles; and the name Epiphany (Ἐπιφάνεια), which signifies an appearance from above, was given to it in allusion to the star described in Holy Writ, as the guide of the Magi or Wise Men to the cradle of the Blessed Infant. 'In Italy,' says Mr Leigh Hunt, 'the word has been corrupted into Beffania or Beffana, as in England it used to be called Piffany; and Beffana in some parts of that country has come to mean an old fairy or Mother Bunch, whose figure is carried about the streets, and who rewards or punishes children at night, by putting sweetmeats or stones and dirt into a stocking hung up for the purpose, near the bed's head. The word "Beffa", taken from this, familiarly means a trick or mockery put upon any one; to such base uses may come the most splendid terms!' But what is quite as extraordinary as that the primitive signification of a word not familiarly understood should, amid the revolutions of centuries, be lost in a different or distorted into an inferior meaning, is the preservation in popular rites of trivial details, which, as we have before stated, conclusively identify many of the practices of our modern Christian festivals as echoes of ancient pagan observances. Of this, Twelfth Day presents a remarkable instance.

The more we examine the Saturnalia of the Romans and compare those revels with the proceedings of our Twelfth Night, the more satisfied do we feel of the correctness of Selden's view. 'Christmas,' he says, in his *Table Talk*, 'succeeds the Saturnalia; the same time, the same number of holy-days. Then the master waited upon the servants, like the Lord of Misrule.' There is here a general likeness to the season of which we treat; but, as Mr Brand further states, the Greeks and Romans at this period also 'drew lots for kingdoms, and like kings exercised their temporary authority'; and Mr Fosbroke mentions that 'the king of Saturnalia was elected by beans', which identifies our Twelfth Night characters, as well as our mode of selecting them, with those of the ancients. Through so many centuries has chance decided who should wear a crown! By the French Twelfth Day was distinguished as 'La Fête des Rois', a name of course obnoxious to the revolutionary fraternity of 1792, who caused such feast to be declared anti-civic, and replaced it by 'La Fête des Sans-Culottes'.

However, before entering upon the important discussion of the 'absolute monarchy' of 'the king of cakes and characters', in which, without any reference to profane ceremonies, there was sufficient found to offend puritanical ideas, we must be allowed to mention some customs observed on the vigil or eve of the feast of the Epiphany. Amongst these was the practice of wassailing the trees to ensure their future fruitfulness, mentioned by Herrick:

> Wassail the trees, that they may beare
> You many a plum, and many a peare;
> For more or lesse fruits they will bring,
> As you do give them wassailing.

The merry bowl which, notwithstanding that it had been so often drained, was still kept brimming throughout all the Christmas holidays, was now when they were drawing to a close actually flowing over; and the warm heart and jovial spirit of the season, not content with pledging all those who could drink in return, proceeded to an excess of boon-companionship, and after quaffing a wassail draft to the health and abundant bearing of some favourite fruit-tree, poured what remained in the cup upon the root, as a libation to its strength and vitality. Here, also, we cannot fail to recognise the rites of classical times lurking in the superstitions used in the cider districts of England. A pleasant custom of this kind is mentioned in the *Gentleman's Magazine* for 1791, as existing in certain parts of Devonshire. It is there stated that 'the farmer, attended by his workmen with a large pitcher of cider, goes to the orchard on this evening; and there, encircling one of the best bearing trees, they drink the following toast three times:

> Here's to thee, old apple-tree!
> Whence thou mayst bud, and whence thou mayst blow!
> And whence thou mayst bear apples enow!
> Hats full! caps full!
> Bushel, bushel-sacks full!
> And my pockets full too! – Huzza!'

This done they return to the house, the doors of which they are sure to find bolted by the females, who, be the weather what it may, are inexorable to all entreaties to open them till someone has guessed at what is on the spit, which is generally some nice little thing difficult to be hit on, and is the

Twelfth Night in London Streets

reward of him who first names it. The doors are then thrown open; and the lucky clodpole receives the titbit as a recompense. Some, it is added, 'are so superstitious as to believe that if they neglect this custom the trees will bear no apples that year'.

> Health to thee, good apple-tree!
> Well to bear, pockets full, hats full,
> Pecks full, bushel-bags full –

is another version of the address used on these occasions, preserved by Brand. We find recorded in one quarter or another a variety of analogous and other customs observed in different parts of England on this vigil; but our diminishing space will not permit us to enter upon a description of them.

To illustrate Twelfth Night, our artist has made two studies of the scenes it presents in London – abroad and at home; and these involve our consideration of the subject, accordingly.

During the entire twelve months, there is no such illumination of pastry-cooks' shops as on Twelfth Night. Each sends forth a blaze of light; and is filled with glorious cakes, 'decorated', to use the words of Mr Hone, 'with all imaginable images of thing animate and inanimate. Stars, castles, kings, cottages, dragons, trees, fish, palaces, cats, dogs, churches, lions, milk-maids, knights, serpents, and innumerable other forms, in snow-white confectionery, painted with variegated colours.' 'This "paradise of dainty devices",' he continues, 'is crowded by successive, and successful, desirers of the seasonable delicacies; while alternate tappings of hammers and peals of laughter, from the throng surrounding the house, excite smiles from the inmates.' This last observation requires explanation, for our country readers.

Let all idle gazers, then, in the streets of London beware of Twelfth Night! There is then that spirit of mischievous fun abroad, which, carried on without the superintending power of a Lord of Misrule, exhibits itself in transfixing the coat-skirts of the unconscious stranger to the frame of the door or window, at which he may have paused to stare and wonder. Once fairly caught, lucky is the wight who can disengage himself, without finding that, in the interim, his other skirt has been pinned to the pelisse or gown of some alarmed damsel, whose dress is perhaps dragged, at the same moment, in opposite directions, so that he can neither stand still nor move, without aiding the work of destruction. These practical facetiæ are the performances of that class of nondescript lads, 'perplexers of Lord Mayors and irritators of the police', whose character Mr Leigh Hunt has as truly drawn as our artist has depicted their persons: 'those equivocal animal-spirits of the streets, who come whistling along, you know not whether thief or errand-boy, sometimes with a bundle and sometimes not, in corduroys, a jacket, and a cap or bit of hat, with hair sticking through a hole in it. His vivacity gets him into scrapes in the street; and he is not ultra-studious of civility in his answers. If the man he runs against is not very big, he gives him abuse for abuse, at once; if otherwise, he gets at a convenient distance, and then halloos out, "Eh, stupid!" or "Can't you see before you?" or "Go and get your face washed!" This last is a favourite saying of his, out of an instinct referable to his own visage. He sings "Hokee-Pokee", and "A shiny Night", varied, occasionally, with an uproarious "Rise, gentle Moon", or "Coming through the Rye". On winter evenings, you may hear him indulging himself, as he goes along, in a singular undulation of yowl, a sort of gargle, as if a wolf was practising the rudiments of a shake. This he delights to do, more particularly in a crowded thoroughfare, as though determined that his noise should triumph over every other and show how jolly he is, and how independent of the ties to good behavior. If the street is a quiet one, and he has a stick in his hand (perhaps a hoop-stick), he accompanies the howl with a run upon the gamut of the iron rails. He is the nightingale of mud and cold. If he gets on in life, he will be a potboy. At present, as we said before, we hardly know what he is; but his mother thinks herself lucky if he is not transported.'

Of Twelfth Night, at home, when 'the whole island keeps court – nay all Christendom', – when 'all the world are kings and queens, and everybody is somebody else', a huge cake, the idol of young hearts, is the presiding genius of the evening. The account given by Nutt, the editor of the *Cook*

Twelfth Night

and Confectioner's Dictionary, of the twelfth-cakes and dishes in vogue a hundred years ago, proves the nursery rhymes of –

> Four and twenty blackbirds baked in a pye,

who

> When the pye was opened all began to sing,

to be no such nonsense as was generally supposed. He tells us of two great pies, made of coarse paste and bran, into one of which, after it was baked, live frogs were introduced, and into the other, live birds; which, upon some curious persons lifting up the covers, would jump and fly about the room, causing 'a surprising and diverting hurly-burly among the guests'. What feeble imitations are the castles, ships, and animals that now adorn our Twelfth Night cakes, to the performances of Nutt! How much, every way, inferior are the specimens of art produced, even by the renowned author of the *Italian Confectioner*, the illustrious Jarrin! On the battlements of the castles of former days were planted 'kexes', or pop-guns, charged with gunpowder, to be fired upon a pastry ship, with 'masts', ropes, we doubt not of spun sugar, 'sails, flags, and streamers'. Nor was the naval power of England lost sight of; for the 'kexes' of this delicious ship were, also, charged with gunpowder, and, when she was fired upon from the castle, her guns were able to return the salute. Then, to take off the smell of the powder, there were egg-shells, filled with rose-water, for the spectators to break, 'and throw at one another'. Nor must a stag of pastry filled with claret be forgotten; which, when wounded, poured forth its blood, free and sparkling as a ruby, for those whose nerves were delicate and needed the refreshment of a glass of wine. Such were the 'subtilties', as these jugglings in confectionery are called, which we now behold represented by the painted figures, 'so bad to eat, but so fine to look at', that adorn our twelfth-cakes.

'How to eat twelfth-cake,' says Hone, 'requires no recipe; but how to provide it, and draw the characters, on the authority of Rachel Revel's "Winter Evening Pastimes", may be acceptable. First, buy your cake. Then, before your visitors arrive, buy your characters – each of which should have a pleasant verse beneath. Next, look at your invitation list, and count the number of ladies you expect, and afterwards the number of gentlemen. Then, take as many female characters as you have invited ladies, fold them up exactly of the same size, and number each on the back, taking care to make the king No. I, and the queen No. 2. Then prepare and number the gentlemen's characters. Cause tea and coffee to be handed to your visitors, as they drop in. When all are assembled, and tea over, put as many ladies' characters in a reticule as there are ladies present; next, put the gentlemen's characters in a hat. Then call on a gentleman to carry the reticule to the ladies as they sit; from which each lady is to draw one ticket, and to preserve it unopened. Select a lady to bear the hat to the gentlemen for the same purpose. There will be one ticket left in the reticule, and another in the hat – which the lady and gentleman who carried each are to inter-change, as having fallen to each. Next, arrange your visitors, according to their numbers; the king No 1, the queen No. 2, and so on. The king is then to recite the verse on his ticket, then the queen the verse on hers; and so the characters are to proceed, in numerical order. This done, let the cake and refreshments go round; and hey! for merriment!'

As *our* contribution towards the merriment of this evening, we cannot do better than present our readers with a copy of the following letter, respecting the manufacture of Twelfth Night characters – which document was handed to us by the artist to whom it was addressed:

> Sɪʀ – As I am given to understand that you are an artist of celebrity, I will thank you to make me a hundred and forty-four different charac-ters, for Twelfth Night, the entire cost not to exceed two shillings and sixpence each, say three plates at two pounds ten shillings a plate, including the poetry, which you can, I am told, get plenty of poets to write for nothing, though I should not mind standing a trifle – say twopence more, if the verses gave satisfaction. You will please do your best for me, and, trusting to your speedy attention to this order, I remain your well-wisher and obedient servant, who will furnish the coppers.

Twelfth Night King

Let not a man be seen here,
Who unurged will not drink
To the base from the brink,
A health to the king!

HERRRICK

Though we publish this letter, that is no reason why we should publish the writer's name. It is evident he was a young hand in the trade, and desirous to rival the graphic and literary talent displayed in Langley's and Fairburn's characters – of which we have preserved specimens in our portfolio. Mr Sandys speaks rather disparagingly of the merit of these productions, and this, considering that gentleman's antiquarian zeal, we must confess, surprises us. In the copy of Langley's characters which we possess, the same love of alliteration, upon which we have already commented as encouraged in the Court of Misrule, is observable. We have, for instance, 'Bill Bobstay', 'Prudence Pumpkin', 'Percival Palette', 'Judy Juniper', 'Peter Puncheon', 'Simon Salamander', 'Countess Clackett', 'Leander Lackbrain', 'Nelly Nester', 'Felicia Frill', etc.

Where the monarch of the evening and his queen are not determined by this kind of pictorial lottery, a bean and a pea are put into the cake; and whoever finds them in the pieces taken, he and she become the king and queen of the evening. Other matters, such as a small coin, a ring, etc., are often introduced into Twelfth Night cakes, and give to the finders characters to be supported for the evening. In some countries, says Sandys, a coin was put 'instead of the bean, and portions of the cake assigned to the Virgin Mary and the Three Kings, which were given to the poor; and if the bean should happen to be in any of these portions, the king was then chosen by pulling straws.'

The three kings mentioned in the above extract are those worthies commonly known by the title of the Three Kings of Colen (Cologne), identified by old legends with the Wise Men of the East, who did homage to our Saviour on the day of which the Epiphany is the anniversary celebration. They are stated to have been Arabians; and are distinguished in the traditionary tales of the Early Church by the names of Melchior, Balthazar, and Gasper. Their bodies are said to have been finally deposited at Cologne, after several removals; and the practice of electing a king on the evening of the Epiphany has been, by some, thought to have a reference to their supposed regal characters. We imagine, however, it will be sufficiently evident to our readers, after what we have formerly said, that it is not necessary for us to seek further than we have already done for the origin of the Twelfth Night king.

St Distaff's day
7th January

Conclusion   The day which precedes this is, as we have already informed our readers, the last of the twelve days which constitute what is emphatically the Christmas season; and with the revelries of Twelfth Night the general holiday is in strictness considered to be at an end. As, however, we found it necessary to approach the throng of its celebrations with some degree of preparation – to pass through some of its lighted antechambers, before we ventured to trust our eyes amid the blaze of the temple itself – so also we dare not step at once from its thousand lights into the common air of the everyday world without a previous subjecting of our imaginations to the diminished glare of the outer chambers which lie on this other side. And this it is the more incumbent on us to do, because the revellers whose proceedings it is our business to describe take the same course in returning to the business of life.

It is not, as we have said, to be expected that after the full chorus of increased mirth which has swelled up anew for the last of these celebrations, the ear should all at once accustom itself to a sudden and utter silence – should endure the abrupt absence of all festival sound; nor can all the laughing spirits of the season who were engaged in added numbers for the revelries of last night, be got quietly laid at rest in the course of a single day. One or other of them is accordingly found lurking about the corners of our chambers after the ceremonies for which they were called up are over, encouraged to the neglect of the order for their dismissal by the young hearts, who have formed a merry alliance with the imps which they are by no means willing to terminate thus suddenly. And sooth to say, those youngsters are often able to engage heads who are older, and we suppose should know better, in the conspiracies which are day by day formed for the detention of some one or more of these members of the train of Momus.

Even in rural districts, where the necessary preparations in aid of the returning season are by this time expected to call men abroad to the labours of the field, our benevolent ancestors admitted the claim for a gradual subsiding of the Christmas mirth in favour of the children of toil.

Their devices for letting themselves gently down were recognised; and a sort of compromise was sanctioned between the spirit of the past holiday and the sense of an important coming duty to be performed. The genius of mirth met the genius of toil on neutral ground for a single day; and the two touched hands in recognition of the rightful dominion of each other, ere they severally set forth in their own separate directions.

Thus, on the day which followed Twelfth Night, the implements of labour were prepared and the team was even yoked for a space; but the business of turning the soil was not required to be laboriously engaged in until the Monday which followed, and which therefore bore (and bears) the title of Plough Monday. After a few hours of morning labour, a sort of half-holiday was the concluding privilege of this privileged season; and the husbandman laid aside his plough, and the maiden her distaff, to engage in certain revels which were peculiar to the day and to the country districts. From the partial resumption of the spinning labours of the women on this morning, the festival in question takes its name; and it is (or was) sometimes called also 'Rockday', in honour of the rock, which is another name for the distaff. It is described as being 'a distaff held in the hand, from whence wool is spun by twirling a ball below'.

Of the sports by which this day was enlivened, we doubt if there are any remains. These seem to have consisted in the burning, by the men who had returned from the field, of the flax and tow belonging to the women, as a sort of assertion of the supremacy of the spirit of fun over his laborious rival for this one day more, and a challenge into his court; and this challenge was answered by the maidens, and the mischief retorted, by sluicing the clowns with pails of water. It was, in fact, a merry contest between these two elements of water and of fire; and may be looked upon as typical of that more matter-of-fact extinction which was about to be finally given to the lights of the season when the sports of this day should be concluded. Of these merry proceedings our artist has given a very lively representation; and Herrick's poem on the subject, which we must quote from the 'Hesperides', includes all that is known of the ancient observances of St Distaff's day.

> Partly work and partly play,
> You must on St Distaff's day;
> From the plough soone free your teame,
> Then come home and fother them,
> If the maides a spinning goe,
> Burne the flax, and fire the tow;

Returning to school

> Bring in pailes of water then,
> Let the maides bewash the men –
> Give St Distaffe all the right,
> Then bid Christmas sport good-night:
> And next morrow, every one
> To his own vocation.'

Our Revels now are ended; and our Christmas prince must abdicate. In flinging down his wand of misrule, we trust there is no reason why he should, like Prospero, when his charms were over and he broke his staff, drown this, his book, 'deeper than did ever plummet sound'. The spells which it contains are, we believe, all innocent; and, we trust, it may survive to furnish the directions for many a future scheme of Christmas happiness.

And *now* Father Christmas has at length departed – but not till the youngsters had got from the merry old man his last *bon-bon*. The school-boy, too, has clung to the skirts of the patriarch's coat, and followed him as far as he could. And farther had *he* gone, but for a clear and undoubted vision of a dark object, which has been looming suspiciously through the gloom, for some weeks past. He first caught a glimpse of it, on stepping out from amongst the lights of Twelfth Night; but he turned his head resolutely away, and has since looked as little in that direction as he could. But there is no evading it now! There it stands, right in his way, plain and distinct and portentous! the gloomy portal of this merry season, on whose face is inscribed, in characters which there is no mystifying, its own appropriate and unbeloved name – BLACK MONDAY!

And, behold! at the gloomy gate a hackney coach! (more like a mourning coach!) – *Black Monday*, visible in all its appointments, and *black Friday*, looking blacker than ever, this black Monday, frowning from its foot-board!

And lo! Through its windows, just caught in the distance, the last flutter of the coat-tails of old Father Christmas!

OUR REVELS ARE, INDEED, ENDED!

The Folklore Society

What is folklore?   Folklore has been defined as 'traditional culture', but no one phrase can do justice to the subject. It embraces music, song, dance, drama, narrative, language, foods, medicine, arts and crafts, religion, magic and belief. Folklore is the way that people fill their lives with meaning, through the stories they share, the daily rituals they perform. Folklore can be both the expression of our individuality and give us a sense of community. From standing stones to biker gangs, from ancient riddles to the latest joke craze, from King Arthur to the playground, from birth to death, folklore is the stuff of life.

The Folklore Society: Who we are   Since 1878 The Folklore Society has provided a meeting-ground for both academics and enthusiasts eager to learn about popular culture and traditional life. The Society promotes awareness of folklore within universities, museums, festivals, in fact wherever traditional culture is discussed and researched.

The Society has an elected committee which aims to be responsive to its members' needs It therefore embraces a number of specialist groups and regional sections, such as the East Anglia Folklore Group, to make the Society accessible to all.

The Folklore Society: What we do   In order to encourage awareness of folklore the Society organises events, prizes and research projects. It runs at least one conference a year, and hosts the annual Katherine Briggs memorial lecture.

The Society publishes its own academic Journal, *Folklore*, in association with Routledge. It also produces numerous monographs and pamphlets either under its own imprint *FLS Books* or in conjunction with other publishers.

In addition to the journal *Folklore*, members receive a regular newsletter *FLS News*, through which they can call on the expertise of the entire Society. They also have access to a specialist library with both reference and lending facilities and a substantial archive. The library constitutes a unique resource for the study of folklore, old and new. Members may also join one of the Society's special interest groups or regional sections.

The Folklore Society: How to contact us   For details about how to join The Folklore Society, about our forthcoming activities and publications, contact:
The Folklore Society, University College London, Gower Street, London WC1E 6BT

Telephone: 020 7862 8564 (with voice mail) or 020 7862 8562
E-mail: folklore.society@talk21.com

The Folklore Society is a Registered Charity No.1074552